THE
STONEHENGE
PEOPLE

THE
STONEHENGE PEOPLE

AN EXPLORATION OF LIFE IN NEOLITHIC BRITAIN 4700-2000BC

RODNEY CASTLEDEN

ILLUSTRATED BY THE AUTHOR

London and New York

To Professors Stuart Piggott, Colin Renfrew and Sir Harry Godwin, three pioneers of modern neolithic studies without whose research this book could not have been written.

First published 1987
by Routledge & Kegan Paul Ltd

Paperback edition first published 1990
by Routledge
11 New Fetter Lane, London EC4P 4EE

Simultaneously published in the USA and Canada
by Routledge
29 West 35th Street, New York, NY 10001

Reprinted 1993, 1994, 1998

Text and illustrations © 1987, 1990 Rodney Castleden

Typeset in Sabon 10 on 11pt
by Columns of Reading
Printed and bound in Great Britain by
T.J. International, Padstow, Cornwall

British Library Cataloguing in Publication Data
A catalogue record for this book is available from the British Library

Library of Congress Cataloging in Publication Data
A catalog record for this book is available from the Library of Congress

ISBN 0–415–04065–5

CONTENTS

ILLUSTRATIONS

PLATES

FIGURES

FOREWORD

By Sir Michael Tippett

I live near to the Avebury stone-circle. A new neighbour has appeared this year out of the ground at Windmill Hill, the farming settlement attached to the huge sanctuary complex. He is provisionally called (locally) George and is a complete skeleton. He lived about five-and-a-half thousand years ago. His possible grandson, the child Charlie, is on display on the floor of the splendid little museum at Avebury, where the engaging custodian, Peter Tate, will tell you all about him.

These two skeleton ancestors are rare, because the folk of that 2,000-year-long period dis-articulated their corpse skeletons, once cleaned by the weather, then buried some of the bones in their mortuaries. Some skeletons have been re-made from these bones, but still intact skeletons are virtually non-existent.

My interest in the stone monuments is instinctive, not archaeological. What I now know about them I have read in Rodney Castleden's books. He sent me *The Wilmington Giant* when it came out, because he thought my intuitions of the life-style of these ancestors, as implied in my opera, *The Midsummer Marriage*, and in what I said, standing among the Avebury stones, once, on BBC television, were perceptive. Maybe.

Their life has been called 'brief, savage and fearful'. Castleden thinks it was brief, pacific and joyful. So do I.

The smaller, more spectacular circle at Stonehenge lies 23 miles on foot due south of Avebury. I saw it first in 1913, when I was eight. It was empty, solitary, un-fenced; and, to a totally ignorant small boy, immense. I *know* it better now, but no more poignantly now than then.

Here is a visionary, dramatic account of a dawn at Stonehenge by someone who knew the stones intimately all his life:*

'One of my mother's people was a shepherd hereabout, now I

---

* Thomas Hardy, *Tess of the D'Urbervilles*, 1891.

think of it. And you used to say . . . that I was a heathen so now I am at home.'

He knelt down beside her outstretched form, and put his lips to hers. 'Sleepy are you, dear? I think you are lying on an altar.'. . . .

He heard something behind him, the brush of feet. Turning, he saw over the prostrate columns another figure; then before he was aware, another was at hand on the right under a trilithon, and another on the left. The dawn shone full on the front of the man westward, and Clare could discern that he was tall, and walked as if trained. They all closed in with evident purpose. . . .

'Let her finish her sleep!' he implored in a whisper of the men as they gathered round.

When they saw where she lay . . . they showed no objection, and stood watching her, as still as the pillars around. He went to the stone and bent over her, holding one poor little hand. . . .

Soon the light was strong, and a ray shone upon her unconscious form, peering under her eyelids and waking her.

'What is it, Angel?' she said, starting up. 'Have they come for me?'

'Yes, dearest,' he said. 'They have come.'

'It is as it should be,' she murmured.

That is imagination fired by ancient, palpable and crafted stone. Rodney Castleden goes another way. After the chapters of scholarship in *The Stonehenge People*, he allows himself, as he must, *his* vision. That is why we can profit so much from his double-book, and why I am so delighted to preface the new edition.

Michael Tippett
Nocketts, 1988

ACKNOWLEDGMENTS

I have to thank Zillah Booth for explaining the intricacies of compound interest to me and so enabling me to make sensible estimates of population changes in prehistory; the Revd Allan Wainwright for prompting new lines of thought on neolithic religion and making useful comments on Chapter 14 in particular; Dr Tony Champion for his constructive criticism of my ideas on neolithic transport; Mollie Gledhill for her thoughts on neolithic pottery; Robin Ruffell and Margaret Hunt for reading the manuscript and suggesting changes that, we hope, have made the book more readable; Andrew Wheatcroft at Routledge for editorial work on the book and for his enthusiastic encouragement.

I should also like to thank Dr Allan Thompson of the Institute of Archaeology in London for coming down to Sussex to verify the chalk object I discovered on Combe Hill as an authentic neolithic carving, and for a very stimulating conversation about excavations in Sussex.

I owe a particular debt to Sir Harry Godwin, who died in the summer of 1985, for his kindness and for encouraging me to press ahead with my plan to bring the secrets of the neolithic before a wider audience.

I must also thank those friends whose support and encouragement have enabled me to complete a daunting task – especially Kit Dee, for coming to Stonehenge with me on the winter solstice and to Avebury with me at dusk, when the stones seemed about to come alive and the neolithic age seemed so much closer. I have to thank Aubrey Burl for his kindness in sharing his ideas with me after the appearance of the first edition of the book, all the more since our two books – both, coincidentally, called 'The Stonehenge People' – might have seemed set to make us rivals.

The lines from 'Hurrahing in Harvest' are reproduced from *The Poems of Gerard Manley Hopkins*, edited by Gardner and MacKenzie and published by Oxford University Press for the Society of Jesus.

R. C.
Brighton, 1990

PRAYING MAN

You are a glass
Tilting at the sun

When he catches you
You are transfixed with light

You hold yourself stilly

You draw him down
Through your own transparency

You focus him
On the dark spots of the earth
And kindle his fires.

SUSAN NORTON

INTRODUCTION

CHAPTER 1

THE MYSTERIOUS MONUMENT

The mysterious monument of Stonehenge, standing
remote on a bare and boundless heath, as much
unconnected with the events of past ages as it
is with the uses of the present, carries you
back beyond all historical record into the
obscurity of a totally unknown period.

JOHN CONSTABLE, 1836

Of those great and ancient mysteries that lie at the foundation of
the British consciousness, Stonehenge is the greatest, most ancient
and most mysterious, a kind of *omphalos* or earth-navel. It has
always held a special position in our culture because a hundred
and fifty generations of people have regarded it, sometimes with
shame or resentment but more often with awe and admiration, as
the beginning of our national heritage. In one of the earliest
written records of Stonehenge, in the twelfth century, Henry of
Huntingdon named it as one of the wonders of Britain. In the
third millennium BC, when it was newly built, it was held in
similarly high regard, as we can tell from the extraordinary
concentration of neolithic monuments aggregating round it; it was
the focal point of the densest concentration of ceremonial
structures to be found anywhere in Britain and it remained the
centre of intense ritual activity for two thousand years.

Some of the ochre sarsen stones have fallen, some have been
pushed over: only five of the thirty lintels that originally crowned
the sarsen circle are still in place. As Inigo Jones observed, both
standing and fallen stones are 'exposed to the fury of all-
devouring age'. When complete, the central stone doorway or
trilithon would have been 7·8 metres (more than 25 feet) high yet,
in spite of their huge size, the stones do not dwarf the landscape of
the open chalk plain. Rather they mark off and make special a
particular place within it. The stone rings and the earth circle
round them seem to turn inwards and upwards to brood upon

some ancient secret wrapped in eternal mystery.

Since the people who made Stonehenge died and their entire culture dissolved into oblivion, succeeding generations have speculated endlessly about the purpose of the monument and the identity of its builders. In his *History of the Kings of Britain* of 1135, Geoffrey of Monmouth recounted, as a matter of historical fact, that Stonehenge was a war memorial raised at King Vortigern's command to commemorate the massacre of four hundred British chieftains by Hengist in AD 490. The prophet Merlin was brought in to build it and at his suggestion the Giants' Ring in Killaraus (possibly Kildare?) was transported to Salisbury Plain and re-erected there. Since 1135 dozens of alternative theories have been advanced, involving Belgae, Phoenicians, Danes, Romans, Minoans, Greeks, Egyptians and druids. King James I was curious about the monument and set Inigo Jones to solve the mystery. Jones wrote off the druids and their 'execrable superstition' with gusto and chose a classical origin: for him, Stonehenge was a Roman temple. Walter Charleton, writing in 1663, thought Stonehenge was a Danish parliament-house. John Aubrey (1626-97) and William Stukeley (1687-1765) were Freemasons and both successfully promoted the idea that Stonehenge was a druid temple.

Although we may smile indulgently at some of the more bizarre misconceptions of past centuries, there are still modern misconceptions – widely held – that need to be dispelled before we can unravel the secrets of the Stonehenge people. To begin with, the monument could not have been built by the druids. It was built more than a thousand years earlier by the people of an altogether different culture, although possibly the druids used it as a temple and may even have claimed deceitfully that they had built it. A very widespread misconception concerns the Heel Stone as a midsummer sunrise marker. It may come as a shock to some readers to learn that the Heel Stone did not mark the position of the midsummer sunrise at the time the monument was raised (see Chapter 9). Our view of Stonehenge also changes very significantly when we realise that its design was radically altered several times over, involving not only rebuilding but a rethinking of the mystic symbolism incorporated in the monument's architecture (see Chapter 10). The stone circle is neither the oldest nor the largest part of the monument: it is the final embellishment – a kind of summary – at the centre of a large and slowly-evolving ceremonial precinct.

But what did Stonehenge mean to the people who designed it and why were they prepared to expend so much energy in building it? Why did they build trilithons there, yet nowhere else? What was the meaning of the stone circle, a type of neolithic monument that was built at hundreds of other sites too? What was the purpose of the outlying Heel Stone? Is it possible to explore the minds of a long dead, alien people and unravel their inmost thoughts on the nature of life and death? Is it possible to discover their relationship with the spirit world and the passage of time? I believe it is possible to find answers to these and related questions, but only by looking far beyond the origins of Stonehenge itself to the origins and development of the culture that produced it.

In 7000 BC, the ice that had held the whole of Britain in its grip for seventy millennia melted finally from the highlands, to leave a gradually warming landscape sparsely peopled by hunting, fishing and gathering communities. These people of the middle stone age, or mesolithic period, scratched a living along the encroaching shoreline and among the pine and oak woods for some two thousand years before the beginning of the era that forms the focus of this book. In 4700 BC a significantly different way of life began, with tamed animals and ploughing, sowing and harvesting ensuring a reliable food supply. The mesolithic inhabitants were converted to it by unknown numbers of mysterious immigrants from the European mainland.

The lifestyle of the neolithic or new stone age included many distinctive revolutionary elements, including farming, pottery and the building of elaborate ceremonial monuments: chambered tombs, earthen barrows, earth circles and stone circles. A surprising number of these monuments have survived more or less intact to the present day, and it is largely because of this that there is so much interest now in the people of the neolithic. The tombs and stone circles in particular prove that they had a developed technology, strength of purpose and an elaborate and deeply-held system of beliefs. Most archaeologists have shaken their heads and despaired of ever understanding what was in the minds of the megalith builders, thinking that their thoughts, beliefs and aspirations were strange secrets that they carried with them into their exotic tombs long ago.

Stonehenge itself has attracted an enormous amount of interest, with some researchers, theorists and dreamers devoting decades of their lives to unravelling its secrets, mostly to little effect. The way to the truth is to try to forget Stonehenge in the first instance, to study the archaeology of other sites and to try to piece the whole culture together like a jigsaw puzzle, starting with the corners and edges and working gradually in towards the centre; the most interesting parts of the puzzle-picture come last. This is the approach I have followed, with Parts 1 and 2 of the book dealing with the material culture and Parts 3 and 4 going into the more difficult areas of social and political structure and religion; the method seems to have worked. The principal secrets of Stonehenge and the people who built it are, after all, accessible to us even though the culture came tragically to an end four thousand years ago. It is perhaps what we should have expected all along of a culture so rich in subtle allusion and metaphor. The direct question goes unanswered, yet a whole series of elliptical questions gives us the answer to the riddle, albeit an answer so startling that we can scarcely believe it.

Over the last two hundred years the preoccupation with the well-documented classical civilisations has given way to a growing interest in the mysteries of ancient Egypt, Mesopotamia and Crete. Yet there is still a popular tendency to begin the history of Britain with the Romans, even though the ruins of Stonehenge demand recognition that something very important – whatever it was – was going on here long before the Roman invasion. A prefatory remark about Stonehenge is now usually made in school textbooks as a concession to the native culture, though far from sufficient. The streams of visitors to Stonehenge find very little in the way of explanation when they arrive there and many naturally assume that it is all a matter of speculation and imagination. 'I guess they were just slaves,' said one American woman as she assessed the effort needed to raise the stones. 'They just built this and died.'

The problem is exacerbated if Stonehenge is visited in isolation or, worse still, treated as a stop between Salisbury Cathedral and Georgian Bath. The monument has a cultural context and it makes sense only when viewed in that context. One purpose of this book is to show the geographical and economic continuum within which Stonehenge and the other monuments contemporary with it were built; the monuments are far easier to understand when we see the links that connect them. Another purpose is to emphasise the people behind the monuments. Archaeologists have traditionally been preoccupied with stones and potsherds, the solid finds that have to be the starting point, and I hope it will become clear quite early in the book that all other inferences are ultimately based upon them. But now, with the 'social archaeology' of the 1980s to help us, more ambitious reconstructions may be attempted: flesh, warmth, muscle and breath can be added to re-animate the skeletons.

It is a long time since a synthesis of the neolithic culture of Britain was attempted. I think I am right in saying that *Neolithic Cultures of the British Isles* by Stuart Piggott, sometime Professor of Archaeology at Edinburgh, was both the first and the last attempt at such a synthesis – and that appeared in 1954. Piggott's excellent book displays all the concern with hard evidence that we would expect from the professional archaeologist, but unfortunately it makes rather dull reading for the layman. I hope that this attempt at a new synthesis, which is certainly overdue, will be more accessible to general readers: it is for them that this book has been written.

The timing of Piggott's book was perhaps rather unfortunate, in that radiocarbon dating was in its infancy. Piggott's assumption, which was very general at the time, was that the neolithic was quite a short period of about five hundred years. The first radiocarbon date for Stonehenge was produced during the writing of his book and he quotes it in the closing pages with evident disbelief. Since then many more radiocarbon dates have been produced and their accuracy has been improved. The recalibrated or corrected dates have been used everywhere in this book; since they are intended to represent calendar dates as closely as possible, they are followed by 'BC' rather than 'bc', which is conventionally used for uncorrected dates. The Appendix shows in table form the conversion of uncorrected to corrected dates for the neolithic period.

One very important result of the new dates is that the neolithic turns out to be much longer, a period of some 2700 years, which in itself requires that we pay closer attention to the events of the neolithic. Given the enormous span of prehistory that we are now confronting, it may be useful for the reader to have some simple subdivisions in mind from the outset. The basis of the following chronology will, I hope, become evident during the course of the book;

– 4700 BC	Mesolithic (the preceding period)
4700 – 4300 BC	Pioneer phase
4300 – 3600 BC	Early neolithic
3600 – 3200 BC	Middle neolithic
3200 – 2000 BC	Late neolithic
2000 BC –	Bronze age (the succeeding period)

Modern archaeological techniques, such as those applied so expertly by Colin Renfrew, Professor of Archaeology at Cambridge, have also yielded an enormous quantity of new information about material life styles, as well as new evidence of social and political relationships. Renfrew's work on Orkney in particular has provided several ideas that are central to this book. Toiling away in his laboratory in Cambridge and offering a chronological and ecological framework for the archaeologists has been Sir Harry Godwin, Emeritus Professor of Botany. He pioneered the technique of radiocarbon dating in Britain and supplied the date for Stonehenge that caused so much consternation in the 1950s. Although not himself an archaeologist, Godwin has made an incalculable contribution to our perception of British prehistory, not least by quadrupling the length of the neolithic.

His initiative in developing the microscopic analysis of pollen trapped in ancient peat layers also enabled him to reconstruct for us the character of the virgin forests and to trace the progress of forest clearance and agriculture.

In his active 'retirement' years, never far from the centre of things at Cambridge, Sir Harry was good enough to discuss with me some of the ideas that have found their way into this book. He was always kind and encouraging; it is a great sadness to me that I was unable to show him the book in its finished form before his unexpected death in August 1985.

These three pioneers of neolithic studies – Piggott, Renfrew and Godwin – have been supported by dozens of other worthy researchers, who have posed one of the most serious problems I have faced in writing the book. I naturally wanted to credit each and every researcher for the work he or she had done on a particular site and often a detailed discussion of the excavation would have been useful, but I realised early on that, because so many sites and so many archaeologists were involved, the book would have become clogged up with references, footnotes and discussions of archaeological technique and interpretation; it would have become unreadable. The book addresses itself specifically to the layperson who is likely to be more interested in the results of archaeology than its processes. I hope that those who seek further detail will be able to find what they need in the Chapter References at the end. I am not an archaeologist and I am not in a position to disagree with the raw archaeology of any site, although my interpretation of its implications is very often different from that of its excavator. In reconstructing the prehistory of the era, we want to go well beyond the purely concrete and material aspects of the culture to reach the economic, social, political and religious aspects. It is in this difference of emphasis that the prehistorian parts company with the archaeologist.

Another problem has been the amount of available data, which is now enormous. In order to reduce the scale of the problem and also in an attempt to achieve objectivity, I initially collated all the evidence I could find on a particular cultural area, such as the disposal of the dead, and wrote an essay synthesising it. Only after I had completed the whole sequence of separate essays did I start to look for links among them to check for compatibility and consistency. What surprised me more than almost anything else was that there were very few inconsistencies and contradictions, and even those turned out to be more apparent than real. This encouraged me to think that the synthesis is very close to the reality. I found that, working on individual essays, the limited field of view gave me a rather two-dimensional picture but, once the essays were juxtaposed and the links connecting them became apparent, the whole matrix of ideas developed a third dimension and sprang into relief. I hope that, while journeying through the book, readers will have the same exciting sensation and that by the end they will have acquired, as I did, a very real sense of a living people and a culture brought back to life.

My own journey began a long time ago when, in the mid-1960s, I went into the Newgrange passage grave in Ireland with Professor Michael O'Kelly. I understood little of what I saw then, but the carved spirals inscribed on the stones seemed, in spite of the vertiginous remoteness and strangeness of the carvers, to be trying to tell me something. O'Kelly, who was at that time in the middle of excavating the monument, was intensely excited by his discoveries and I felt when we were standing on the Hill of Tara later that day, and his leprechaun eyes danced distractedly round the wide horizon, that his thoughts were far away in time and space: he was in the fairy mound, the Mansion of Oengus, the Youthful Hero, and re-living the mystic lives of men who had been dead five thousand years; he was seeing in his mind's eye the old kingdoms as they were long before the Celts.

No books existed then to explain why the passage grave was built or to bring alive the people who made it and the other monuments of the same period, and I was anxious to know more. This book is for people, like that nineteen-year-old youth, who need a mental picture of those two-and-a-half thousand years of lost history and who want to understand what was in the hearts of the Stonehenge people. There is an entire lost heritage waiting to be regained.

PART 1

SETTLEMENT AND AGRICULTURE

CHAPTER 2

HERE IN THIS MAGIC WOOD

Behold! This is the announcement of much to do:
To invoke Tu, Tu of the outer space,
Tu, eater of people.
Streamer! Streamer for us, streamer for the gods,
Streamer that protects the back, that protects the front.
The interior was void: the interior was empty.
Let fertility appear and spread to the hills.
Grant the smell of food, a portion of fatness,
A breeze that calls for fermentation.

Polynesian first fruits feast

When we reconstruct in our mind's eye the virgin forest that stretched from one end of Britain to the other at the beginning of the neolithic, we have a measure of the magnitude of the neolithic enterprise. Little else, after all, could be done until substantial areas of the forest had been cleared. When the great forest developed, Britain was a moister and a warmer land, warmer than today by two degrees Celsius. The temperature had risen gradually since the end of the Ice Age some two thousand years before and cold-tolerant trees like the pine were in retreat, making way for warmth-loving deciduous species. The pine had virtually disappeared in England and only remained as a major element in the forests of the eastern Scottish Highlands, where as many as 40 per cent of the trees were pines. The birch too was in retreat and only made an important constituent of the forests in the northern half of Britain (Figure 1).

Huge tracts were mantled by deciduous forest and there were few open spaces to attract colonists. Above 750 metres there were patches of high, montane grassland; unstable land surfaces like screes were without vegetation; limestone areas such as Upper Teesdale were sparsely vegetated with low-growing herbs. Apart from these limited and unattractive areas, the only two kinds of open habitat remaining were the coastline and the lower slopes of the valley sides. These ecological boundaries were magnets to pioneer settlers as little work was needed to clear sites for houses and gardens and on each side there were contrasting habitats offering a variety of foodstuffs.

There were some pure oakwoods but in most places the forest was a complex mosaic of deciduous trees, with oaks, elms, alders and limes making a canopy and hazels composing the understorey. Limes, which are warmth-loving, were confined to southern

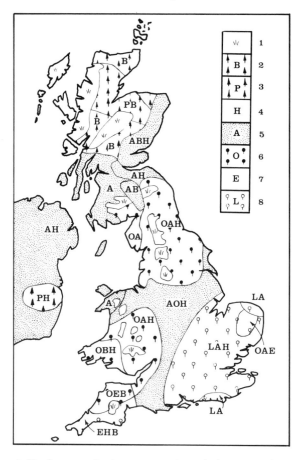

1 The forest: predominant tree species at the beginning of the neolithic.

1 montane grassland and open shrubland	4 hazel
	5 alder
2 birch	6 oak
3 pine	7 elm
	8 lime.

Where two or three letters are shown, they are arranged in order of precedence, the first indicating the dominant species

Britain, where they accounted for as many as one-tenth of the forest trees.

As the pioneers trekked through the forest searching for suitable areas to clear, they would have seen significant variations from region to region. The oakwoods of the Midland claylands were much denser than the oak-hazel woodlands of the chalklands of Dorset. Pine-birch forests covered the north-eastern highlands of Scotland. On the exposed, windswept, salt-sprayed islands of the far north there was a shrubland of birch, willow and hazel with a ling field layer; Orkney seems never to have held a true woodland cover, although isolated yews, oaks and hawthorns managed to gain a foothold. By contrast, the oak-alder forests of East Anglia had many elms and birches in it, as well as a few limes and pines, making a dense, closed forest with a poor field layer under its deep shade.

In the early neolithic, the Fens were dry enough to support an oak forest, but as the ground became more waterlogged the vegetation thinned out into a tract of sedge fen with a light canopy of alder, birch and sallow. Similar vegetation was found in the Somerset Levels, the lowlands flanking the Humber and Firth of Forth, and numerous other ill-drained sites.

In the south-west there was mixed oak forest everywhere except on the high moors. There, on the flat summits, blanket-peat formed, with only cotton-grass and sphagnum moss growing. Blanket-peat formed in the other mountain areas too, wherever

Plate 1 The primeval oakwood. Much of Britain looked like this at the beginning of the neolithic

there were level surfaces higher than about 360 metres. On sloping ground the forest went on up to at least 750 metres and at the outset even the flatter raised bog areas were covered by alderwoods.

In spite of all these variations, the early neolithic forest was more continuous and more homogeneous than it was ever to be in later times. Although there were local changes in its composition and quite important differences in density, the forest when seen from a high mountain top would have appeared uniform and virtually continuous, with far less distinction between highland and lowland zones than we can see today. It is said that a squirrel could have crossed the country from one side to the other without ever setting foot on the ground, so continuous was the canopy. The forest smothered Britain like a vast green sea; as it existed in 5000 BC it presented a formidable challenge to the earliest neolithic farming communities.

FARMING IN THE PIONEER PHASE

When the first settlers arrived in about 4700 BC, they chose the easier, open sites. In the following phase of prospection, they assessed and then exploited the environment with a blend of mesolithic and neolithic techniques. The open, ecological boundary zones offered wide possibilities for hunting, fowling, fishing and gathering. At the same time, small garden-like plots were opened up in the lighter woodland for cultivation. A temporary clearance was made by felling and burning, followed by a few years of crop cultivation. After that the soil was exhausted and crop yields sank so low that the forest was allowed to regenerate. As each clearing was abandoned, it was overgrown first by grasses and weeds, then by bracken and small trees such as birch or hazel, and finally by tall trees. The sequence was repeated endlessly as the pioneers moved on through the forest to make one new clearing after another.

The pioneer phase as we see it here is close to the traditional view of neolithic farming as a whole; small, primitive groups scratching a precarious living in clearings in a vast primeval forest. The land clearance in the lowlands of Cumbria involved several successive temporary clearance episodes, reminiscent of the 'slash-and-burn' techniques of present-day tropical cultivators. Similarly, at Llyn Mire in the Wye valley there were at least two phases of cereal cultivation followed by soil exhaustion and woodland regeneration in only twenty years.

THE EARLY NEOLITHIC

During the next phase, beginning in about 4300 BC and continuing until about 3500 BC, forest clearance was on a larger scale and of longer duration. A Danish experiment in forest clearance followed by cereal cultivation showed that the yield of emmer wheat fell rapidly; by the third year, cultivation was no longer worthwhile. This suggests that the pioneer clearance episodes were very short. The later clearances were more substantial. Several places in East Anglia, such as Hockham Mere and Seamere, give evidence of a landscape kept open for up to three hundred years. At Hockham Mere where the soils are light and friable the initial clearance was in 3770 BC: by 3450 BC the forest had closed in again to remain untouched, apparently, for another four hundred years. The forest covering the Wessex chalklands was opened up for cultivation in much the same way. The pollen and snail record at several Wessex monuments shows that the forest was cleared and then cultivated; after that there was often a change of land use from cultivation to pasture. The same record of clearance is repeated at site after site and by 3500 BC large tracts of chalk hill country were open.

The clearance may have been done with stone axes mounted in wooden hafts. We know from modern experiments in Denmark that three men can clear 500 square metres of forest in four hours using polished flint axes; working for a week, they can make a substantial clearing of about a hectare. Even so, a good deal of sweated labour is involved and the neolithic farmers may not have been in such a hurry. Tree-ringing could have been used instead; left for a year until they had died and dried out, the trees could then have been destroyed by firing. Alternatively, or in addition, livestock could be used. If turned into a woodland in sufficient numbers, cattle can destroy it by trampling the seedlings. This method would take much longer, as it would only prevent the forest from regenerating: the existing trees would be relatively undamaged. It is possible that the man-made clearings gradually expanded because of this type of interference.

We know that fire was used to clear some sites, such as the pinewoods of Great Langdale in Cumbria and Ben Eighe. In a gravel pit at Ecton in Northamptonshire I have seen charred tree trunks 30 centimetres and more in diameter preserved horizontally in neolithic peat layers. The blackened, crazed tree trunks are clear proof of forest clearance by fire on the gravel floodplain of the River Nene; the clearance was right beside a neolithic occupation site and almost certainly contemporary with it.

The chalk uplands of southern and eastern England were among the first areas to attract farmers, because the soils were light and easy to manage with simple implements and also because they were loessic and very fertile. Much has been made in the past of the chalklands as a focus for neolithic agriculture, but a wide range of landscapes was brought into the economy. The calcareous uplands of the Cotswolds were used for pasture and cultivation. The heavy soils of the lowlands round Bath produced wheat. In Wales there was pastoral activity on upland sites while cereals were grown in the Wye valley. The lowlands surrounding the Lake District produced cereals while the forested lakeland valleys were used for collecting leaves for fodder, and temporary clearance of oakwoods, e.g. in Ennerdale between 4000 and 3400 BC, may have provided summer grazing. Why the higher pine and birch woods in the Great Langdale area were cleared by firing in 4600 and 3460 BC is not at all clear. The gritstone moors of the Pennines were cleared in a small way for summer grazing on the Nidderdale Moors near Ripon and also to the west of Sheffield, presumably by transhumant farmers based on the lowlands to the east.

Most of the farmers were based in the lowlands. Detailed studies of Orkney and Penwith show that at one site after another the megalithic tombs stand just above and overlook a patch of fertile arable land. Even though commanding hillside and hilltop sites were often chosen for the monuments, they marked the upper margins of the farming territory, the wilderness edge.

There was a flurry of activity in the Midlands too. Far from remaining a huge and intractable expanse of continuous oak-alder forest, the Midlands had a substantial farming population exploiting the easily managed and fertile soils of the terraces along the sides of the major valleys. In East Anglia, away from the western chalklands, the farmers again focussed on the low, flat, fertile terrain of the river terraces, such as Eaton Heath on a low terrace of the River Yare. The claylands of East Anglia seem to have been left alone; Buckenham Mere, only 10 miles east of Hockham Mere but on heavy clay, was left forested until the bronze age.

Large areas of forest were left untouched right through the neolithic in North Yorkshire, East Durham, the claylands of East Anglia and the Midlands, the New Forest and probably the Vales of Kent and Sussex. The abundance of game for hunting shows that forest was widespread. Yet by 4000 BC there were already countless small clearings, many of them temporary but an increasing number permanent. By 3500 BC much of the chalkland of southern and eastern England was open, while much of the rest of Britain was a mosaic of clearings for cultivation and pasture, open woodland, closed forest, montane grassland, fen and raised bog.

The apparent contrast between south and north is slightly puzzling. Far more land remained open, though not necessarily under cultivation, in southern Britain than in the north. It may be that the chalkland pastures were easy to turn over to sheep and cattle, whose grazing would have maintained a permanent grassland over wide areas. But why was this not happening, as far as we can judge, in northern Britain? Maybe the population density and thus the food requirements were greater in the south. Maybe the gently undulating plateaux that make up most of the chalk country made better livestock ranching terrain than anything that could be found in the highland zone. More likely it was both, a result of population pressure and natural advantages inherent in the landscape.

Generally, farmers did not clear level ground as this could raise the water table and lead to the formation of bogs. This shows an awareness of environmental processes surprising at such an early date. Although some have argued that neolithic people were partly responsible for the formation of raised bogs, there is no real evidence that they were. In some areas peat was forming in the uplands well before the neolithic, whilst in Northern Ireland it was developing in the bronze age; it really seems unrelated to culture.

Clearance in northern England was not so extensive as in southern England, and here too there was a concentration on the lighter calcareous soils. In East Yorkshire, barrows and settlements cluster on the alkaline soils of the Tabular Hills and Yorkshire Wolds, avoiding the clay and sandstone areas. In Cumbria, clearance focussed on the coastal lowlands, while the mountainous interior was left largely uncleared, though used for fodder-gathering, hunting and axe factories.

As yet there is little evidence for clearance in Scotland. At Pitnacree in the Tay valley, the forest seems to have been cleared when the barrow was built, in 4080 BC. The same thing happened at Dalladies in Kincardineshire five hundred years later. The distribution of the Scottish tombs, very close to the present upper limit of arable farming, suggests once again that farmers were selecting the warmer and more fertile lower slopes. The idea that chambered tombs and earthen long barrows should command the farmed territory from its upper boundary seems to have been widespread.

On Orkney, land clearance phases of the pioneer type did not occur; trees were never dominant and once cleared the islands seem to have remained open. Farmers selected the lower slopes for agriculture, areas coinciding broadly with those in use at the present day for arable farming. On both Rousay and Mainland Orkney, each farming territory was overlooked by its own territorial chambered tomb standing on slightly higher ground.

CROPS AND LIVESTOCK

In some areas, pasture for livestock grazing was established very early on, perhaps immediately after clearance, but the farmers' first priority was to grow cereals, which are known from as early as 4200 BC at Hembury in Devon. The main cereals were emmer wheat, naked six-row barley and hulled six-row barley: all three were common in neolithic Europe generally. Some farmers were growing einkorn wheat and club wheat, and their fields were dotted with knotweed, chickweed, bindweed and burdock. Flax may have been grown for its seeds, which could be pressed for linseed oil, or its fibres, which could be used to make linen. So far, no trace has been found of any vegetables and it may be that this area of the diet was filled by gathered food such as blackberries, barberries, sloes, crab apples, haws and hazel nuts.

Fields on the lower slopes were generally used for extended periods of cultivation, whilst those at higher altitudes deteriorated quite quickly and sustained only short-term cultivation. The Danish pioneer clearance experiment showed that only three consecutive years of cropping emmer wheat were needed to reduce a field to low fertility. Since the temporary clearances lasted ten times as long, some form of land mangement was probably employed, perhaps a system of fallowing, with wheat sown only in alternate years. In addition, farmers are known to have used manuring. At the Links of Noltland on Westray, Orkney, both animal manure and composted domestic refuse were deliberately spread on cultivated land as fertiliser.

Farmers prepared the ground for cereals with an ard drawn by an ox or a pair of oxen, as shown in Italian rock engravings. The ard looked something like a primitive plough, but with no mould-board so that the ground was broken up with a hoeing action. The earliest ards may have been crook-ards, with the beam and share in one angled piece of wood. To the rear end of the beam, the ard-maker attached a stilt, a forked timber that enabled the ardman to guide the ard. He also fitted replaceable stone ardshares to the toe, some of them double-pointed so that they could be turned round when they were worn out.

As the ardman walked slowly back and forth across the field, he took care that his parallel furrows were no closer than 30 centimetres or else the share slipped sideways into the previous furrow. Often he took the ard back along the same furrow deliberately to improve the break-up of the soil, but it was in any case necessary to cross-ard a second set of furrows at right angles to the initial set to finish the job well. The furrows are asymmetrical, showing that the ardman tilted his stilt at 10 or 15 degrees to make the soil turn over. Even heavy soils could be arded; old assumptions about neolithic farmers being confined to the lightest soils can be discarded, as claylands were certainly cleared and ploughed. The evidence of cross-arding is very widespread, from Skaill on Orkney to Carrawburgh in the Tyne valley and Rudgeway near Bristol.

Harvesters painstakingly reaped the cereal crop with little flint sickles. Occasionally they used very fine, large curved sickles and the one found at Chelsea is a masterly piece of craftsmanship. The grain was later ground on saucer-shaped querns with a stone grain rubber; it was milled with a circular movement, rather as in a pestle and mortar. The saucer querns gave way in the late neolithic to saddle-shaped querns, in which the rubber was pushed backwards and forwards.

Mixed farming was the norm right from the beginning and as the period wore on livestock became more important. Once a clearing was made over to pasture it was impossible to break it up with ards to return it to cultivation. The turf had first to be stripped off using wooden turf spades (Figure 28c), which meant a lot of extra work. Farmers must often have been tempted to leave the pasture alone. On the other hand, turf frequently was removed, presumably for the purpose of returning to cultivation. The turves were used for house- and barrow-building, so when pasture was restored to crop production there was a by-product, but additional work was needed to achieve this and much will have depended on local conditions and human choice. If, for instance, there was a convenient area of untouched forest nearby, the group may well have decided to clear that for cultivation rather than retrieve the old land under pasture.

Large areas of the chalkland had been turned into pasture by 3500 BC. Once farmers had turned sufficient numbers of cattle onto the land, they could have maintained the grassland indefinitely. Sheep were easier still to farm extensively in this way and, although cattle remained the most important type of livestock, sheep numbers increased slightly in the later neolithic.

The use of turves in building the Lambourn long barrow shows that pasture was established in the Berkshire Downs as early as 4250 BC. The little farmstead at Bishopstone in Sussex was sustained in 3220 BC by cereal farming and later by pastoral farming. The increasing area under pasture does not mean that the area under arable was declining; the focus of arable farming shifted continually as old land became exhausted and new land was taken in from the forest. The pattern in southern England seems to have been an altitudinal shift, from middle slopes down to foot slopes, from hill country out into lowland. The shift of emphasis (see Chapter 4) from generally hilltop and hillside locations for causewayed enclosures to generally lower locations for the later neolithic henges fits in well with this shift in the arable areas. So we can assume that the area of land under crop production was at least maintained and may have increased slightly in absolute terms. But the proportion of the landscape under pasture went on increasing.

The emphasis on pig-rearing at Durrington Walls – an exceptional site in so many ways – is puzzling. It may point to the existence of extensive woodlands near Durrington since woodland was needed for pannage, or it may mean that eating pork held some significance; certainly pigs were unpopular nearly every-where else. They were not unlike wild boar and it is possible that the two were crossed inadvertently when domestic pigs were left to run with wild boar while foraging in the forest. They may alternatively have been crossed deliberately to increase the strength of the domestic stock. The animals at Durrington stood 70 centimetres high at the shoulder and were smaller and longer in the snout than modern pigs.

Far and away the most important animals in terms of numbers were the cattle. The breed the early stockmen favoured was a large beast, *Bos frontosus*, with long horns and fairly close to the wild *Bos primigenius* that still roamed, fearsome, through the forest. The stockmen evidently did not regard overwintering the stock as a problem as they kept many of their animals through two winters before slaughtering them by pole-axing. They slaughtered them as they reached maturity, showing that they were keeping them for meat not milk. Butchering seems to have been rather wasteful: in some cases only 22 per cent of the possible joints of beef were taken from carcases. At least that shows that food was plentiful.

The sheep were similar to Soay sheep or the long-tailed Drenthe heath-sheep of the Netherlands. They were small, scrawny animals and it is not surprising that the very low numbers only picked up in the late neolithic as the area of chalk pasture became very large and the quality of the turf became too poor for cattle.

There were horses, a small breed of only 12 or 13 hands, like the modern Exmoor pony, but they have usually been dismissed as 'wild'. Even so it is just possible that horses were, after all, domesticated at this early date. If so, it was probably for their meat rather than for riding or farmwork. There were already two breeds of dog at Star Carr in 8000 BC and there may have been several more breeds by the late neolithic period. At Ram's Hill and Durrington there were big dogs like Labradors, standing some 50 centimetres high at the shoulder; at other settlements there were smaller dogs like rather long-legged terriers. They were probably used for guarding, hunting, shepherding and as pets. Some dogs lived to be old, beyond their useful working lives, so their owners kept them out of affection.

It is likely that transhumance was practised in some areas, especially if population increased and the area of usable new land

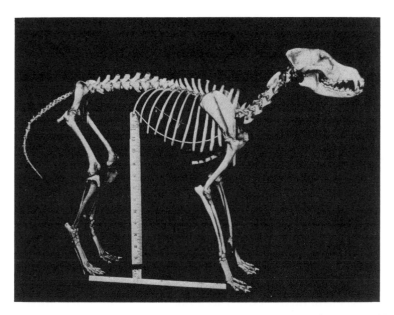

Plate 2 A little dog that lived in the earth circle at Windmill Hill in about 3300 BC

decreased during the later neolithic. The seasonal movement of cattle and sheep could have been the best way of exploiting poor, marginal lands in the mountain areas. The Pennines may have been used for summer grazing by cattle herders based in the neighbouring lowlands of Yorkshire, Lancashire and Durham. The mountains of eastern Wales could have been used in a similar way by herders based in the Severn valley. Short-distance transhumance may have been common even in lowland Britain. Stockmen wintered their cattle and sheep down on the valley floors, took them up the hillsides in spring, across the chalk and limestone hilltops in summer and back to the lower slopes again in autumn. Barker and Webley also believe that pigs were moved backwards and forwards seasonally, but this seems less likely; anyone who has tried driving a pig will know that it is to be attempted as infrequently as possible. In the Somerset Levels cattle were grazed on the north-east footslopes of the Polden Hills. These hangings were and still are very fertile and would have provided excellent summer grazing, but in winter they were flooded. So it looks as if an inverted transhumance was employed, taking the cattle up onto the higher slopes of the Poldens in winter. The heavier timber trackways across the Levels, like Abbot's Way, are thought to have been used for the seasonal movement of cattle.

THE MID-NEOLITHIC CRISIS

Before going on to discuss the economic crisis that developed in the mid-neolithic, it may be useful to discuss the possible reasons why the area under pasturage was extended, since the swing to pastoralism was an integral part of the crisis. First, as we have already seen, it was difficult to plough up established pasture with the ard: the turf had to be removed first. Second, there were still large tracts of virgin forest that could be cleared for cultivation when old fields were exhausted. A third and more controversial view is that soil fertility ran down and, since the outcome of cultivation was proving so unsatisfactory, farmers saw livestock-rearing as a safer option. A fourth possibility is that the population was increasing, creating a greater demand for housing, some of which used turf as a raw material.

There are all sorts of assumptions implicit in these views, not all of them justified by firm evidence. One complication already hinted at is the compatibility of pastoralism, arable farming and the supply of turves. As turf is stripped from a meadow to supply building materials, the site is in effect being made ready for cultivation. Perhaps we should visualise a cycle in which cultivation gave way to a lengthy period under pasture, followed by turf-stripping and a further period of cultivation. This may account for the truncation of many neolithic soils. Another assumption that may be called into question is that population levels rose sufficiently fast to strain resources. We will return to this much larger issue later, but the concept of a mid-neolithic crisis leans heavily on assumed significant increases in the population.

A moderate view of the crisis comes from Whittle, who sees it as an economic standstill evidenced by widespread forest regeneration in about 3500 BC. Although much of southern England remained open after that time, especially on the chalk, over the country as a whole the forest was encroaching on land cleared in the early neolithic. Even on the chalk there were areas not just turned over to pasture but reverting to scrubland. Jullieberrie's Grave in Kent is an undated long barrow built in just such open scrub country. At Windmill Hill, cleared land was recolonised by woodland in 3650 BC, woodland that remained in 3300 BC when the causewayed enclosure was built. Whittle interprets this countrywide change in terms of an enlarged population that had expanded on resources that were initially rich but were now depleted. People had to adjust to declining resources.

How convincing is this? The evidence is not easy to interpret because much of it comes from special sites that are almost by definition not going to be representative of the landscape as a whole. The monuments may have been taboo places in whose vicinity certain activities such as cultivation were precluded. Alternatively, the monuments may have been built on land already cleared and regarded as exhausted. Either way, the evidence entombed in the monuments is not necessarily typical of the landscape as a whole. In any case, stagnation or reversion to scrub and woodland at the older sites does not rule out the possibility that farmers were simultaneously taking in new land from the forest elsewhere. Clearance and cultivation on lower ground could easily make good the losses on higher ground, once the farmers had the confidence to attempt the heavier soils. All the evidence from the pioneer phase, through the early neolithic and including the alleged crisis, can be seen in terms of extensive farming methods – provided that population levels were still fairly low and there was still a large untapped reserve of forest.

But the mid-neolithic crisis is an event referred to by several other archaeologists, so we ought to explore it a little further. Paul Ashbee attributes this neolithic crisis to soil impoverishment and erosion resulting from deforestation and cultivation over a long period. The farmers neither foresaw nor understood the loss of soil fertility, so they resorted inevitably to magical rites to restore fertility. Pursuing this line of thought, Ashbee sees the votive deposits of occupation debris in long barrows and enclosure ditches as symbolic manure. The long barrows were built across the chalklands as poignant appeals to some deity for improved soils. The building of the monuments is thus associated with group awareness of the ecological crisis. If Ashbee is right, the dates when the barrows were raised should coincide with the crisis period.

I looked at the radiocarbon dates for those long barrows that have been dated, and causewayed enclosures too, since Ashbee includes them, and there is indeed an increased frequency in the period 3600-3200 BC. During that time twenty-one chthonic shrines were raised, compared with nine in the preceding four hundred year period and seven in the succeeding period. So there may be something in Ashbee's argument. Even so, there is good reason to be cautious: most long barrows have yet to be dated, so the pattern is very incomplete. In addition, at least fourteen of the shrines were built before the crisis period so, although they may relate to the enterprise of agriculture and the sustenance of fertility in a very general way, they cannot convincingly be used as an argument for a particular period of crisis.

Colin Burgess uses words like 'calamity' to describe the economic changes of 3600-3200 BC, using as evidence the degradation of the soils of the Wessex chalklands and the reversion of arable to scrub or grassland. He acknowledges that the centres of cultivation had moved to the lower slopes of valleys fringing the chalklands and his idea of a growing separation and social distinction between lowland farmers and upland stockmen in the later neolithic is an extremely useful one. Where his view is inconsistent is in attributing greater power to the pastoralists than to the cultivators, when we know that the pastoralists were operating in a deteriorating habitat. The location of the great, sprawling henges in the depleted pastures is not really much good as evidence of a 'power base'; such modern concepts seem in any case out of place in the neolithic context. In many cases the new henges were located close to the original centres, the causewayed enclosures. It was natural enough in that they were associated with the tribal identity. There was a strong element of geographical inertia in the location of the later neolithic centres. The one conspicuous locational difference between the causewayed enclosures and the henges is that the henges tend to be on lower ground. That implies that so far as there was a migration of the tribal centre it was down towards the lands of the cultivators. It tells us that the cultivators and pastoralists remained integrated in one society and the cultivators still had pull.

Burgess assumes that population growth outstripped agricultural resources, but his estimate for the population of Britain in 2000 BC is 500,000. This is substantially higher than other estimates, such as 2,000 for England and Wales from Atkinson, 200,000 from Green and something between 10,000 and 100,000 from Fowler. Burgess is assuming that there was a natural increase in the population, an excess of births over deaths, of 0·6 per cent per year right through the prehistoric period. He argues that in a thousand years a small group of initial immigrants would multiply, at that rate, to some 10 million or so; therefore self-adjustment in the form of famine, war or pestilence must supervene. As we now know that the neolithic was a very long period, we must assume that catastrophes of this kind occurred and kept the population down. The grassland phase is seen as an attempt to evade the disaster, an act of desperation that failed, since even the pasture ultimately reverted to forest in many places.

Possibly the strongest argument against Burgess's extreme view of the crisis period is the absence of any evidence of social or religious upheaval. There does not seem to have been any increase in territoriality, defensive or aggressive fortifications, or warfare. There is no sign of religious hysteria in new types of fertility monument or more extravagant forms of existing monument. His initial assumption that population was increasing at 0·6 per cent per year may well be false. The age structure of the population was very youthful and life expectancy low. Population growth may have been very low indeed, perhaps only 0·1 per cent per year. If so, a group of 500 immigrants arriving in Britain in 4700 BC would only have trebled in number by 3500 BC and by 2000

BC they would still have numbered only 7500.

It looks very much as though the Burgess-Ashbee picture of an agricultural economy in a state of collapse is too lurid. There is nevertheless evidence of soil truncation, soil depletion and podsolisation. Farmers in this critical phase were learning that pastures as well as arable fields can eventually lose their fertility and that new techniques of land management would need to be developed. We should regard the crisis as a phase of growing self-awareness in the farming communities. Farmers came to realise that they would need to husband their resources if food supplies were to continue. It was a coming-to-terms, not a calamity.

LATE NEOLITHIC RECOVERY

From 3200 BC onwards, new techniques were adopted. It was easy to pull back from the brink of ecological disaster because the population density was still very low by modern standards. The major environmental change that marks the start of our late neolithic recovery phase was the abrupt drop in the level of elm pollen, not just in Britain but across the whole of Europe. Initially, it seemed to Harry Godwin that a change in climate must be responsible for a such a widespread and synchronous change in vegetation, but there are no other indications of a major climatic change. Troels-Smith put forward the idea that when grazing was in short supply farmers stall-fed their livestock on nutritious elm leaves gathered in the forest. When Godwin first drew attention to the elm-decline, it was generally thought that the neolithic started relatively late and that even clearance for farming, let alone any other environmental impact of man, could not possibly have been on such a large scale at that early date. We now know that both settlement and farming were widespread and well-established in Britain and Europe by 3200 BC. The scatter of radiocarbon dates for the elm-decline has also become wide enough for Godwin himself to think man a more likely cause than climate.

The elm-decline cannot be due to forest clearance as we know that the major clearance phase was between 4300 and 3500 BC; indeed it came at a time when much of the evidence points to forest regeneration. The selection of elm in particular has made some think in terms of disease, with the recent alarming rapid spread of Dutch elm disease across Britain. Yet the idea of selective leaf-picking is very persuasive. Regular cropping could dramatically affect the number of flowers on the elms and thus the amount of pollen released. Cropping elm leaves at that time fits in well with the idea that farmers were looking for new styles of land management; farming the forest took pressure off overworked pastures. The grass and arable land meanwhile had suffered a considerable amount of damage. Rain seeping down through the poorly protected soil was washing away the soluble bases and leaving the soil more acid. The leaching process happens without any help from man in fast-draining sandy soils, where the effect is to return acid-tolerant species to dominance, in other words, birches, pines and ling become commoner. The clearance of the forest accelerated this process and from 3000 BC onwards there was more birch and ling. But we must not blame the farmers entirely. There is evidence that in the last interglacial, a hundred thousand years ago, there was progressive leaching and a deterioration in the vegetation without any interference from man.

From 2500 BC onwards the environment became wetter and this too had an effect on the decisions made by the late neolithic farmers. The wetness caused blanket-bogs to form across wide areas on the high moorlands. Wetter conditions on the uplands and lowlands encouraged farmers to go in for stock-raising rather than crops, reinforcing the trend towards livestock farming.

Another aspect of the new, later neolithic land management was the organisation of some of the farmland into systematic large-scale field systems. On the Nene river terrace at Fengate, stockmen laid out a network of straight ditches, probably originally with banks and hedges to control the cattle more effectively. The long parallel boundaries marked out field corridors that were sub-divided by offset ditches 50-100 metres long. The Fengate system was laid out in 2750 BC and was used for over five hundred years for highly organised cattle ranching and beef production. Similar field systems, doubtless used in a similar way, stretched away from Fengate for at least 32 kilometres along the Fenland edge.

Such large-scale, orderly field systems were probably organised only in the late neolithic, but we must not attribute too much significance to the absence of evidence from the early neolithic. The survival of ancient field boundaries is likely to be a rarity; most have been obliterated by later ploughing, by natural weathering in the uplands and by the burial of the ancient land surface on parts of the lowlands. Freak survivals of a few field systems nevertheless prove that some were laid out in the middle neolithic. The Behy-Glenulra field system in County Mayo has been preserved under blanket peat; its slightly curving stone walls built in 3220 BC enclose fields 200-350 metres long and 160 metres wide.

There are possible neolithic survivals among the so-called 'Celtic' lynchets of the southern English chalklands. A lynchet with a bronze age barrow built on top of it at Winterbourne Abbas in Dorset appears to be neolithic. The general feeling among archaeologists is that most of the lynchets are no older than early bronze age, but not so long ago the prevailing view was that they were no older than iron age. The fields at Itford Hill in

Sussex have only recently been recognised as bronze age rather than iron age. One lynchet at nearby Bishopstone has been positively proved to date from the neolithic, associated with the farmstead dated 3220 BC. Eventually, more of the 'Celtic' field systems will probably prove to be neolithic, especially those that have the 'swathe-and-offset' pattern seen at Behy-Glenulra and Fengate.

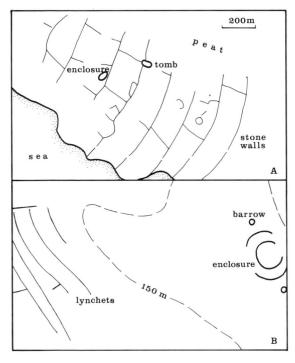

2 Field systems
A – Behy-Glenulra in County Mayo
B – Combe Hill in Sussex

Often the fields were irregular in shape. The late neolithic village at Brouster in Shetland is surrounded by farmland divided up by drystone walls. Each house had up to six fields, each field being 18-29 metres across, so that holdings were about 2500 square metres. Surface stones were carefully picked out and built into heaps. Some archaeologists are disparaging about the Brouster fields, dismissing them as mere gardens farmed by hand, but they are important in showing order and organisation even at the smallholding level. It may well be that the garden system we see at Brouster was characteristic of agriculture in the early neolithic generally.

OVERVIEW

The evolution of neolithic agriculture fell into four phases. The process began with a pioneering phase (4700-4300 BC), when the early colonists settled the fairly open sites, prospected for areas suitable for cultivation and made small temporary clearances for cereals and grazing. The second phase, the early neolithic (4300-3600 BC), saw larger clearances that were of longer duration. Mixed farming, with cereal cultivation and livestock-rearing, was normal. In the third phase, the mid-neolithic crisis (3600-3200 BC), the deleterious effects of farming on the landscape became evident. A combination of deforestation, farming practices and climatic conditions caused the soils to deteriorate physically and chemically. Over large areas, the loss of soil fertility and an increase in population of unknown scale made the farming communities reconsider their approach to land management. In the fourth and final phase, we see a late neolithic recovery (3200-2000 BC). There was a shift in emphasis away from cultivation towards pastoralism and a more intensive aproach to farming in general with, for example, experiments in fodder-gathering for livestock and large-scale field systems. With population levels rising and areas of unproductive raised bog and leached heathland increasing, farmers tended to focus on specific areas of farmland to which they applied more careful management methods. Meanwhile in the marginal lands there was something of a regression to near-mesolithic life styles. At Skara Brae people depended increasingly on the older practices of hunting, fishing and fowling. In the uplands, they made forays into the mountains where they used temporary camp sites and specialised tool kits for hunting.

Although Burgess has given us a dismal view of the mid-neolithic crisis, farmers seem to have avoided the very worst mistakes. They did not, for example, attempt to farm the high sandstone areas of the North York Moors, but used them instead for hunting. They somehow sensed that farming there would not be worthwhile; it was their successors, the farmers of the bronze age, who made the spectacular gaffe of clearing the woodland and farming it. The result was rapid leaching and the formation of the degraded, podsolised soils that are still almost completely unproductive today.

The overall picture of agriculture in Britain is one of diversity and dynamism. In England in particular farming went forward with vigorous momentum in a wide range of environments and using a wide range of soils. There were large differences in farming methods from region to region and from valley to hill within each region. It was a more varied scene than was found in

Europe, where cultural styles seem to have been homogeneous over larger distances. The greater variety was partly due to the sharp contrasts in soils and relief that are found over quite short distances in Britain. But it was also due to insularity. As with other techniques, the island people borrowed farming practices piecemeal from other cultures, combining and adapting them to suit the varying conditions of the island.

Local mesolithic practices were incorporated into the local economy where appropriate. The wooden trackways across the Somerset Levels (see Chapter 8) were constructed in the early neolithic to connect diverse habitats and facilitate the exploitation of fish, fowl, field and pasture. As the availability of fish and waterfowl fluctuated seasonally, the marsh people evolved a seasonal rhythm of alternating mesolithic hunting and neolithic farming practices to suit the local conditions. At coastal sites, fishing was an important part of the economy. People of the highland zone developed the seasonal migrations practised by mesolithic communities into transhumance, with stockmen taking herds of cattle and flocks of sheep up into mountain pastures for summer grazing. Everywhere, hunting and gathering contributed something to the economy.

Agriculture was not a doctrinaire technique imposed by bigoted incomers, but a flexible and sensitively applied technique carefully and continually modified to suit local resources. The development of agriculture in neolithic Britain shows a growing knowledge of ecology and a great capacity for learning. The willingness to learn turned the early neolithic environmental exploiter into the late neolithic environmental manager. This characteristic of the neolithic spirit transformed the mid-neolithic crisis from a potential disaster into a coming-of-age. As if by adoption, the Stonehenge people made themselves the children of the ever-fruitful earth.

CHAPTER 3

HEARTH AND HOME

Thus the Druids contented themselves to live in huts and caves, whilst they employ'd thousands of men, a whole county, to labour at these publick structures.

WILLIAM STUKELEY

The retrieving of these forgotten Things from oblivion in some sort resembles the Art of a Conjurer.

JOHN AUBREY

When we look at the wreck of Stonehenge, open now to the ravages of the weather as it always was, it seems to epitomise the traditional image of the material culture: roofless and wind-blown, frazzled by frost, sleet and beating sun. We tend to picture the people living rough, perhaps in caves, perhaps in makeshift and rickety shelters that were cramped, damp and draughty, creaking in the wind. When Curwen excavated Whitehawk camp at Brighton in the 1930s, he saw its squalid inhabitants crouching in dank, windswept ditches for shelter, living out an abject existence at the lowest imaginable level of barbarism. His view was not unlike that of John Aubrey, who described the Avebury people as 'almost as savage as the Beasts, whose Skins were their only Rayment. They were 2 or 3 degress I suppose less savage than the Americans.' But life was not so wretched. What emerges from the archaeological evidence is that people made a variety of types of houses, each carefully built, probably quite comfortable and in some instances surprisingly large.

STONE HOUSES

The most substantial remains are those of stone houses. In Devon and Cornwall there are several small stone rings, the footings of circular houses, on Dean Moor and Stannon Down, and at Rider's

Rings and Grimspound on Dartmoor there are even ruined villages. At the moment there are no firm dates for these West Country remains: they may belong to the neolithic or to the bronze age, so we must treat them with caution.

Firmer evidence of neolithic stone architecture comes from Orkney and Shetland. In 1850 a storm took the top off a high sand dune called Skara Brae on the shore of the Bay of Skaill on Mainland Orkney. It exposed an immense midden and the ruins of ten stone houses jutting out of it. The earlier houses at Skara Brae measure about 4 metres across inside, the later ones about 5 metres. Their roughly square plan with rounded corners is marked out with drystone walls rising vertically for a metre or so, then oversailing as if to minimise the roof area. The roofs are missing, though the walls of the splendidly preserved House 7 survive almost to roof height at 3 metres. There is a doorway above the entrance and an upper level passageway to provide access to it, so there is every reason to suppose that this house had an upper floor. A fallen pillar in House 7 probably supported this floor. The roof above that was probably a shallow cone of timber covered with turves. Orkney is virtually treeless today and standing timber would have been in equally short supply in the neolithic. Perhaps the villagers went beachcombing for driftwood: trunks of conifers can float from North America in the Gulf Stream. One neolithic building at Stanydale in Shetland used some 700 metres of dressed timber, so there can have been no shortage of driftwood.

3 Skara Brae. The earlier stone houses, dating to about 3100 BC, are shown black. The later houses, dating to about 2800 BC, are shown stippled. The site was abandoned 300 years later. Stone beds (b) and dressers (d) are shown

Each hut has a single doorway fitted with holes for draw-bars to secure the doors. Further protection from the weather was achieved by clustering the houses so that their doorways opened into narrow passages between them (Figure 3). At the outset the houses stood separate from one another: later the passages were given slab roofs. It is not clear why these slabs were set only 1.3 metres above the paved floor, and the entrances to chambered tombs were often built just as uncomfortably low. There is a grain of truth in the traditional explanation that people in those days were smaller, but it is clear from their skeletons (see Chapter 12) that they were not pygmies. Instead we should treat the low passage ceiling as an architectural curiosity that may help us to gain an insight into the neolithic psyche: but this is a larger question to return to later.

The high quality of the interior finish of a Skara Brae house really has to be seen to be appreciated. The close-fitting corbelled masonry flows in soft curves round the walls. Small beehive cupboards are let into the thickness of the walls and tiny keeping-places like stoups were used for storing personal belongings such as beads and charms.

The Shetland people built their houses to an oval plan and their walls are generally thicker, which may relate to the cooler climate (Figure 4). The walls of the Skara Brae house are 1 metre thick, whilst those on Shetland are up to 5 metres thick. The Shetland houses differ in lacking stone furniture; perhaps they had wooden

Plate 3 Skara Brae. The dresser, a deliberately ostentatious feature, faces the door across the big square hearth. The square tanks on each side of the dresser may have been used for storing water or shellfish

furniture that has perished. Directly opposite the doorway is a cell, usually in the form of a circular or semi-circular apse, made either by recession into the thickness of the wall or by projecting piers. The doorway is approached along a passage that is straight, slightly curved or dog-legged. Stanydale, which has a dog-leg passage, also has a curious feature shared by the Skara Brae houses, an alcove outside the door, interpreted by some as a guardroom, but possibly a dog kennel.

Some of the Shetland house-builders varied the basic ground plan into a heel shape. This design was borrowed from the plan of a local type of chambered tomb, a circular cairn with one side flattened off to make a façade. There is a significant association in Shetland between houses for the living and houses for the dead. Another variation in Shetland is the figure-of-eight plan, an enlarged form made by adding a horned forecourt (without a roof) or anteroom (with a roof) to a heel-shaped or oval house. All these houses show care and forward planning in their design. For instance, only small areas of the interior are paved and they are the areas that would suffer most wear: the doorways, connecting passages and forecourts. The absence of holes in the floor implies that stone, wooden or pottery vessels were used for storage, as we would expect from the more complete furnishings at Skara Brae.

The overall impression is that the people of Orkney and Shetland enjoyed a high level of domestic comfort. Living conditions for ordinary people were apparently at least as good

Plate 4 Skara Brae. A stone bed in House 5

as they were in medieval Britain over four thousand years later: at Skara Brae probably rather better. Euan MacKie has developed an ingenious theory that Britain was dominated by a priestly caste housed in special élite villages like Skara Brae, while other dwellings, for ordinary folk, were distinctly inferior. The evidence emerging from Orkney and Shetland, though, as more and more stone houses are discovered, is to the contrary. Even so, we must allow that over much of Britain the dwellings were not made of stone but of wood.

TIMBER AND SOD HOUSES

One of the greatest problems for archaeologists has been the prevalence of perishable materials in the main tradition of domestic architecture. Since builders preferred to use timber, thatch and turves for their houses, nothing at all remains above ground. Ploughing during later centuries has at most sites removed all traces of post-holes in the subsoil. In spite of these adverse circumstances, we are gradually building up a picture of a widespread tradition in the lowlands and uplands of rectangular timber houses constructed more stoutly than archaeologists of the 1930s would have believed, yet much lighter than the massive hyperborean stone houses. The rectangular timber house was an enduring feature of the period and may, as more case studies emerge, eventually prove to be diagnostic.

We could not expect any part of a timber house built five thousand years ago to survive, yet some timbers have been found that seem to belong to just such a house. When the planks of the timber trackways in the Somerset Levels are examined closely, holes and joints can be seen that have nothing to do with the engineering of the trackways. These planks are apparently recycled timbers from houses on the higher ground at the margins of the Levels.

The design of the timber house can be reconstructed from the pattern of surviving post-holes, which commonly shows a rectangular plan 4 or 5 metres wide and with a length varying from 5 to 9 metres. Often there was a row of posts down the centre of the house to support the ridge pole. Sometimes there were two rows of posts, presumably to support the centres of the rafters and prevent the sagging that must have led to the collapse of many other roofs. This second design also left a central aisle clear of posts: presumably beds and other furniture and equipment were pushed back into the side aisles. Often the posts were set in a 1-metre wide foundation layer of gravel set in clay, making a footing for the wattle-and-daub wall that was fixed to the vertical posts. These quite spacious and stoutly made rectangular houses were built right through the neolithic.

When the people of Fengate near Peterborough built their houses, they used a different construction method. For one such house, dated to 3700 BC, they excavated a bedding trench in a 7-metre square and then set posts vertically in it, side by side, to make a continuous wooden wall with a 2-metre wide doorway in the middle of one side. The roof was presumably supported by internal posts that may have stood on socketted stones. Projections from the walls suggest eaves that overhung by a metre or so, creating shallow verandahs at the front and back of the house.

Quite a lot of occupation sites in the lowland zone have few or no post-holes. Instead there are concentrations of hearths, tools, fragments of pottery and 'storage' pits. The use of these pits actually varied widely; some were used as ovens and kilns, others as stands for round-bottomed pots, but most were used for storing food. The pits are concentrated in south-east England, specifically south and east of the Jurassic Way, and they represent a practice that did not transfer well to the wetter and thinner soils of the north and west.

At some of these postless settlement sites the house floors can be detected as discoloured, darkened patches with concentrations of tools and broken pottery. A cluster of oval floors, each about 3 by 2.5 metres, at Honington in Suffolk can be interpreted as a hamlet of sod houses. They were defined by a low wall of turves, perhaps a metre high. Long flexible branches of alder or willow could then be stuck vertically into the turf wall and bent over in semicircular hoops to be planted in the wall opposite. Alternatively, stouter, more rigid poles could be planted diagonally into the upper course of the turf wall to make a conical roof frame. The roof frame was covered with greased skins or turves. Because all the materials used rot and the entire structure was above ground, all that is left is the enigmatically discoloured floor. The origin of the sod house is unknown, but it probably developed out of a type used by the native mesolithic people. The turves became available only after neolithic people cleared the forest and established pasture, but the superstructure could originally have been planted straight into the soil.

The sod house is the ultimate nightmare for the archaeologist yet, elusive though it is, it represents a parallel tradition to the rectangular timber house tradition and probably ran right through the neolithic period.

TIMBER ROUNDHOUSES

In the later neolithic, round timber houses made their appearance. The fairly small circles of post-holes at Meldon Bridge in

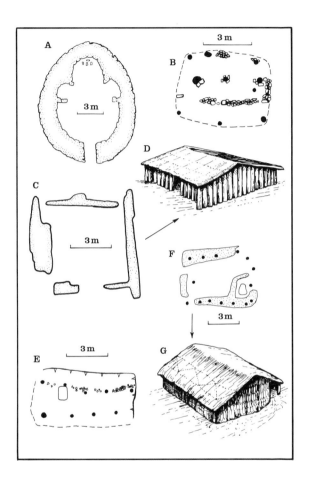

4 Family dwellings

A Plan of stone house at The Gairdie, Shetland
B Plan of wooden house with stone footings at Nottage, Glamorgan
C Plan of wooden house at Fengate, Peterborough
D Reconstruction of Fengate house
E Plan of rectangular wooden house at Clegyr Boia, Pembrokeshire
F Plan of wooden house with stone footings at Haldon, Devon
G Reconstruction of Haldon House; the walls were probably wattle-and-daub, the roof probably thatched

Peeblesshire and Thirlings in Northumberland are the remains of houses built in the same way as the rectangular timber houses but with a conical timber-framed roof covered with turf, skins or reed-thatch according to local custom. It is not yet clear where, when or how the new tradition began. It may have evolved in the middle neolithic out of the rounded plan of the sod house, which was circular, oval or square with rounded corners, but however it began the new tradition gained momentum during the late neolithic. In the third millennium BC many villages, such as Barford in Warwickshire and Willingdon in Derbyshire had both rectangular and circular houses, and by the start of the bronze age circular houses had become the norm.

There was an unusual variation among the smaller round-houses. At Grovehurst in Kent, for example, round wooden houses 4 metres across with wattle-and-daub walls were built round shallow hollows extending across the whole floor area of the house. The floor was evidently sunk 60 centimetres below the land surface to create more headroom; similar modifications are often made to sixteenth- and seventeenth-century cottages in order to make them roomier.

One of the many mysteries of the neolithic is that builders in Britain did not develop the long-standing tradition of rectangular timber houses to produce any very large structures. On the European mainland, there are many examples of large wooden longhouses often built, Fengate-style, of contiguous vertical timbers set in bedding trenches. It is strange that British buildings did not extend the rectangular house in the same way. The design of the long barrows may throw some light on the problem (see Chapter 11). The Fussell's Lodge long barrow, shown reconstructed in Figure 48, was evidently intended to look like a European-style longhouse. Even so, the visual reference may itself be an import and it does not prove that longhouses were built in Britain. As far as I know, only one timber longhouse has come to light in Britain, at Balbridie in Grampian. Remains of timber posts dating from 4000 to 3500 BC show the ground plan of a large building 25 by 14 metres with bowed end walls. This has been seen as evidence that neolithic chieftains were living in some style, like the chiefs of the dark ages, but there is no reason to suppose that the building is anything other than a communal dwelling, just like its European counterparts. The three internal walls could have been used to divide the building into four terraced houses, although the large floor area of the subdivisions (about 85 square metres) implies that even these would have been shared by two or more families.

But Balbridie seems to be a solitary example. What developed in Britain in place of a fully developed longhouse tradition? In some areas, builders took up the circular design instead and enlarged it

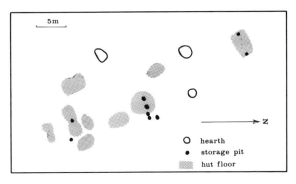

5m

O hearth
• storage pit
░ hut floor

5 Plan of a farming hamlet at Honington, Suffolk. There were probably thousands of such settlements in Britain.

– to staggering proportions. The typical house of 5 metres diameter was adequate for a small family and many prehistorians assume that any structures larger than this must have been temples or cult-houses. In fact there is every likelihood that they too were domestic buildings, designed to be used as communal dwellings in the same way as the European longhouses.

The misleadingly named Sanctuary near Avebury (Figure 29) is the site of four successive circular wooden buildings raised between 3200 and 2270 BC. The last of them was a house 12 metres in diameter surrounded by a circular wattle fence 20.5 metres in diameter that may have served as an animal pen. Sometimes it is said that the post-holes held free-standing posts, a wooden version of the stone circles, but it is more likely that the posts supported a conical thatched roof with a raised central lantern. Four of the post-pipes (casts of the original posts) slanted outwards as if forced out by the weight of a roof. The shells of freshwater molluscs may have been brought to the site accidentally in bundles of reeds carried up from the river shallows to thatch the roof.

At Marden, 11 kilometres south of the Sanctuary, lies one of the four Wessex superhenges. Inside the great enclosure and close to its north entrance stood another large roundhouse, its diameter exactly half that of the Sanctuary.

Sixteen kilometres south-south-east of Marden lies the greatest of the superhenges, the embanked and ditched enclosure of some 12 hectares called Durrington Walls. When a small part of it was excavated, the post-holes of two large roundhouses were revealed (Figure 16). The southern roundhouse at first consisted of posts arranged in four concentric rings, the largest being 23 metres across. When this structure decayed it was replaced by a six-ring building 39 metres in diameter. This very large building is thought to have been covered by a thatched timber-framed conical roof.

The centre of the roundhouse was probably open to the sky and contained a ring of carved ritual posts or totem poles. The single doorway, marked by two massive and presumably very tall doorposts, faced the south-east entrance to the henge. Inside, enormous wooden columns made of great tree trunks soared 9 metres into the gloomy roof and must have created something of the atmosphere of a medieval cathedral, with the dramatic light-well reminding us of the lantern at Ely. The interior must also have had something of the atmosphere of a circus tent. For its neolithic inhabitants, who knew nothing of cathedrals or circuses, it must have been the epitome of the great mother forest beyond the town gate, an ordered microcosm of the natural world, with a symbolic clearing at the centre letting in the slanting shafts of sunlight.

Just to the north of the huge southern roundhouse stood a smaller building. The four massive posts at its centre may have been supporting pillars for a square lantern. It has been suggested that these big rotundas may not have had simple conical roofs; instead the buildings may have been built tower-shaped, but we could speculate endlessly about the precise form of the super-structure. The sarsen circle and trilithons of Stonehenge III were raised at the same time as the Durrington Walls rotundas and only a mile away. The sheer exoticism and intellectual daring of Stonehenge must be kept in mind in any consideration of Durrington. It was the people living at Durrington who built Stonehenge as their ceremonial centre and there is little doubt that they applied the same exuberant virtuosity when they designed and built their dwellings.

Woodhenge was a third large roundhouse, built just outside the enclosure (Figure 6). It was the first to be discovered, spotted from the air by Squadron-Leader Insall in 1925. Like the other roundhouses, it was a large communal dwelling, even though it

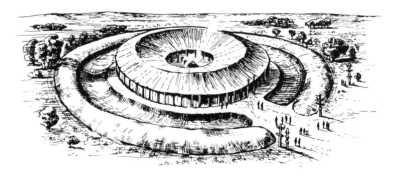

6 Woodhenge. A reconstruction of the large wooden roundhouse that stood outside the gates of Durrington Walls

has always been assumed, right from the moment of its discovery, that it was a temple precinct. Those who wish to interpret it as a temple can point to its special extramural position and to its unique plan with six elliptical post rings. But its sophisticated shape is better explained by its later date, 2340 BC, and its location can easily be attributed to overcrowding inside the henge. In the absence of any strong evidence to the contrary, we should interpret Woodhenge as a domestic building. The overspill dwelling, raised two centuries after the other roundhouses, had its own ritual ditch because it was outside the protective earth circle of the main enclosure. Its most outstanding characteristic was its enormous size – 44 metres along its main axis. It has been interpreted as a ring-shaped building with an open courtyard or impluvium in the middle; this seems quite possible, but it is curious that there are no traces of gullies or drains in the central area and some such arrangement would have been necessary to carry away rainwater.

The roundhouse at Mount Pleasant, the superhenge near Dorchester, was 37 metres in diameter and in some ways more impressive than the Durrington rotundas. Its five concentric rings of posts were divided into equal quadrants by radial corridors; the

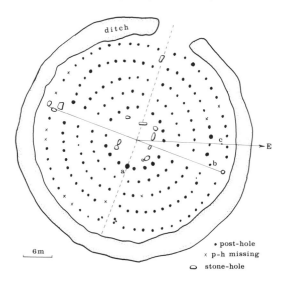

7 Plan of the large roundhouse in the Mount Pleasant superhenge. The posts were arranged in a very orderly way with the same number of posts in each quadrant, e.g. four in the innermost ring. When the building finally collapsed and decayed, it was commemorated by a cove-like sarsen setting at the centre, other stones marking the axial aisles. Additional posts, a, b and c, were probably added at this stage. Post c may have been a marker for the equinox sunrise.

north and south corridors were parallel-sided, whilst the east and west corridors had sides that were radii. The house was built in 2600 BC and when it eventually collapsed and decayed the occupation of the site was commemorated by an elaborate ritual structure. A large cove of sarsen slabs was erected in the centre, with pillars at certain points on the rotunda's perimeter, one of them marking the equinox sunrise position.

The Avebury people commemorated their Sanctuary with another stone ritual structure. After the last of the roundhouses collapsed and decayed, a circle of sarsen slabs was erected on the site. The conversion of domestic sites into ceremonial centres is not so strange if we make the analogy with ancestor worship. A father or grandfather who is treated only with secular respect in life may be reverenced in death. The same process of spiritualisation may have occurred with the tribal dwelling-places, inhabited as they were for many generations, and growing to symbolise the collective identity of the people.

TWO CONVERGING TRADITIONS

Through the long centuries of the neolithic period, people were living in dwellings that belonged to one of two pervasive traditions. One tradition was that of rectangular ridge-roofed timber houses, the other that of roughly circular sod houses. In the middle neolithic, house-builders developed this second tradition a stage further into circular timber houses, and these became commoner in the late neolithic. The average floor area of all these dwellings is about 23 square metres, quite adequate for a nuclear family.

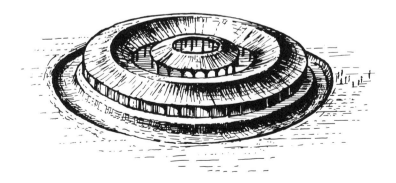

8 The Mount Pleasant roundhouse: a possible reconstruction

Out of the circular timber house tradition sprang a very special development, a group of spectacular roundhouses with a maximum size, at Woodhenge, of 44 metres across. The largest in terms of floor area were Mount Pleasant (over 1000 square metres), Durrington southern roundhouse (over 1100 square metres) and Woodhenge (over 1500 square metres). These huge structures were littered with domestic debris showing beyond question that they were dwellings. We should remember that some of the European longhouses were also very large and that they were used as communal dwellings. One of the longhouses at Sittard in Holland was 32 by 6 metres; its floor area of 192 square metres was equivalent to that of a Wessex roundhouse with a 16 metre diameter. In other words, we can point to domestic buildings on the continent that are actually larger than the roundhouse at Marden and the northern roundhouse at Durrington. Woodhenge may have housed as many as forty families if it was used exclusively for residential purposes. It is likely, though, that parts of these great buildings were set aside for special communal functions, so twenty or thirty families seems more probable.

Our fresh look at the evidence shows us, perhaps rather surprisingly, that even the major timber edifices were domestic in function. Antiquarians have understandably been swept along by the ritual preoccupations of the neolithic people, identifying too many sites as temples. Not all the buildings were used primarily for ritual by any means. There has for a long time been a popular tendency to ascribe ritual functions to sites or objects that are difficult to explain. This is unfortunate because, as this book reveals, the Stonehenge people were strongly oriented towards ritual and symbolic gestures. To add in extra, spurious ritual elements only impedes our understanding of the culture. What we glimpse in the sites discussed in this chapter is a fundamentally strong and comfortable domestic stratum on which the rest of the culture – tombs and stone circles and all – could grow: the hearths and homes of the Stonehenge people.

CHAPTER 4

THE BROKEN CIRCLE

You make the seasons for the sake of your creation,
The winter to cool us,
The summer that we may taste your heat.
You have made far skies that you may shine in them,
Your circle in its solitude looks on all that you have made,
Appearing in its glory
And gleaming both near and far.
Out of your oneness you shape a million forms –
Towns and villages,
Fields, roads and river.
All eyes salute you, bright Disc of Day.

THE PHARAOH IKHNATON, 'Hymn to Aton', c.1365 BC

SETTLEMENT IN THE EARLY NEOLITHIC

When the first European migrants sailed across the sea to colonise the island, they did not straight away mark out the magic circles of earth and stone that now epitomise their culture. Out of the sun's oneness they did indeed come eventually to shape a million forms, ringing the changes with inexhaustible virtuosity on the circle and the spiral, but important preliminaries were necessary before they could build the great disc-shaped enclosures. The island with its dense cover of forest was a daunting prospect. Small wonder that the first settlements were modest affairs close to the sea coast. There were hundreds of attractive coastal inlets, many of them long since silted up, offering them harbours for their fragile vessels and sheltered waters for fishing. Immediately behind the high water mark, the salt wind maintained an open habitat where people could walk and work without first having to clear away the woodland. In the early neolithic, following the pioneer phase, there were still many settlements on and near the coast, such as Eskmeals and Ehenside Tarn in Cumbria, the village of sod houses at Ehenside dating to 3750 BC. A mixed economy

45

based on farming and fishing persisted at many coastal home-steads into the middle neolithic too as, for instance, at Bishop-stone in Sussex (3250 BC).

Away from the coast, early neolithic farmers preferred light and well-drained soils, probably because they were only lightly wooded and therefore easy to clear. Generally, alkaline soils were chosen; in Yorkshire, the burial mounds and storage pits are concentrated on outcrops of chalk and corallian limestone. But there were many exceptions. Farmers on Anglesey, for example, were tackling heavy clay soils.

In the early stages some colonists may have used caves, but not to any significant extent. Even in the colonisation stage, neolithic man set himself higher standards of living than cave-dwelling could ever allow. Most early neolithic people lived in open stances, i.e. unenclosed homesteads or groups of dwellings, and contrary to popular beliefs many of them were on low ground. In the Midlands and East Anglia, low river terraces were settled in the valleys of the Yare (3940 BC), Nene (3700 BC) and Trent (3480 BC). Other settlements were akin to the coastal sites of the pioneer phase in that they stood at the boundaries of strongly contrasted habitats, such as Shippea Hill in Cambridgeshire (3710 BC). It is well known that there were settlements in the hills too, and even there new sites are being discovered. Open stances stood on Windmill Hill in Wiltshire in 3670 BC and Hambledon Hill in Dorset in 3500 BC, before enclosures were built on their sites.

Here and there, more detailed settlement patterns have come to light. In the Isle of Man over twenty-five individual settlements have been identified, each one a separate homestead. This complete dispersion of settlement was typical of the early neolithic. It is what we should expect, given the circumstances of a low initial population density, extensive farming methods, limited technology and friendly relations with the native people and fellow colonists.

In Yorkshire there were many farmsteads on the chalk Wolds and on the limestone area of the North York Moors, yet none that have been traced in the Vale of York. It is possible that sites await discovery there, given the pattern emerging in the Midlands, but a similar discrepancy exists in Sussex. Farmsteads or farming hamlets were spaced on average 2 kilometres apart in the east Sussex Downs (Figure 63), whereas very few are known from the low-lying Weald to the north and north-east; sites such as Playden (2200 BC) may represent a late movement down to begin to clear and farm the dense Wealden forest. Round Week on the north-eastern edge of Dartmoor there were sixteen small late neolithic open settlements, each built round a spring on a warm south-facing slope. Flint flakes and pot boilers show that tool-making and cooking went on at each farmhouse.

Dispersed open settlement seems to have been very widespread. Although the settlements mentioned so far were small, they were nevertheless fairly close together and their tools and pottery show that they were in continual contact with each other. They were also spread across a wider variety of landscapes in Britain than in Europe generally. Population densities may have been rising by the middle of the neolithic, at least in the kinder lowland zone. In the north and west of Britain, where environmental conditions were less favourable, settlement was at a lower density overall, with large empty areas between one farming community and the next.

The early pattern of small scattered farmsteads housing family groups was the dominant and prevailing pattern for over three thousand years after its inception by the neolithic pioneers. The pattern was remarkably persistent through time and space; a very similar scatter of homesteads and hamlets evolved over wide areas of the British Isles, which is surprising in view of all the local variations in economy. It seems to make little difference what the local balance was among crop-farming, livestock-rearing, fishing, hunting, mining or manufacturing – the pattern of small dispersed settlements was found almost everywhere in the early and middle neolithic.

Honington in Suffolk shows us the sort of informal collection of houses that made up a farming hamlet. There was no trace of the rigorous organisation and implied authority that lay behind the regimented layout of the typical Danubian village of mainland Europe. Another small village at Hurst Fen near Mildenhall was apparently just as informal as Honington.

The best examples of villages are the stone villages of Orkney and Shetland. Skara Brae was occupied in three phases, 3180-3160 BC, 2900-2200 BC and then sporadic reoccupation after the mysterious disaster that led to the village's abandonment. Substantial and impressive though Skara Brae is as a display of neolithic thought, technology and society, the surviving part of it probably had a population of only thirty. There is no way of knowing how much of the village has been lost to the sea. Similar stone villages existed at Rinyo, Knap of Howar and Links of Noltland in Orkney and Brouster in Shetland.

THE FIRST MAGIC CIRCLES?

Some distinctive and original landmarks began to appear early on in the woodland clearings, landmarks that were to have important repercussions on the dynamics of the culture in the later neolithic. These were large enclosures marked out by earth and stone banks and ditches. The simplest form was a discontinuous, roughly circular bank inside an even more discontinuous chain of quarry ditches. The many gaps in the ditch-rings led to the name 'causewayed enclosures'. The area enclosed in the centre varied, with a long axis as small as 75 metres (Windmill Hill) or as large as 225 metres (Barkhale); the mode was 95 to 105 metres (Trundle, Combe Hill, Whitehawk, Robin Hood's Ball, Whitesheet and Orsett). The overall size varied more because some enclosures consisted of a single bank and ditch ring (Whitesheet, Barkhale), whilst others had two (Staines), three (Windmill Hill) or even four (Whitehawk and Trundle). As a result the total area could be as small as 1 or 1.5 hectares (Combe Hill and Rybury) or as big as 8.5 hectares (Windmill Hill).

The earliest radiocarbon dates, a sequence from 4930 to 3210 BC at Abingdon, imply that the causewayed enclosures were being built right from the very beginning of the pioneering phase. The Abingdon dates may be reliable, but they do seem incredibly early; dates clustering in the period 3600-3300 BC for six other enclosures imply that that was the main phase of causewayed enclosure building.

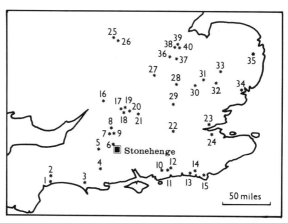

9 Causewayed (and closely related) enclosures

1 High Peak	15 Combe Hill	28 Cardington
2 Hembury	16 Crickley Hill	29 Maiden's Bower
3 Maiden Castle	17 Eastleach	30 Melbourn
4 Hambledon	18 Broadwell	31 Great Wilbraham
5 Whitesheet	19 Langford	32 Kedington
6 Robin Hood's Ball	20 Aston	33 Fornham
7 Rybury	21 Abingdon	34 Freston
8 Windmill Hill	22 Staines	35 Broome Heath
9 Knap Hill	23 Orsett	36 Southwick
10 Trundle	24 Chalk	37 Tansor
11 Barkhale	25 Mavesyn Ridware	38 Uffington
12 Bury Hill	26 Alrewas	39 Barholm
13 Whitehawk	27 Briar Hill	40 Maxey
14 Offham		

The role of these important monuments is very controversial. Gordon Childe (1940) interpreted them as fortified villages. More recent prehistorians have been dissatisfied with this view because no remains of houses were found in them and because of the large number of gaps in the alleged defences; one ditch at Whitehawk, for instance, has fifteen causeways through it. At most enclosures, there were no signs of palisades or gateposts, either. Stuart Piggott (1954) suggested they were stock enclosures, where cattle could be penned and surplus animals slaughtered each autumn. Case (1962) thought they were used for periodic fairs and ritual feasts. The apparently votive offerings of pottery and food found in the ditches led Smith (1971) to interpret the circles as cult centres.

Although some enclosures are relatively clean of domestic debris and contain only odd bones, suggesting a funerary function, others contain a lot of domestic rubbish implying at least seasonal and possibly permanent occupation. The absence of houses from an enclosure can be accounted for in several ways. The circle may have been visited only on feast days; farmers and their families could have gathered there in a temporary camp just for a few days at a time for social or religious gatherings. Alternatively, people may have been living there continuously but in sod houses that have left no trace. It is possible that, on the exposed chalk hilltop sites where weathering and erosion have lowered the surface by up to 60 centimetres in the last five thousand years, even the post-holes of quite substantial wooden houses will have been destroyed. In fact, storage pits and post-holes *are* found in some of the circles.

So, without rejecting a ritual function for the enclosures, there is every reason to suppose that settlement was the common, everyday function for most of them. Most have been only partially

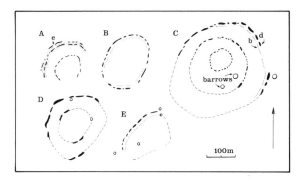

10 Plans of causewayed enclosures

A – Orsett; B – Whitesheet Hill; C – Windmill Hill; D – Robin Hood's Ball; E – Knap Hill; b – bank; d – ditch; e – entrance.

excavated, so the existence of houses in them could yet be proved. Excavation in the very large enclosure on Hambledon Hill has already revealed structures that could well have been houses. Orsett has post-holes showing that complex structures stood at the north-west entrance and just inside. The gate was an impressive free-standing monument of curving palisades, whilst the structure inside could be interpreted as an irregular rectangular house 11 by 8 metres. Orsett was unique in having a palisade set in a bedding trench as an additional barrier (Figure 11).

11 The entrance to the Orsett causewayed enclosure. This is one possible reconstruction of the entrance from a maze of post-holes

The ditches and banks of the enclosures provided them, like the more solid barrier of the Orsett palisade, with a kind of ritual protection. In fact, the design of the enclosures' boundaries makes far more sense in terms of ritual protection than any type of military defence. They were magic circles – the beginning of a long European tradition that persists down to the present day. The magic circles had to be large enough to contain all the members of the group for seasonal feasts. A few households would have been established there permanently to act as hosts, custodians and caretakers, possibly with some special functionaries such as shamans or wise men as well. We do not know how significant the size of the circle may have been. Possibly the more elaborate designs, such as Whitehawk with its four concentric rings, palisades, gateposts and outworks (Figure 12), were an expression of tribal pride. Size may relate simply to size of territory; the 2-hectare Whitesheet enclosure served a territory with only 7 long barrows in it, whilst the 8-hectare Hambledon Hill enclosure served a much larger territory with about 35 long barrows.

As a focus for tribal gatherings, the causewayed enclosure had a major function to fulfil in welding the scatter of farming families into a tribal group. It aided social integration by enabling people to exchange family news and providing opportunities for them to arrange formal contracts such as marriages. Above all, it became a symbol of the tribe's identity.

Throughout the lowlands of southern England, the causewayed enclosures were major features of the physical and social landscape. The long barrows (see Chapter 11) were more numerous and more local, corresponding to the parish churches that formed the foci of the medieval villages. The causewayed enclosures were more widely spaced and fewer in number: the nearest medieval parallel would be the cathedral. The people of the highland zone did not make enclosures as a rule, so some other monument must have served as a tribal symbol. It seems that the large chambered tombs fulfilled this function and it may explain why domestic debris is frequently found round them. Many of the chambered tombs have façades and forecourts (Chapter 11) which were arenas for ceremonies that may well have involved whole groups. We can see now why the great passage grave of Maes Howe stands in the centre of a large earth circle: it is a symbol for the identity of the tribe, with a magic ring to protect it.

The neolithic pioneers were establishing themselves all over Britain from about 4700 onwards. Yet, with the single exception of Abingdon, the causewayed enclosure did not appear until 3600 BC. This gap has not been satisfactorily explained. One explanation that has been put forward relates to the number of innovations that were under way during the pioneer phase. Whether we are considering colonists trying their skills out in a new and unfamiliar landscape or the indigenous people experimenting with new styles of living, the first few centuries were concerned with getting the fundamental living skills right. Another, separate, explanation could be that increasing population density brought people into social contact more and more frequently until a time came when they felt it was desirable to make the meetings more orderly and more formal. We could also argue that a critical density would have to be reached before sufficient numbers of people could be called together to construct such monuments. Whittle argues that lower densities in the north and west of Britain explain the absence of enclosures, but the amount of labour and organisation involved in building a chambered tomb was at least as great.

I think the delay in the building of earth circles is best explained in the following way. In the very early days of the pioneering phase, the colonists and their native 'converts' would have been too preoccupied with solving the basic problems of building a farming economy from scratch to spend time and thought on a ritual precinct. On the other hand, that does not explain the length of the delay, a period of between five hundred and a thousand years, so presumably very low population played a role. There is almost certainly a third factor, that is too often overlooked. The neolithic people were as subtle of thought and feeling as we are and we should not forget that national, regional or family groups seek different foci, different endeavours to express their identity, at different times. In western Europe, national ideals and aspirations are expressed in very different ways now from, say, two hundred or even fifty years ago. Even allowing for a slower pace of change, it is clear that the way in which group identity was expressed in the neolithic could have undergone a marked change after five hundred years.

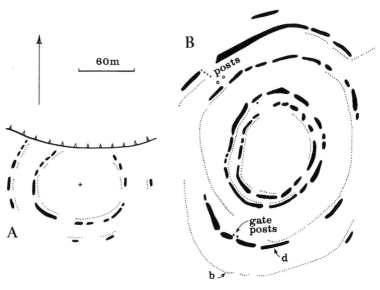

12 Plans of two Sussex causewayed enclosures

A Combe Hill, on the South Downs escarpment. The cross indicates where I found the chalk talisman shown in Figure 71c.
B Whitehawk. The posts in the north-west entrance suggest an orientation to the midsummer sunset.

Not all the early neolithic earthen enclosures were circles. Broome Heath in Norfolk was horseshoe-shaped. Part of the ditch and bank was followed by a second unit of ditch and bank. The inner bank was revetted with a timber wall and the crest of the bank topped by a palisade. It looks like a defensive work until one sees that it only half surrounded the village; it can only have had a ritual purpose. The excavators of Orsett causewayed enclosure felt that it had always been open to the south and that it had been deliberately left incomplete. If so, it may be that the c-shape was symbolic. It may be that the Arminghall monument, also in East Anglia, was a reworking of the same symbol.

HENGES

In the middle neolithic, the design of the ceremonial tribal centre was changed. The most distinctive alteration was the switching-round of the internal bank and external ditch arrangement to an external bank and internal ditch. At the same time, the ditch was turned into a more formal and continuous feature as more importance was attached to it. These 'henges', as they are called, are circular but with far fewer breaks in the perimeter than the earlier enclosures. Henges usually have only one or two diametrically opposed entrances with a flat central area, although there were as many local variations on the henge idea as there were on the causewayed enclosure. Some henges have a second ditch outside the bank and so continue the causewayed enclosure tradition. Stonehenge I (Figure 32) is a curiosity in that it has an external ditch, eight breaks in the ditch ring and six in the bank ring. It is in effect nearer to being a causewayed enclosure than a henge, so it is ironic that it has lent its name to the whole type of henge monuments. The external bank is usually taken as the main diagnostic feature of the henge.

The function of henges has been widely discussed, but there is little reason to suppose a significant change of intention accompanying the change of design. The builders reduced the number of entrances, implying that they wished to increase the ritual strength of the bounding ditch and bank. The simplification of the shape into a double circle implies that the idea of the protective power of the magic circle had come into sharper focus. But there is no reason, in the majority of henges, to suppose that the multifunctional use of the enclosure had changed. As before, the earth circle was a focus for tribal ceremonies and meetings. As before, it symbolised the identity of the tribe and its pride in that identity.

Thornborough Circles, 8 kilometres north of Ripon, are three large henges arranged in a line with a gap of 0·8 kilometres between each circle and the next. Each circle is 244 metres across with diametrically opposed entrances to north-west and south-east, each apparently leading on to the next. How this huge complex of precincts was used can really only be guessed at, but the alignment of their entrances shows they were used together in some way. The sheer size and formality of Thornborough imply that ceremony was more important there than mere settlement.

Arminghall in the Tas valley in Norfolk was a rough circle 80 metres across overall, but the small diameter inner ditch enclosed

13 The distribution of henge monuments

1 Ring of Brodgar	6 Marden
2 Stones of Stenness	7 Durrington Walls
3 Thornborough Circles	8 Mount Pleasant
4 Priddy Circles	9 Knowlton Circles
5 Avebury	10 Waulud's Bank

an area only 26 metres across, which was mostly taken up by a horseshoe setting of eight massive posts, each a metre in diameter (Figure 14). The 10-metre span would have been too large to roof, so the posts are usually interpreted as free-standing and possibly elaborately carved totem poles. But there is an alternative. The posts could easily have supported a horseshoe-shaped wall made of either horizontal timbers lashed to the uprights or hurdles coated with wattle-and-daub. Since the size of the post-holes implies very tall timbers, perhaps over 10 metres high, the structure envisaged would have looked very imposing – a tall cylindrical tower, open to the south-west. The c-shape reminds us of Broome Heath and Arminghall too may have been an occupation site. The predominantly ritual character of the site need not preclude some form of settlement if only for a handful of custodians.

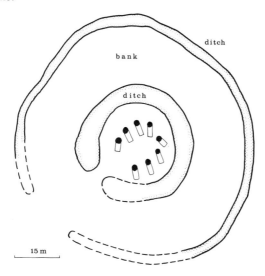

14 Plan of Arminghall, a Norfolk henge built in 3300 BC. The post-holes in the centre held large oaken posts; each hole has an access ramp

When Arminghall was excavated first, in 1935, it was thought to be a late monument, but the radiocarbon date shows that it was built in the middle neolithic, 3300 BC. Few henges have been dated and, in view of Arminghall, it is wise to concentrate on the half dozen that have been radiocarbon dated. Among these is the little-known site at Barford in Warwickshire, where there were several phases of development within the middle neolithic. The first stage consisted of an interrupted ring of pits with the excavated material piled up to form an outer bank; the discontinuous ditch shows a link with the causewayed enclosure tradition, as does a second ring of pits in the interior. At the centre was a hole that could have been for votive offerings if we wish to see the site as a straightforward ritual centre, or for storage or for a post to support a conical building if we admit that this 'proto-henge' could be a domestic occupation site.

The Barford people later dug a large continuous ditch with a single entrance outside the earlier earthworks. At the centre they raised a great post, which they afterwards burned. Again, we can interpret this as a totem pole or as a roof support for a conical sod house. In a third and final phase, between 3350 and 3000 BC, the Barford henge was further enlarged. The early date of this henge is interesting. For a long time it was thought that henges were begun in the late neolithic and developed into stone circles in the bronze age. Isobel Smith doubts whether two traditions of circular enclosures would have developed independently; she thinks it far more likely that the henge tradition evolved out of the causewayed enclosure tradition. The evidence suggests that the reality was more complex.

The causewayed enclosure tradition began in the early neolithic and in general the henge tradition took over from it in the late neolithic. Nevertheless we can point to areas like Sussex where the causewayed enclosures apparently continued in service right through to the end of the period, were not supplanted by henges, nor even modified to make them more henge-like. We can also point to the surprisingly early appearance of henges in some places. At Barford we can actually see how a monument very like a causewayed enclosure was transformed into a henge before 3300 BC. It is exactly what we should expect in a small-scale cellular society; some groups seized on a new idea immediately and rang the changes on it, while others rejected it and clung to older customs. Some took on the henge idea in a small way, building only small henges of limited variety, while others after apparently resisting change suddenly started developing the idea with great virtuosity right at the end of our period. There are huge regional and local variations (Figure 13).

Stonehenge is not, as we shall see later, in Chapters 7, 9 and 10, by any means a typical henge. Yet, however untypical it may be, it is the one henge that we simply cannot ignore because it has come to exemplify the culture. Visitors to the monument usually concentrate their attention on the great stone settings in the centre and overlook the henge proper. The stone circles and horseshoes were added at the very end of the neolithic to what had been up to that point a fairly unimpressive earth circle. The circular bank and external ditch enclosing a precinct 93 metres across were created in 3000 BC with a single entrance to the north-east. The beaded external ditch is a clear reference back to the causewayed enclosure tradition. We have no evidence for any occupation at Stonehenge I and plenty of evidence for other activities (see Chapter 9). In the later stages of development, the special non-domestic functions became so conspicuous that now nobody seriously doubts that it was anything less than a temple precinct.

This leads to an important new conclusion. Henges could evidently be used in the same multifunctional way as causewayed enclosures, but along with the greater clarity and definition of the design came a tendency towards specialism. Some were laid out as great social meeting-places, doubtless for livestock fairs, trade, political meetings, feasts and religious ceremonies, but others were designed – as Stonehenge pre-eminently was – to celebrate major calendrical events. Some were sacred precincts, but others had a secular element, albeit protected by the magical power of the earth circle.

Most henges were of a similar size to the causewayed enclosures. The average overall size of the causewayed enclosures was about 220 metres as compared with an average of 105 metres for henges. Causewayed enclosures often had two or three boundary rings with gaps of five metres or more in between, so the average size of the central precinct, within the innermost rings, was much less, about 120 metres. In other words, there was a general similarity in the dimensions of the central precincts.

THE GIANT HENGES

I have deliberately left out of these calculations the select but very important group of giant henges built in the late neolithic. Avebury is the best known of them but because it is very different from the others and its function was predominantly religious it is better dealt with separately as far as detail is concerned. Even so, its site, size and earthwork design are of the same general type as those of the three other Wessex superhenges (Figure 15). Avebury consists of a roughly circular bank with an internal ditch enclosing a huge flat precinct some 420 metres across and 11 hectares in area. The ditch and bank are impressive (Plates 12 and 13); the bank was originally 28 metres wide at the base and 6 metres high and the ditch 9 metres wide and 10 metres deep. There were four entrances dividing the circle into roughtly equal arcs. The site is a low-lying one on a broad shelf of Middle Chalk, slightly above the floodplain of the little River Kennet, which passes just to the west of the enclosure.

Marden was on an even lower-lying site in the Vale of Pewsey, next to a tributary of the River Avon: indeed the edge of the narrow floodplain forms the western boundary of the enclosure. Marden had (still has) a very large irregular oval precinct 450 by 330 metres, with entrances to the north and east. The precinct contained a large ritual mound (see Chapter 14) and at least one roundhouse (see Chapter 2).

Durrington Walls, on low ground beside the River Avon, was 480 metres across with entrances to the north-west and south-east. In a precinct of this size (10.1 hectares) there was ample space for a variety of activities. Only a narrow strip has been excavated, so we know only a small part of the precinct's original contents. The remains of the roundhouse (Chapter 2) confirm that

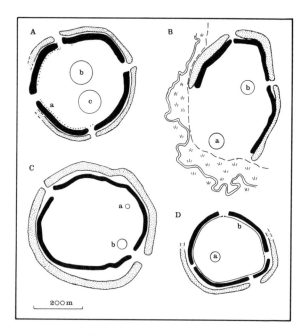

15 Plans of the Wessex superhenges

A Avebury;
   a Great Circle; b North Circle; c South Circle

B Marden (2500 BC); a low round barrow; b Hatfield
   barrow

C Durrington Walls (2500 BC); a Northern Roundhouse;
   b Southern Roundhouse

D Mount Pleasant; a roundhouse; b massive palisade raised
   in the early bronze age.

in 2500 BC Durrington was a substantial settlement. An almost
identical date, 2560 BC, came from Marden, so we know that
these two great settlements flourished at the same time. Yet the
giant henges are strangely ambiguous. Most writers have assumed
that they functioned as metropolitan centres or regional foci for
large territories and, as such, housed a ruling élite. They may be
right, but there are other possible interpretations. It is, for
example, equally possible that certain groups decided to invest
much more time, work and ingenuity in designing and building
their tribal centres. They were investing much more in a concrete
expression of their group identity, an archaic equivalent of the
Sydney Opera House. As I shall try to show later, some groups
outside Wessex, especially in the highland zone, were doing the
same but in stone instead of timber and earth.

    The location of the superhenges implies that, for Wessex at

least, the foci and therefore also the boundaries of the tribal territories did not shift very far (Figure 64). In each case the giant henge was built on a low site not far from the old causewayed enclosure, which may still have been visited out of sentiment. The Dorset Downs, once served by Maiden Castle, were now served by Mount Pleasant and Maumbury Ring. Euan MacKie suggests that the two sites represent a division of functions: that Mount Pleasant was the settlement for a theocratic élite and Maumbury Ring was the ceremonial centre. The old site was not modified because, for probably metaphysical reasons, the new henges were built on low sites close to streams. So Maiden Castle on its 130-metre summit was abandoned in favour of a site 66 metres lower and within 300 metres of the River Frome. The move was made by 2600 BC, although the henge ditch was apparently not dug until 2170 BC.

In a similar process, the early neolithic enclosure of Robin Hood's Ball with its waterless, near-summit location on Alton Down became unsuitable and was replaced by a valley floor site at Durrington, 45 metres lower and beside the Avon. As with Maiden Castle, it looks as if the original functions were divided between two sites, the purely ceremonial centre here being Stonehenge. Durrington is 5.2 kilometres and Stonehenge 4.4 kilometres from the earlier centre.

Marden in its turn replaced Rybury, 5.6 kilometres away to the north. Rybury stood on a dry hilltop at 240 metres, whilst Marden was beside a stream at 105 metres. It seems quite likely,

Plate 5 Avebury. The huge portal stones marking the south entrance of the henge

given the incredibly high level of ritual activity at Avebury only 11 kilometres distant, that local small-scale religious centres were overshadowed.

Avebury at about 155 metres beside the Kennet, succeeded Windmill Hill, 1.6 kilometres away on a 180-metre high hilltop. Avebury was the religious centre, so where was the settlement? The Kennet Avenue, a ceremonial way flanked by rows of sarsen stones, leads from the south entrance of the henge towards the answer. Two and a half kilometres away it comes to an end on Overton Hill at the Sanctuary. As we saw in Chapter 2, the Sanctuary was a communal dwelling and as such it almost certainly housed the host group acting as custodians of the henge. Where the larger numbers of people came from that would be needed to create the henge at the outset is a question that needs to be treated separately, with the larger issues of social and political organisation. One point that perhaps could be made in advance of that discussion is that the Avebury henge stands in a relatively small peninsula of chalk downland served in the early neolithic by three causewayed enclosures. If Marden replaced one, Avebury replaced the other two.

But what of the settlements? What kind of settlement was Durrington? The southern roundhouse could have housed fifty families if we assume that the average size of a dwelling was 23 square metres and that this was designed to house a family. If a family consisted of 4, 5 or 6 people, the roundhouse could have housed up to 300 people. The enclosure offers space for perhaps five more similar buildings if they were spaced out in the same way as the two that have been excavated. If we assume again that they were all residential, we arrive at a startingly high total population for the settlement of between 1200 and 1800. In practice, corridors and probably the central lanterns would have been left unoccupied to allow freedom of movement, so the figure was probably much lower than the theoretical maximum. But even if we halve it we are dealing with a very substantial township of 900 people.

The scale of the engineering works involved in digging the ditch, building the bank, felling the trees, trimming and shaping the timbers, raising the roundhouses and thatching them speaks of an industrious and well-organised community. It was apparently able to call on specialists outside the settlement to take on some of the tasks, unless all the skills were mastered by the inhabitants. Some writers, such as Euan MacKie, have been worried by this; they have thought it impossible that a farming community could undertake such large-scale works without full-time specialists. The question is closely linked with the nature of neolithic society and it is sites like Durrington Walls that will test the workability of any theoretical model we try to develop for that society (see Chapter

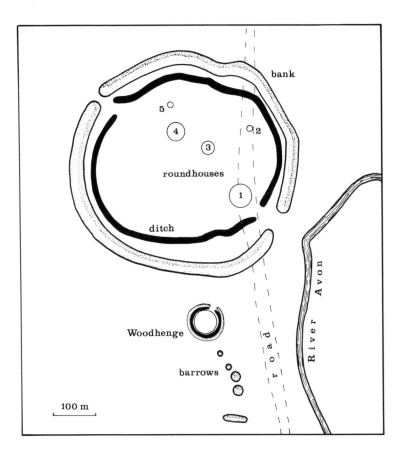

16 Durrington Walls
1 – Southern Roundhouse (excavated); its massive dipylon doorway faced the
   midwinter sunrise through the south-east entrance of the henge
2 – Northern Roundhouse (excavated)
3, 4, 5 – roundhouses detectable on air photographs, but not yet excavated
Unfortunately the re-routed road still goes through this important monument

13). For the moment, it is enough to say that we have no evidence
for interpreting Durrington as a religious centre of any kind. Conversely there is a midden behind one of the roundhouses, telling us
emphatically of its domestic function. Nor is there any reason to
regard the settlement as the power base of a theocratic sect. There
seems to be no reason to regard it as anything other than a full-
scale proto-urban settlement. The laying-out of the large enclosure in the late neolithic has been taken by some to indicate
sudden expansion and importance, but the site was already settled
to an unknown extent before the henge was built.

Plate 6 Durrington Walls. The bank along the western perimeter is well preserved. The precinct in the foreground shows no visible trace of the many timber buildings that once stood here

Sadly, the rest of England and Wales has yet to yield anything on the scale of the giant henges of Wessex with their great wooden rotundas. Two recently excavated sites in Scotland have shown that the idea nevertheless travelled far, and it may be that other comparable sites will eventually be uncovered.

Forteviot, near Perth, was a hyperborean transformation of Durrington Walls. A river cliff cut by the Water of May formed the settlement boundary to the south-west: the rest was marked by a curving palisade forming a perfectly circular enclosure 245 metres in diameter. A circular building 30 metres across stood inside whilst another of about the same size stood outside, making an interesting parallel with Woodhenge. There were also three smaller ring-ditches 10-20 metres in diameter outside the enclosure and two of small diameter inside, close to the large building. The enclosure gateway was approached from the west by a ceremonial entrance passage about 40 metres long. The general concept is similar to that underlying Durrington and it argues for a long-distance exchange of ideas interpreted in different ways according to local customs, geology and materials.

THE BREAK WITH THE CIRCLE

The L-shaped palisade erected at the larger site of Meldon Bridge in the Southern Uplands of Scotland is one stage further removed from the superhenge tradition of Wessex. Like Forteviot, Meldon Bridge was built in the late neolithic. This time a valley floor site was chosen, at the confluence of two streams that form the boundaries to the east and south. It seems entirely natural in a water-oriented mystery cult that, in the end, running water itself should be used to create the margins. The boundaries to the north and west are marked by the L-shaped palisade. Once again, the entrance is marked by a passage approach in the west wall.

Meldon Bridge introduced an important conceptual departure from the older tradition. We have seen how the circle had been used repeatedly as a symbol of unity, of wholeness, of the sun, of the earth: it was a many-sided symbol. It appears singly or twofold or threefold; it appears misshapen, as incomplete arcs or fragmented by causeways; it appears embellished by one, two or four henge entrances; it appears climactically at Stonehenge formed into a continuous stone ring, the lintels of the sarsen circle.

But at the end of the neolithic the circle tradition that evolved through the causewayed enclosures, henges and superhenges came to an end. It was replaced by a haphazard attempt at straight-sided or irregular enclosures. At Hunstanton in Norfolk the enclosure became a rectangular stockade; at Belle Tout in Sussex and Sonning in Berkshire, a rectangular bank and ditch. The break with the circle brought with it the end of the neolithic period. The transition into the bronze age was under way.

One by one the great roundhouses at Durrington Walls, abandoned and silent for a hundred years, collapsed in ruins. Ivy

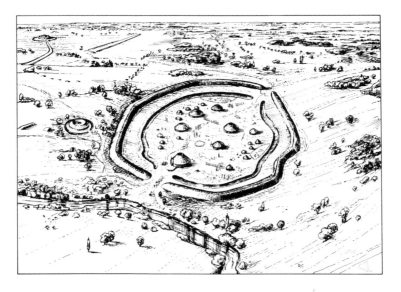

17 Durrington Walls in the later neolithic: a reconstruction. In the distance from left to centre are Stonehenge with its Avenue, the Cursus and Lesser Cursus. In the middle distance from left to centre are a long barrow, a round barrow, Woodhenge and Durrington Walls. In the foreground is the River Avon.

covered the few stout pillars remaining and the wilderness stole in to cover the hearths of the lost town. The handful of splintered stumps still standing in their sockets must have seemed like a satire on the stones of the temple that stood, magnificently complete, at Stonehenge. The town, the people and their strange, exotic way of life have all vanished almost beyond recall. But it is still just possible to visualise the excitement in the pre-dawn twilight as the whole community set off across the fields, in procession, like the figures on Keats' Grecian urn. The difference is that we know to what green altar the procession led; the people were going to celebrate the midsummer sunrise at Stonehenge and take part in ceremonies to urge the spirit of nature to bring forth a full harvest.

> Who are these coming to the sacrifice?
> To what green altar, O mysterious priest,
> Lead'st thou that heifer lowering at the skies,
> And all her silken flanks with garlands drest?
> What little town by river or sea-shore,
> Or mountain-built with peaceful citadel,
> Is emptied of its folk, this pious morn?
> And, little town, thy streets for evermore
> Will silent be; and not a soul to tell
> Why thou art desolate can e'er return.

PART 2

INDUSTRY, TECHNOLOGY AND COMMUNICATIONS

CHAPTER 5

OF THE EFFECTE OF CERTAINE STONES

Man puts his hand to the flinty rock
 and overturns mountains by the roots.
He cuts out channels in the rocks
 and his eye sees every precious thing.
He binds up the streams so they do not trickle,
 and the thing that is hid he brings forth to light.

Job 28: 9-11

Now in this present Chapter, I will speake of certaine Stones, and of their Effecte and marvellous Operations.

ALBERTUS MAGNUS, *The Second Boke: Of the Vertues of Certaine Stones*

Stone was a crucial element in the consciousness of the Stonehenge people. Their greatest monuments were virtual glorifications of the stone out of which they were made and we sense that the builders had a truly unique empathy with whatever rock they elected to use. In some instances, such as the bluestones at Stonehenge, the stone was clearly supposed to possess powerful magical properties, although it is impossible now even to speculate what those 'marvellous Operations' might have been. Often the stone provided more obvious material help, supplying the raw materials for the axes needed for land clearance, house building, fences, palisades, boat building and fuel gathering.

The flint-mining industry in Sussex began very early, indeed almost as early as the first farming communities; it was fundamental to the neolithic way of life. Mining was preceded by gathering and the most likely collecting places for surface flints were the shore platform and cliff foot where the coastline struck across chalk outcrops. The Seven Sisters represent such a site today, though any neolithic collecting place will have been eroded away: the neolithic coastline was a mile away to the south. Although there were plenty of flints along the chalk shore, many

67

were damaged by weathering and water-rolling. It cannot have been long before the collectors started looking for undamaged flints, levering them from the cliff faces where they occur in nodules or seams in the bedding planes.

It was while looking up at these chalk cliffs, I believe, that man first learned geology. Over large areas, the chalk bedding planes are either horizontal or only gently dipping and this would have been, as it still is, very clear in the natural geological sections offered by the cliffs. The applications were obvious. Once an outcrop of a good flint seam had been discovered, it could be pursued inland along the contour of the hillside and, indeed, on neighbouring hillsides at about the same height. That neolithic man understood this principle of applied geology is clearly demonstrated by his activities in the South Downs near Worthing (Figure 18).

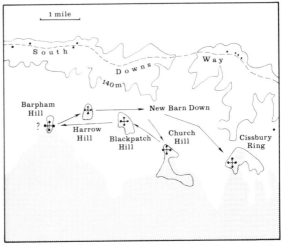

18 Flint mines near Worthing. The stippled area is the outcrop of flint-rich chalk. The arrows show the order in which the mines were worked. There was a settlement on New Barn Down. The black dots are barrows.

The shafts sunk into Church Hill were the earliest, at 4300 BC. The next hill to the west, Blackpatch Hill, came into use in 4100 BC, while the next again, Harrow Hill, was worked in 3700 BC. The little community that specialised in mining as its major sideline was based on a hamlet at New Barn Down. Rather than travel any further to the west, where there was in fact one more hill to exploit, the miners turned their attention to the east, to Cissbury on the far side of the Findon valley. The Cissbury shafts have been dated at 3500-3400 BC. The miners were following from hill to hill the flint-rich layer of chalk known to geologists as the Gonioteuthis quadrata zone, which is hard enough to create a secondary escarpment south of the main one. They were thus developing an awareness of landforms as well as geology.

The solid chalk with its primary deposits of sound flint is only found in southern and eastern England. Elsewhere, glacial deposits contain secondary flints of a poorer quality. The people living in the highland zone and the non-chalk lowlands had no direct access to good quality flint and only mined flints were suitable for crafting into the larger tools. So, when highlanders required good flint, they depended on lowlanders to supply it; this was one of the major stimuli to widespread trade in flint tools.

The technique of flint mining can be illustrated from the early pits in the South Downs. At Church Hill, each circular shaft descends vertically about 5 metres into the crumbly chalk. At the flint seam the base of the shaft flares slightly so that the working floor extends an extra metre in all directions. The bell shape is common in other mines too, where the flint seam is at 5 metres or less. At these depths it was not worth digging horizontal galleries from the foot of the shaft; the time it took a miner to reach the working face and get the flint back to the surface increased as the radial galleries lengthened. The miners thus preferred bell-pits; it was more efficient to dig a new bell-pit a few metres away in spite of the labour involved in excavating a new shaft.

At Harrow Hill the main seam is 6 metres below the surface. At this critically deeper level, the labour invested in excavating the shaft was such that galleries were considered worthwhile (Figure 19). Pit 21, for example, has seven galleries radiating from the shaft foot, some penetrating far enough to require artificial light. The miners worked by the light of little pottery lamps: the soot marks are still there on the gallery ceilings. Above, a second seam of inferior flint was followed along two additional galleries, but the shaft was made with the aim of retrieving the high-grade floorstone. Once again, the time it took the miners to reach and extract the flint became a factor in limiting the extent of the gallery system radiating from each shaft. The spacing of the shafts at 6-10 metres apart implies that a combined gallery journey of about 4 metres and shaft journey of 6 metres was an economic limit for flint extraction. This fine judgment of labour and time inputs results in the summit of Harrow Hill being peppered with over 160 shafts. Many of the radial galleries interconnect and this may have helped in the rapid transfer of flint to the surface. Miners used the worked-out galleries for storing waste rock from new galleries, saving the work involved in taking it up to the surface.

At Blackpatch Hill large numbers of shafts give an impression of large-scale industry, but each of the hilltop sites was used intermittently over several centuries. One new shaft every five

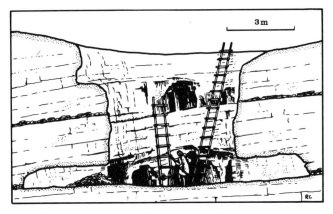

19 A flint mine on Harrow Hill. There are galleries on two levels, following two layers of flint. Unfortunately all the shafts have been back-filled, so there is at present no access

years, for example, would supply the needs of a small community like the hamlet at New Barn Down. But the large quantities of flint delivered to surrounding regions, some even to the highlands, show that the miners were not working on a subsistence level: they were deliberately and systematically over-producing, generating a surplus for gifts, barter or trade.

Cissbury has a similar number of shafts, about 100, up to 15 metres deep, with interconnecting radial galleries that were backfilled as they were exhausted. The tools that were thrown down when worn or damaged give us a good idea of the miners' technique. Deer antlers were trimmed to a single tine to produce a multi-purpose L-shaped tool, sometimes used as a light though not very effective pick. More commonly it was used as a lever: chalk and flint have naturally occurring cracks into which a pointed lever could be inserted. It could also be used as a wedge, hammered home by a second antler or, for a resistant seam, a block of chalk. The miners used their lever-picks in a variety of ways, finally hooking them under large, tabular slabs of floorstone and prising them up like loose paving stones. The waste chalk was scooped up in shallow wicker trays using tiny shovels made from ox shoulder blades fitted with antler handles. This may seem to modern eyes rather dainty and certainly inefficient, but it saved the workers' hands from undue wear and tear and the small-scale method was well-suited to the cramped conditions of the galleries.

Close beside the shafts at Church Hill and Cissbury were the tool factories, patches of open hilltop where craftsmen expertly flaked or knapped the flint to make long narrow axes. The vast quantity of waste flakes found on the ancillary flaking floor at Cissbury shows that the output of axes was very large indeed. The axes were not polished at the South Downs factories and it seems that some customers used their axes unpolished.

It was, incidentally, at Cissbury in the 1870s that Pitt-Rivers tried the first archaeological experiment. He and another man dug out one cubic yard of mine in one-and-a-half hours and deduced that a complete gallery could be excavated in twelve. He also discovered that, at least in the short term, using his bare hands was faster than using a neolithic shovel. The techniques used for excavating the flint mines were fundamentally the same as those used for quarrying the ditches of long barrows, causewayed enclosures and henges, and indeed for digging the stone-holes for Stonehenge.

The flint mines in the Worthing area are of great importance because they are clustered and because they have been excavated and dated. But there are also scattered mines elsewhere in the South Downs at Stoke Down, Lavant and Windover Hill: these have yet to be explored. There were quarries at East Horsley and Farnham in the North Downs and mines at Pitstone Hill in the Chilterns. There were few mines in the North Downs and Chilterns because there was less flint in those areas than further south; the isolated sites may have been trial pits that prospectors felt were not worth developing because there were better sources elsewhere.

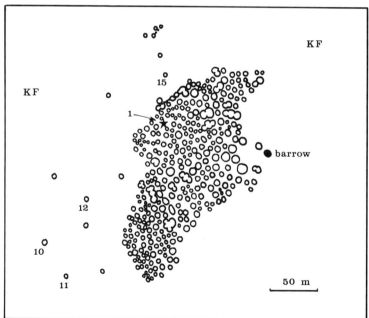

20 Grime's Graves. Shaft 1 is the only one open to the public. Near the shafts are the knapping floors (KF), where flint tools were manufactured. Grime's Graves was a major industrial centre in the late neolithic

The Cornish used beach flints, whilst in Devon fresh flint was quarried from the chalk at Beer Head and exported in a semi-manufactured state to be finished at consumer settlements such as Hazard Hill. The Devon flints were distributed by land and sea, with vessels making landfalls at Mounts Bay and Plymouth Sound. But not all the flint tools in the West Country were local: some axes were imported from Sussex. The major mining centre in the Wessex heartland, at Easton Down in Wiltshire, was opened in 3400 BC, at about the same time as Cissbury, and continued in use into the late neolithic.

By far the biggest centre of flint mining was Grime's Graves at Weeting in Norfolk, where some 700 shafts were opened over an area of 14 hectares between 2840 and 1870 BC. Because of the fractures in the chalk, the tunnel roofs would have collapsed very quickly, so each shaft and its gallery system would have been completely worked out in one season. The miners left only 2 per cent of the chalk supporting the roof and removed up to 80 per cent of the principal flint seam, adapting their methods to the geological conditions.

The sides of the chalk valley were unsuitable for adit mining, because the natural fissures in the chalk tend to gape there, making the roof of a tunnel very unsafe. The vertical shafts sunk into the hilltop are funnel-shaped because frost-shattering had weakened the upper layers of the chalk. At Grime's Graves the chalk is covered with fluvioglacial sands, so the upper slopes are quite gentle; with increasing depth, the rock strength improved

Plate 7 Grime's Graves. An industrial wasteland of the late neolithic

Plate 8 The galleries of Grime's Graves

and a steeper-sided, narrow diameter shaft was possible. In this way, the inverted bell shape was developed. At the bottom of Grime's Graves shafts, the spacing of the fractures in the chalk is at its maximum, so the size and extent of the tunnels are also at a maximum. The joint pattern allowed the miners to open up an extensive tunnel network, whilst the soft chalk allowed them to work it easily with antler tools.

The miners probably descended the shafts by means of ladders or fixed stairways. Gnaw-marks on antler picks in the galleries show that voles were trapped in the mines; without some form of ladder, the voles could not have got to the foot of the shaft alive. Rope marks on the walls show that the flint was hauled to the surface in baskets or bags on ropes.

The large scale of the industry was apparently a late neolithic feature; it clearly served more than local needs. Another late neolithic development was the total concentration on floorstone; the shafts pass through several wallstone seams to reach the best flint. Euan MacKie relates the increase in production at Grime's Graves in about 2500 BC to the building of the roundhouses in Wessex. Enormous quantities of timber were felled and trimmed to create the roundhouses and the increased demand for stone axes was met by intensified activity at Grime's Graves. We can be sure anyway that the mining industry became more concentrated and intensive in the later neolithic.

It is thought that each mine was worked by twenty men, ten toiling in the galleries and ten carrying the prized flint to the shaft and hauling it up to the surface. Probably the same men did the knapping. After the mine had produced about fifty tons of flint and was exhausted it was usually backfilled straightaway as a

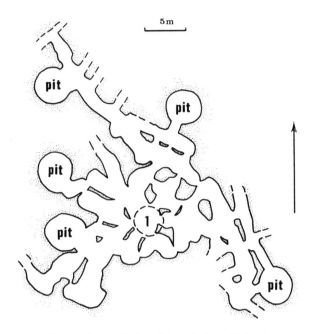

21 Grime's Graves. A plan of the galleries radiating from
Shaft 1. The interconnecting galleries enabled miners to
extract the maximum amount of flint with the minimum of
danger

safety measure, to stop livestock and children from falling down
the shafts; a young girl met her death at Cissbury in just such an
accident, and was buried where she fell.

AXE FACTORIES IN THE HIGHLANDS

In the later neolithic, there was a stepping-up of mining activity in
the highlands of Britain too, where igneous and metamorphic
rocks were quarried. At this time three axe factories became
outstandingly important. Of these, Mount's Bay, a Cornish site
that is now submerged, was probably the last to be developed, in
about 2500 BC. The others, Great Langdale in Cumbria and
Graig Lwyd in Wales, were in use right through the neolithic
(Figure 22). Some flint from the lowlands filtered through to the
highlanders, but in the main they used stone substitutes that
fractured to give a hard, sharp edge. Craftsmen at Graig Lwyd on
the slopes of Penmaenmawr Mountain made distinctive axes out
of augite, known petrologically as Group VII. Axes produced on
the spot out of stones gathered from the scree were exported far
afield, they have been found as far away as Upware in the Fens

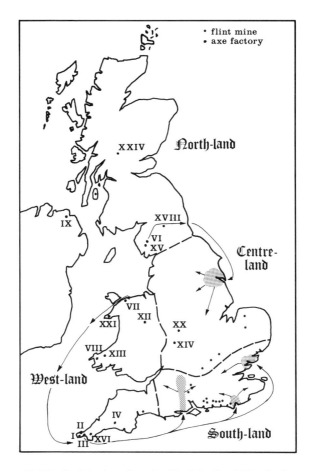

22 Distribution of axe factories. North-land and West-land were producer provinces; Centre-land and South-land were customer provinces. The stippled areas have an unusually high proportion of exotic axe-heads: at the heart of each is an importing harbour.

and Cairnpapple in West Lothian, although the main market was Wessex.

The other big axe factory, active at the same time and dated as early as 3300 BC, was Great Langdale. The main site was on the screes south of the Pike of Stickle, where loose stones of tuff and rhyolite (Group VI) were picked off the scree to make half-finished axes or rough-outs. Axes were exported over an astonishingly wide area from Clydeside to Bournemouth, but once again there was a favoured market, this time including the middle Thames valley, the Cotswolds and Avebury. Some axe rough-outs were finished and polished in Cumbria prior to export. The Low Furness-Cartmel area and the village at Ehenside in particular were tool-making sites closely linked with Great Langdale. Ehenside was settled as early as 3600 BC and may have been involved with the Langdale factory from the beginning.

There were many smaller factories using a variety of rocks, of which the best-known is the dolerite (Group XIII) mined in the Preseli Mountains. The exact location of the neolithic quarries has yet to be discovered, but we know that traders carried axes of the distinctive bluestones as far afield as Northern Ireland and Durrington Walls. The same quarries produced the consignment of bluestone monoliths commissioned for Stonehenge, the most momentous and controversial cargo in British prehistory.

Craftsmen at the little factories of St Ives and Marazion turned out the greenstone axes (Group I) that have been found at Durrington, Avebury and Stonehenge. The Cornish factories are very old and this early start in the south-west may be related to activity in Wessex and Sussex, where flint mining was under way by 4300 BC; coastwise contact and exchanges of ideas among the peoples of the south could well account for this precocity. Many of the major stone mines were closed down once metal became available for tool making, but the bluestone continued to be in demand for ceremonial objects because of its magical properties.

Few sites could produce stone suitable for making axes, scrapers and knives, yet the demand was universal. Every community from Wight to Shetland made efforts to procure the stone tools essential to its way of life. Some of the stone was carried hundreds of miles to find its market and if we can establish the way in which it travelled significant new aspects of the culture may be revealed.

THE MYSTERY OF THE STONE TRADE

One way in which these long distances may have been covered is by a large number of short-distance exchanges. The communities were segmentary, small-scale and self-organising, each small tribal territory running its own economy and its own social system, even though there seems to have been widespread cultural uniformity. In this view, the cultural landscape of the early neolithic is seen as a myriad of cellular units, each territory only a few miles across yet not dependent on any external authority or leadership (see Chapter 13). The people of each territory met their neighbours in adjacent territories to exchange goods, news and ideas. If we draw inferences from archaic societies of the present day, it seems probable that exchanges of goods or even gifts were an integral part of the maintenance of good relations with neighbouring territories. The artefacts themselves might be useful, like the stone tools, or they might be symbolic; we should keep this latter category of gift in mind when we come across objects that are obviously non-functional. The trade in stone tools was not just utilitarian, enabling communities to obtain good quality tools: it also had a valuable socio-political function in cementing friendly relations.

One difficulty in applying this cellular theory of movement to the stone axes is that there are wide swathes of countryside where axes of a particular petrological group are missing. That could be due to archaeological oversight, or to certain communities using their prized axes to destruction: many axes were broken in use and re-flaked into smaller tools. Even so, the distribution of finds (Figure 22) implies another explanation – long-distance trade by land and sea. The idea that peak production at Grime's Graves was related to peak demand in Wessex is given extra force when we realise that the two areas were connected by a ridgetop trackway following the belt of chalk country right across England (Figure 35).

The clusters of 'foreign' stone axes in East Anglia are equally revealing. There is a major concentration of highland axes at Mildenhall to the west of the Icknield Way, between the trackway and the Fenland edge. We can interpret this as the result of long-distance trade along the Icknield Way or by sea, with a landfall in the Fens, which were at that time partly flooded and formed an extension of the Wash. There is a second concentration where the Suffolk-Essex border strikes the coast. The location on the coast and up the estuaries of the Deben, Orwell, Stour and Colne can only be explained in terms of import by sea. The axes came from Cornwall, Wales, Great Langdale, Northumberland and even Ireland.

Trade between highlands and lowlands was a two-way enterprise. Flints from Sussex and Wessex were taken to Cornwall, whilst Cornish greenstone axes were brought to Wessex and Sussex from the Land's End peninsula. The traders may have used the chalk trackways or sailed along the coast. The cluster of greenstone tools at Flamborough Head could have arrived along the chalk trackway network, since the headland is at the north-eastern end of the chalk outcrop, but here an import by sea does seem the most natural interpretation. Isolated boulders of highland rocks found their way to the lowlands in the Ice Age, dumped in glacial deposits, and an unknown proportion of the stone axes could have been manufactured from these glacial erratics. Even so, there are dozens of products from known factory sites in the highlands that are found in one specific area tens or hundreds of miles away and this argues strongly for a purely human explanation.

The two theories explaining the spread of stone axes need not conflict with one another. It is quite possible that traders made long-distance journeys to deliver large consignments of axes while at the same time people were exchanging or giving one another individual tools at their territorial boundaries. The next major question, focussing again on the structure of neolithic society, concerns the status of the traders. It is possible that a few members of a farming community developed the skills to extract and shape stone into implements on a part-time basis, perhaps putting in a month's stint of mining or knapping each year. Many archaeologists think that the mines and tools show evidence of such highly developed skills that the miners and knappers must have been specialists, but it is nevertheless possible to see them as integral members of a farming community, exercising their specialised skills part-time. It is much harder to see how the long-distance traders could be other than full-time specialists, since they must have spent so long away from home.

In a segmentary society, most people would remain at home most of the time and their rare visits further afield would take them only into the neighbouring territories. With no overall authority, there would be no need for people to travel to a capital to offer tribute, nor for officials to journey to the provinces to enforce regulations. In this sort of context, now hard for us to imagine, knowledge of regional let alone national geography would have been very restricted and probably very distorted. Knowledge of long-distance trackway routes and of coast-hugging sea routes and navigation skills would have been the preserve of a specialist minority. At least that is how it appears.

The traders needed to find their way along complicated itineraries passing through lands that were, in socio-political terms, minutely subdivided. They had to carry heavy loads of stone implements without the aid of wheeled transport. They had to know where their customers were and what the likely demand would be when they reached them. That in turn implies that they carried orders for further supplies, and presumably some form of payment, back to the axe factories. Given the complexity of such an operation, it would only be workable if the journeys were undertaken by the same individuals each time. An alternative explanation is that people from the consumer communities went to the axe factories to procure their axes, taking with them both their detailed requirements and payment. This would be more efficient for the industry, but less efficient for the farming communities; it would mean that hundreds more people were travelling footloose about the country instead of contributing directly to food production. In addition, many more people would have needed a detailed geographical knowledge of Britain.

It is a great unsolved mystery. On the present evidence, the exact nature of the trading operations cannot be established. Yet perhaps we can gain an insight into the type of enterprise it may have been by looking at a modern analogue in Papua New Guinea. By the device of substituting space for time, we can sometimes gain a privileged glimpse, as through a window, of the remotest past. The Koita people, who live on the south coast near Port Moresby, trade by barter. Amongst other things, they trade in stone axes of a type remarkably similar to the British neolithic axes. Once a year, in September, specially chosen representatives used to set off after elaborate ritual preparations on the *hiri*, the great trading voyage to the Gulf of Papua. The annual voyage, established by ancient custom, took the Koita navigators on a round trip of over 360 miles. The vessels they used were rafts made of simple dugouts lashed together and powered by lobster-claw sails. On each voyage, four rafts went in convoy with various goods to exchange for ninety tons of sago.

It is quite possible that representatives of coastal communities in neolithic Britain went on similar expeditions to collect consignments of stone axes. Christchurch Harbour at the mouth of the Avon was the main importing and exporting centre for Wessex, with a route northwards following the Avon to Durrington Walls. A round trip along the coast from Christchurch to Mount's Bay, the source of the Cornish axes, is just 360 miles – about the same as the Koita's trading voyage. We can imagine that the great trading expeditions, like all the activities associated with farming, hunting, fishing and religion, were woven into the seasonal rhythm of the community's life. We can also imagine that the adventures took on a powerful spiritual significance way beyond their obvious practical value. The massive accretion of rituals, taboos and charming ceremonies that surrounded the Koita's trading voyages shows that there was far more to the *hiri* than sago.

CHAPTER 6

CLAY CIRCLES: THE FIRST POTTERY

I am always thinking about designs, even when I am doing other things and, whenever I close my eyes, I see designs in front of me. I often dream of designs and whenever I am ready the designs just come to me.

Hopi Indian potter

A lot of the pots are rather crude. Those who want to present the Stonehenge people as primitive savages can smile with satisfaction as they point derisively at their pottery. But we must remember that it was the first pottery and that it was made without the aid of a wheel. Since the wheel was only invented and used to a very limited extent in the later part of the neolithic, it is surprising that circular plans were attempted for all pots throughout the period. It is almost as if the forms the potters chose to make required and conditioned the invention of the wheel. Nowadays we take it for granted that cups, bowls and jars will be circular in plan and are intrigued when we occasionally come across different shapes, but the circle is a tradition that began in the neolithic, before the shape could be produced automatically by a wheel rotating the clay between the potter's hands.

The rounded shape was selected deliberately, possibly because it had a symbolic value, like the earth and stone circles, and probably because it imitated containers already in existence but made of other materials. Basketwork trays were an important part of the tool kit, indispensable in collecting and carrying soil and rock debris for the excavation of ditches and mines and the building of banks and barrows. Baskets of a deeper form for carrying and storing food would almost certainly have preceded the manufacture of pottery, and they are easier to make into rounded forms than straight-sided. Even the decoration of some of the pottery seems to imitate the texture of basketwork (Figure 25). Before the invention of pottery, liquids were contained in leather bags, like biblical wine-skins; when filled, they swelled into rounded shapes. Again, some of the pottery decoration imitates the perforations near the neck that were needed to secure and hang up a leather bag.

We have no way of knowing whether the manufacture of pottery was an exclusively male or exclusively female preserve: perhaps both women and men participated in it. The potter's craft was a simple one. He or she kneaded the clay to soften it and make it workable, then pressed it into the flat pieces from which the base and sides were assembled. When the general shape of the pot was complete, the seams between the patches were smoothed off and obliterated by patting the walls between fingers or knuckles. Often the potter wet his or her hands to finish the

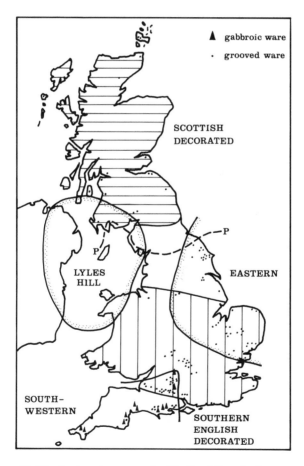

23 Distribution of pottery styles. The line P-P marks the northern limit of Peterborough ware

surface and give it a fine, smooth, leathery feel. Sometimes crushed volcanic rocks were mixed into the clay to prevent the pottery from cracking during firing and when it was later used for cooking – a kind of prehistoric Pyrex. Some pots were dipped into a slip of clay and water to cover up a rough surface. On Orkney, the Unstan ware was then burnished with a bone tool to make the surface shiny and impermeable: there were no glazes in these early days. Many utensils were left plain, but some were decorated by dragging a splinter of bone across the clay (incised decoration) or by pressing fingernails, shells, bird bones or whipped cord into it (impressed decoration); occasionally the potter added appliqué decorations made of clay rolls to give a relief moulding, often in the form of ribs or cordons (relief ornament). Finally, the pottery was baked.

Archaeologists have always been obsessed with pottery. In the days before radiocarbon dating, they seized on it as a means of establishing the chronology and the culture at each site. It now seems that, although the pottery style is intrinsically interesting as an aspect of neolithic cultural development and certainly altered with time, it cannot usually be made to indicate a date. Some pottery styles continued in use for 1500 years and there was a considerable overlap: in the period 3500-3300 BC, for instance, at least four major pottery styles were in use simultaneously. Nor can pottery style be used with much confidence in determining culture. At the Windmill Hill causewayed enclosure, the plain flint-gritted early ware gave way to shell-gritted and ornamented ware later on. In 1954, Stuart Piggott interpreted this as meaning that the site was taken over by a new group of people. Now, we would be more likely to interpret the same evidence in two very different ways: a change of fashion among the local potters or a change in trading relationships with pottery perhaps imported from a different region, but either way the resident group remaining unchanged. We are, in other words, visualising a more sedentary, more adaptable and more eclectic people.

The names given to the pottery styles are another problem. Different archaeologists use different names, and the use of type-sites tends to imply that those places were significant, perhaps as potteries or distribution centres, but they were not. It is beyond the scope of this book to instate new names and it might confuse readers familiar with the old terms, so I reluctantly retain the old ones.

The earliest pottery style to emerge was the Grimston-Lyles Hill style. This is named after sites in Yorkshire and Northern Ireland, but it was the norm for British pottery in the early neolithic. It first appeared about 4600 BC and persisted for some 1600 years, disappearing in 3000 BC. The pottery was undecorated, with shoulders and round bottoms, some of it very finely made (Figure

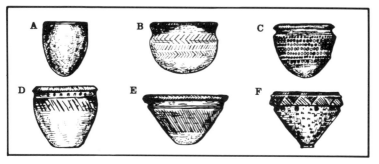

24 Pottery styles

A Grimston/Windmill Hill (plain early neolithic) ware; from the Trundle
B Ebbsfleet; from Windmill Hill   C Mortlake; from West Kennet Long Barrow
D Rudston; from Rudston   E Meldon Bridge; from Northumberland
F Fengate; from West Kennet Long Barrow

24A). During the life-span of this very long-lived ceramic
tradition, other, shorter-lived styles came and went. The Hembury
style, about 4100–3300 BC, has for long been recognised as a
significant early neolithic style. Like Grimston ware it was mainly
simple, undecorated, round-based bowls, but there were some
bowls with big curving lugs that were perforated horizontally for
threading carrying or hanging thongs. Curiously, the Hembury
bowls were of a finer fabric and better made than much of the
bronze age pottery. A sub-type of the Hembury ware was the
special, fine, red ware made on the Lizard: some of this was sent
to Wessex, but the distribution of the Lizard and Hembury ware
as a whole was very restricted. Because Hembury ware was
regionally confined, Whittle has proposed 'South-Western Style' as
a better name.

Plate 9 A bowl in Abingdon style, made in about 3500 BC

The Abingdon style was another short-lived tradition of the early neolithic, about 3800-3200 BC. Found in central and southern England, this type consisted typically of round-based bowls with a band of outside decoration between the rim and the shoulder (Plate 9). The pattern of mutual influences developing in lowland England at this time was very complex. There were, for instance, similarities and overlaps in the styles of pottery called Abingdon, Windmill Hill, Whitehawk, Ebbsfleet, Mildenhall and Broome Heath. The recurring shape, with slight local variations, was the round-based bowl with a shoulder, often with decoration round the rim and sometimes extending below the shoulder as well. Plain round-based bowls remained in use throughout the late neolithic as well, but their relative importance in the pottery assemblage declined as increasing numbers of new decorative forms came in.

The main pottery tradition of the middle and late neolithic was the Peterborough tradition, beginning in 3500 BC and continuing to the end of the period. It developed out of, and overlapped with, the Grimston tradition, beginning as a localised regional style in the lower Thames valley. The earliest stage was the making of the Ebbsfleet bowls, coarse, heavy, round-based vessels with a well-marked shoulder. They had impressed whipped cord decorations in chevrons or criss-cross both inside and outside the rim, on and below the shoulder. There was often a row of pits in the neck suggesting the thong-holes of a leather bag. As the decoration became more extensive and more exclusively whipped cord in type, the pottery became more widespread. By 3300 BC, Ebbsfleet was in use from Dorset to Yorkshire (Figure 24B).

The Mortlake style, fully developed by 2700 BC, was still more

Plate 10 A bowl in Mortlake style, made in about 2700 BC

profusely ornamented, with complicated impressed bird bone and fingernail patterns covering the entire outer surface of the bowl. The shape altered significantly with the development of heavy, hooked rims and deep necks (Figure 24C). A further development into the Fengate style produced a deep, sloping collar and a distinctive conical form taping to a small, flat base; it marks the very end of the neolithic. In northern Britain other Peterborough variants appeared, such as the Rudston and Meldon Bridge bowls, which are similar to Mortlake bowls but with a more conical shape with rims extending further out, sometimes with chamfered outer edges devised to display more decoration.

The Peterborough tradition pervaded much of Britain and underwent many small local variations. There were also substantial areas of overlap among the regional variants that can easily be understood in terms of exchanges or trade. There were long-distance movements of pottery as well that may have been part of a ceramic counter-trade to the trade in stone axes.

GROOVED WARE

Peterborough ware was the standard ware over much of Britain in the middle and later neolithic. The Grooved ware, a new decorative tradition, started later, in about 2900 BC. This too was a national tradition and the two types of pottery were often in use at the same sites. Grooved ware has a flat base and a simple bucket, barrel or flowerpot shape, often 40 centimetres in diameter. The smaller pieces, about 10 centimetres in diameter and 10 high, are simple shallow flowerpot shapes: they are probably drinking cups. The ornament, which is often very elaborate, covering much of the outside and the inner rim, is made of incised grooves in cordons of geometric designs. The potters also added relief ornament in the form of vertical ribs, horizontal cordons and wavy lines. Impressed ornament is used as well to texture zones or panels. The general effect of the decoration is sumptuously rich and varied; it seems odd that some vessels were left completely plain (Figure 25).

Much the same patterns were produced over the length and breadth of Britain. It is one of the strangest features of the British neolithic that the same type of pottery with only slight variations is found in Orkney and in Wessex. The origin of the ware seems to be Orkney, where the distinctive Unstan bowls of the early neolithic mark an early stage in the development of the style. After this period of Hyperborean incubation, the new style broke out and spread with extraordinary rapidity across the rest of Britain, appearing at Stonehenge in 2800 BC, very shortly after its first appearance in Orkney.

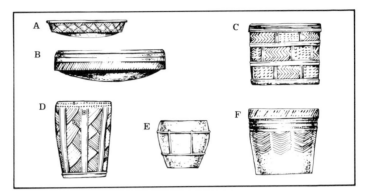

25 Pottery styles

A Unstan bowl; from Midhowe   B Unstan bowl; from Taversoe Tuick
C Grooved ware; from Woodhenge   D Grooved ware; from Wilsford
E Grooved ware; from Woodhenge   F Grooved ware; from Clacton

People living in many southern English villages were using both Grooved ware and Peterborough and this suggests that they had complementary uses. Grooved ware seems to have been used only in domestic contexts, whereas Peterborough pottery is found both at settlement sites and in burials, so there was some distinction in use. This comes out most clearly in Yorkshire, where 80 per cent of the Grooved ware is concentrated in less than 1 per cent of the land area. This remarkable concentration is within a 5-kilometre radius of the Rudston Monolith, an important tribal identity symbol at the centre of a complex of ceremonial monuments. As the mace-heads of the late neolithic also centre on Rudston, the tribal metropolis is seen to have attracted prestige goods and we are justified in identifying the Grooved ware as a prestige commodity.

POTTERS, PEDLARS OR TRADERS?

In 1954, Stuart Piggott linked new pottery with new people and the spread of a pottery style with colonial expansion. More recently, Isobel Smith has unravelled chronological changes and regional variations within the Peterborough tradition and shown that the evolution of a pottery style can be very complex. We cannot assume that a particular style belongs to a particular sub-culture. There are large areas where styles overlap, showing that practices in neighbouring areas frequently influenced one another. Alternatively, the overlap areas can be seen as areas where the potters were in direct competition with one another. Potters may have been itinerant, since clay and firewood, the only raw materials needed, were available nearly everywhere. Whittle suggests that the wandering potters may have produced pottery to local specifications and that each potter may have been able to make pottery to order – in any style. Certainly the movement round the country of highly mobile travelling potters would be more efficient than trade in finished pottery. But if that hypothesis were true, we should expect to see Grooved ware shapes with incised ornaments and Mortlake bowls with relief ornaments – the full range of permutations of forms and ornaments – as virtuoso potters experimented. That did not happen. It appears that certain styles remained mutually exclusive and that there must, at the very least, have been two different groups of potters to explain the separate traditions of Peterborough and Grooved ware. That could be explained by itinerant potters trained in different traditions starting out from different centres but with overlapping circuits.

The alternative explanation is trade in the finished product. The idea at first seems unlikely, since itinerant potters could travel light whereas pots are bulky and awkward to carry. On the other hand, we know that long-distance trade in heavy objects was undertaken. It also seems logical to suppose from the more general availability of clay that shorter distances were involved in the pottery trade than in the stone trade.

The distribution of the fine, red ware from the Lizard across the West Country and into Wessex is easily explained as some kind of trading operation in finished pottery. The pattern of finds is consistent with coastwise trade along to Christchurch Harbour and then up the River Avon – a very similar enterprise to the shipment of Cornish axe-heads, in fact. Although there may have been itinerant pedlars, the mechanism proposed for the movement of stone tools is adequate to the situation. There may have been relatively few centres at which pottery was made, although they would have been more numerous and widespread than the axe factories. Local movements can be explained by exchanges at territorial boundaries, gifts and accidental losses during journeys. Some transfers were incidental to the movement of other commodities. The movement of pots from Cornwall to the interior of Wessex was secondary to the export of salt, which would have to be taken in some form of container.

The main type of pottery movement was nevertheless the larger-scale shipment of pottery for its own sake. The prestige pottery, Grooved ware, is an obvious candidate for this. The origin of the Grooved ware in Orkney and its very sudden introduction into England implies the initiation of a large-scale trading operation from Orkney to Wessex. It is not too fanciful to suppose that Orkney was the centre of a substantial Grooved ware manufacturing industry stimulated by demand from visiting representatives of communities all over Britain. The Orcadians, to judge from the scale of their monuments, held themselves in high esteem in the third millennium (see Chapters 10 and 11). This may in part be explained by the prestige they had gained from the pottery trade. But if the Grooved ware that has been found at Durrington Walls really came from Orkney, it was specially done for the customer in 'Durrington style' which is quite distinctive (Figure 25). There are many more questions than answers here.

Much of the pottery was plain but serviceable. Its form was well-suited to the 'ground-level' life style of the Stonehenge people, as the rounded base could easily be nested between tussocks of grass or in little hollows in the earth, and the unglazed, matt surface was easy to hold securely. Towards the end of the period, a taste for ornament of a particularly earthy and plastic type developed, but in general the pottery remained fairly plain and functional. People evidently preferred it that way. This is in distinct contrast to the people of central Europe who produced very refined pottery in a wide variety of beautiful and exotic forms, often richly decorated in coloured patterns. The British were less concerned with the aesthetic value of their pottery, even though some of it does have a kind of earthy sensuality; their thoughts were elsewhere. The extraordinary wealth of ceremonial monuments in Britain finds no parallel in central Europe. I think we can indulge a certain casualness, a certain haste, in the Stonehenge people's pottery when we realise that they were massively preoccupied with greater projects by far.

CHAPTER 7

BY WHAT MECHANICAL CRAFT

To this day there stand these mighty stones gathered together into circles – 'the old temples of the gods' they are called – and whoso sees them will assuredly marvel by what mechanical craft or by what bodily strength stones of such bulk have been collected to one spot.

HECTOR BOECE, *History of Scotland*, 1527

The scope of neolithic technology was startlingly ambitious, and the more we learn about it from detailed studies of the tools and reconstructions of the way they were used, the more impressive it is that so much could have been achieved with so few and such meagre tools. Often the tools were handled with great dexterity and it is difficult to evaluate experiments with facsimile implements because the modern experimenter starts from scratch without the appropriate conditioning, skills or attitudes. What is truly awe-inspiring, though, is the vast amount of time that many of the techniques required. Two outstanding qualities of the Stonehenge people, qualities they possessed limitlessly, were patience and perseverance.

STONE, BONE AND ANTLER

The stone axe, perhaps their best-known implement, has already been mentioned in Chapter 5, but it was only one of a range of tools produced from skilfully flaked stone (Figure 26). Among the principal users of stone tools were the leather workers, who turned the hides of cattle slaughtered for meat into leather and made clothes, footwear, thongs and rope. Scrapers and knives were essential for butchering, skinning, cleaning fat and hair from the hides and cutting the finished leather into required shapes. Burins were used to perforate the edges of hide so that they could be sewn together. The first stages in the process of leather making, as reconstructed by Aubrey Burl, involved scraping the fat off the hides and then soaking them in urine to make the removal of the coarse hair easier. The hair was scraped off with scrapers and combs, then the hides were soaked in cow dung to make them swell, tanned in an infusion of oakwood and finally softened by rubbing in animal brains. This awful technique produced a pale and supple leather that could be made into a wide range of comfortable garments.

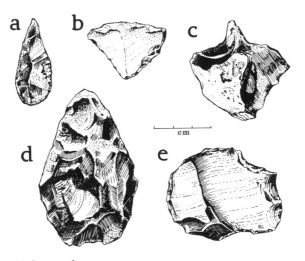

26 Stone tools.
a leaf-shaped arrowhead
b transverse arrowhead
c burin
d spearhead
e scraper

Another important by-product of slaughtering livestock was bone. Red deer antler, a rather similar material but more porous, was gathered from the forest floor. Small bones could be made into pins, needles and awls. Large bones could be made into chisels and gouges for carpentry. Less commonly, large bones like femurs were made into adzes; the femur was sawn in half lengthways, the marrow hollowed out and a wooden haft fitted to make a roughly L-shaped tool. Scapula shovels were in use everywhere; a simple little shovel was manufactured out of the complete shoulder blade of an ox, pig or deer with an antler handle. Smaller bones were often turned into beads by notching them at intervals and snapping pieces off; the marrow was hollowed out to make the perforation for stringing.
Yet another almost universal tool was the antler pick (Figure

27 Pick and shovel. The antler pick and ox scapula shovel were standard equipment in the flint mines

27). A shed deer antler made a useful rake, pick or hoe without any modification, but usually all except the brow-tine (the lowest tine) was sawn off leaving the beam as a handle. These simple picks were used in countless thousands for excavations of all kinds: the ditches of earth circles, long barrows, chambered tombs and passage graves, the stone-holes of stone circles and standing stones, the post-holes of palisades and roundhouses, and the shafts and galleries of the stone mines. Single tines made punches for splitting timber and stone or light hammers. The cut end of a tine was often notched with radial grooves to make a comb with a ring of pointed teeth; these were used for removing hair from animal hides and for carding wool. We know that in the bronze age both men and women carried combs to comb their own hair with and it is likely that the people of the neolithic used their antler combs in the same way.

Sometimes antler was used to sleeve a stone axe-head. The axe-head was fitted into a short length of hollowed-out antler and this in turn was fitted into the socket in the wooden haft. Often the fit was strengthened with birch-bark resin. More commonly, short lengths of hollowed-out antler were used as handles for other tools. A cache of antler fragments found at Fletton near Peterborough included several pieces 10 centimetres long that had been carefully smoothed off and were clearly intended for use as handles. I have held these and was surprised at how firm, smooth and comfortable they were to grip, infinitely better than most modern handles. Experiences like this bring us suddenly very close to the Stonehenge people. They have an immediacy that is vital in any real appreciation of the nature of the culture. More specifically, handling the antler fragments proved to me how sensitive the workmen were in their choice and treatment of their materials.

TIMBER, ROPE AND BASKETWORK

A great deal of the perishable equipment that was used has inevitably not survived. Among the exceptions are some basket-work trays that were used for carrying waste rock during excavations. We can infer woven floor matting, too, from the impressions it left on the bases of pottery. A similar weaving technique was used with twigs and branches to make hurdles, fences and the trackways across the Somerset Levels. Ropes were made out of a variety of materials such as twisted heather and wild clematis, whilst strips of leather or rawhide were plaited to make the very strong hawsers needed for hauling and raising megaliths. At the other end of the scale, finely made plaited cords were used to fasten cloaks and other garments: they were part of the everyday equipment available to the potter for making patterns on clay.

Very little wooden equipment has survived, yet a range of objects has come down to us from just three sites: the Somerset Levels, Ehenside in Cumbria and North Ferriby on Humberside. That this tiny sample of neolithic sites should produce so many different kinds of artefacts tells us that wood was absolutely vital to the culture. Hunters in the Somerset Levels had beautifully made bows that mark the beginning of the English longbow tradition. The Ashcott bow, dating to 3400 BC, is very slender, 1·95 metres long, with a roughly square cross section and made of yew wood. The Meare bow, dating to 3425 BC, also of yew and the same length, may well turn out not to be typical (Figure 28E). To begin with, its shape is without parallel anywhere in Europe; it is broad (7 centimetres) and flat (only 1½ centimetres thick), with a discreet keel to give it a little more strength. In addition, it is elaborately carved. There are six carved parallel bands on each side of the grip and a complicated decorative pattern of transverse and diagonal webbing made of rawhide strips. The Meare bow is a marvellous piece of craftsmanship and it is hard to believe that weapons of this standard were part of the hunter's normal equipment. The outstanding quality of its finish may be an expression of a particular hunter's personality: although we cannot distinguish individual people by name in prehistory, on occasions we can sense that they existed.

At Ehenside, the hunters used oak throwing sticks to bring down small game, as well as clubs and fish spears – or are they pitchforks? In Somerset, non-hunting wooden equipment included dishes, mattocks, turf spades, wedges and toggles. At North Ferriby, apart from the boats, which will be mentioned in Chapter 8, there was an elaborately designed winch 0·7 metres high and 1·7 metres long; this windlass was hauling boats up on to the

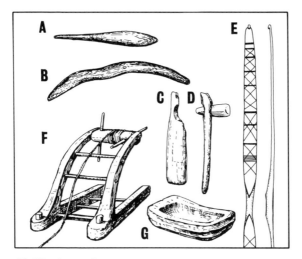

28 Wooden artefacts.

A club; B throwing stick; C turf-spade or paddle;
D axe-haft (A-D from Ehenside Tarn); E the Meare bow
(from Somerset Levels); F windlass (from the Humber);
G bowl (from Ehenside Tarn)

foreshore in the Humber estuary right at the end of the neolithic.

The great roundhouses of the Wessex superhenges were really virtuosic displays of carpentry and show that by the late neolithic woodworking techniques had reached incredible heights. It is sad that virtually nothing remains of these consummate achievements except the post-holes. The techniques of the master carpenters were nevertheless imposed in a quite extraordinary way on a more durable material that *has* survived. The sarsen circle and trilithons of Stonehenge are remarkable in so many ways that it is easy to overlook the most curious feature of the monument: the way in which pure carpentry techniques have been translated into stone. The lintels are supported on uprights by mortice and tenon joints and the lintels of the great ring are interlocked by means of tongue and groove joints. As we shall see later, the cross-reference is far more than merely technical.

THE STONES OF AVEBURY

Avebury and Stonehenge are the most spectacular surviving examples of neolithic technology in southern Britain: in northern Britain they are only rivalled by the Orcadian monument complex that includes the Ring of Brodgar and Maes Howe. The two southern centres, of near-neighbouring territories, provide us with an excellent illustration of the ways in which simple equipment was used to achieve great ends. The two sites also illustrate two important general characteristics of the culture: the large-scale and self-confident view of man's relationship with nature and the almost manic tenacity of a people gripped by an obsession.

Let us start with Avebury (Figure 30). The monument is older than the stones of Stonehenge and it looks as though, in their stone circles and stone horseshoes, the Stonehenge people were developing an idea that the Avebury people had already initiated. Indeed, many of the misconceptions that surround Stonehenge have arisen because theorists have studied it and speculated about it in isolation; it can only be understood in the context of the monuments and occupation sites around it. The big sarsen stones were an obvious choice for a megalithic structure. The stones were already quarried in the sense that nature herself had weathered them out of an ancient sandstone layer that formerly covered the chalk. The sarsens were also flattish, which made them far easier to transport and handle than rounded boulders. In addition, the stone could be smoothed to an extent, it was extremely durable, it could be split into rough pillars and – most important of all – it was to be found very close to Avebury. The main disadvantage was that its immense hardness made it very difficult to work. It was and still is three times harder to work than granite. So, in spite of the benefits of sarsens, the people of Avebury were setting themselves a daunting task. The final form of the stones as they stand incorporated in the monument is a moving compromise between man and earth. The inward-facing surfaces have been painstakingly smoothed but the outer surfaces retain their grotesquely gnarled natural skins.

The source of the sarsens was Overton Down (Figure 29). Although they were already quarried, they were half-buried in soil, so the first task was to lever them out onto sledges using stout timber beams. Rollers made of tree trunks have often been proposed as a way of moving megalithic stones, but they would have been less efficient than sledges. Rollers would reduce friction slightly but against that we have to set the disadvantage that men would be continually running backwards and forwards, fetching rollers left behind by the moving stone to set in its path again. On skewed slopes, there would also be a danger of the stone sliding sideways off the rollers altogether. These problems would not occur with a sledge, as nothing was left behind and the runners would tend to make it move in a straight line; if well-designed, it could reduce the friction by 90 per cent. A hundred people could pull a twenty-ton sarsen on a sledge all day without undue exertion.

Although still relatively rare, the wheel was known throughout Europe at the time Avebury was built. Solid wooden disc wheels

29 The Avebury area, including some destroyed monuments.

1 Beckhampton Avenue 2 Kennet Avenue 3 Falkner's Circle 4 Waden Hill barrows 5 Sanctuary 6 Old Chapel mortuary enclosure 7 Huish Hill mortuary enclosure. Long barrows a Mill; b Shelving stones; c Monkton d Old Chapel e Horslip f South Street g Longstones h Beckhampton i Avebury j West Kennet k East Kennet. Silbury's moat is shown black

and even clay models of waggons have been unearthed, so the concept of waggon transport was certainly available to the Avebury people. On the other hand, the enormous weight of the sarsens would probably have broken apart any wooden bearing, even if we envisage the weight distributed across as many as four axles. All things considered, the sledge still seems more likely.

The route taken from the hilltop to the henge-site is uncertain, but sledges would be far easier to manage on level ground or on very gentle gradients than on steeper slopes. The best route was to the south along the crest of the chalk escarpment. At Overton Hill, a short one-in-fifteen gradient to the west took the sarsens down on to the low chalk shelf where the monument was to stand. This is the route to be preferred on purely geomorphological grounds; it offers the most favourable slopes and avoids the obstacle course of sarsens littering the floor of Clatford Bottom.

As if confirming this hypothesis, the route follows an established neolithic trackway along the north-south stretch; it turns sharply from the Ridgeway at the Sanctuary, a neolithic roundhouse; from there to Avebury it follows the West Kennet Avenue. The Avenue was probably built at the end of the enterprise as a triumphant celebration of the sarsen path. A similar origin has been proposed for the Avenue, marked by ditches only, leading to Stonehenge. The Stonehenge Avenue is thought to celebrate the way the bluestones were brought up from the River Avon: certainly the central and eastern sections of the

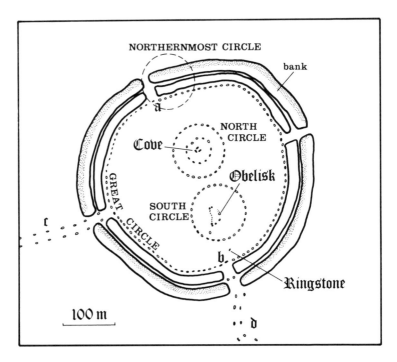

30 Plan of Avebury. Surviving and visible stones, whether standing or fallen, are shown in solid black. Stone-holes and presumed stone-holes are shown as open ellipses.

a North Portal Stones: the Swindon Stone survives
b South Portal stones; both survive
c Beckhampton Avenue;
d Kennet Avenue

Avenue, which were constructed late, can be interpreted this way (Figure 41). The Avenues at both sites can be seen as ways made sacred by the passage of the monument stones.

The level site at Avebury had already been cleared and farmed for some time when it was chosen as the place where the monument would stand. It was marked out with two rings of wooden pegs, and the sarsens arrived on their sledges, one by one. The undertaking was spread over a long period, fitted in between farming and hunting. Perhaps only two stones were brought down from the hills each summer. The holes were prepared one by one, as each stone arrived. The stone was tilted into its hole and erected by a combination of pushing with levers from the back and pulling with hawsers from in front. The erection probably took a week. There are several thick stake holes near each stone, showing how the leaning, half-raised stones were left supported overnight while the workmen went off to eat, drink and rest. When the stone was finally vertical, the gap between it and the sides of the socket was filled with sarsen packing stones, hammered in to ensure that the stone stood firm.

31 Stukeley's drawing of the Obelisk at Avebury. This monolith formerly stood at the centre of the South Circle and was probably the first stone to be raised at Avebury. It was felled by the villagers in the fourteenth century and broken up shortly after William Stukeley drew it in 1723

When the two inner stone rings, the North and South Circles, were complete work was begun on a third, further to the north. It was never finished. Changes of plan were characteristic of the great engineering projects, as we might expect when they were drawn out over decades or centuries. At Avebury, the change was to an even more ambitious plan: a huge threefold third circle consisting of a stone ring, a ditch and a bank, all encompassing the first two circles. Because the third circle, the Great Circle, is

Plate 11 Three stones of the Avebury South Circle

not a true circle, a great deal of futile speculation has gone into its supposed trigonometry, but it was simply not practicable to draw a true circle. The first two circles were drawn true using a stake, a rope and a sharpened wooden peg. That was easy, but once the North and South Circles were in position a surrounding ring could only be put in by eye. It looks as if a few radii were threaded among the obstructing stones to get an approximation to a circle, but it was evidently the overall effect of circularity that was important to the designers and that certainly has been achieved. An additional reason for non-circularity at Avebury, Stonehenge and a host of other ditched enclosures, was the method for ditch-digging. The ditches were dug in segments by separate work gangs and each segment displays a certain independence of mind, being straighter or more curved, wider or narrower, deeper or shallower

Plate 12 The east entrance at Avebury. The outer bank is to the right, the silted ditch is in the centre and the precinct is to the left

Plate 13 The Avebury ditch. The excavation of 1922 revealed its true depth

than adjacent segments. So it was quite usual for causewayed enclosures and henges to be deformed circles.

The Great Circle consisted of some 98 sarsen stones standing 7 metres inside a steep-sided and flat-bottomed ditch 21 metres wide, 9 metres deep and 427 metres in diameter. The ditch was excavated painstakingly with antler picks. It is thought that the solid chalk was first cracked by fire and then smashed with hammer stones. The resulting rubble was raked up with antlers and scapula shovels and loaded onto wicker trays. The ditch was made particularly deep beside the South Entrance causeway in order to impress visitors: on one side it was as much as 11 metres deep. On a project of this scale, some division of labour was used and while some people were hammering, others were raking and shovelling and still others were carrying trays of rubble to the ditch corner where it was hauled up in baskets or leather bags on ropes. The rope-marks and the wear of foot-traffic along the inner edge of the ditch shows how highly organised the project was. Given its scale, it had to be.

The rubble taken from the ditch was carried a short distance outside across a level berm to the lower marker bank that had been laid out at the start of the Great Circle phase. The amount of work involved in excavating the ditch meant that it was to be many decades before the whole circle could be completed, so the line of the 5-metre high great bank was fixed at the outset by a small marker bank. The line to be followed by the ditch was probably marked by pegs. Like the ditch-digging gangs, the gangs building the great bank worked on a particular segment. The result was a rather uneven crest line. The same sort of effect is seen in some long barrows; Holdenhurst in Hampshire has a series of roughly conical dumps as its foundation. Once again we see a method employed at Avebury that was part of the general fabric of the culture permeating lowland England. The only difference was one of scale. The average long barrow is 45 metres long, 18 metres wide and 2 metres high, and the 1000 cubic metres of material would have involved some 4000 man-hours of labour. The volume of material excavated from the Avebury ditch and transferred to the outer bank is equivalent to that of the average-sized pyramid of the Fifth Dynasty, raised at about the same time, in 2600 BC.

MOVING THE STONES OF STONEHENGE

There was an earth monument at Stonehenge several centuries before the Avebury circles were drawn. Indeed, the story of Stonehenge's development straddles that of Avebury, starting earlier, ending later and using ideas and materials from Avebury on the way. If we leave aside for the moment the enormous posts that once stood on the site of the car park, the earliest coherent design that we can decipher was Stonehenge I. This was laid out in a huge woodland clearing that seems to have been made especially for the monument: the site has never been ploughed. In 3000 BC, the mean of the latest corrected radiocarbon dates, the monument consisted of a low white circular bank of chalk rubble thrown up from a surrounding ditch. A single entrance on the north-eastern perimeter gave access to a circular precinct 93 metres across (Figure 32). It owes something to the causewayed enclosure tradition, with its ditch outside the bank. Avebury, which was built later, has the more usual henge arrangement of ditch within bank. Avebury is remarkable in other ways: in being stupendously large and in having four entrances. Stonehenge I was a modest affair by comparison, using mainly the techniques of the causewayed enclosure tradition, with fairly shallow, flat-bottomed ditches laid out in an irregular plan and made of about a hundred adjacent oval pits. A hundred or more people were involved in the digging, with as many more basket-carriers, if all parts of the ditch were being worked at the same time. In fact it is more likely that, as at Avebury, the line of the ditch was initially marked out with pegs and then dug piecemeal by quite a small group of people. We need not assume they were in a hurry.

Where Stonehenge I differs significantly from the causewayed enclosure we think it replaced (Robin Hood's Ball) is in its

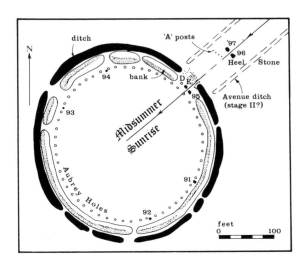

32 Plan of Stonehenge I. The earth circle was laid out in about 3000 BC. The bluestone setting (Stonehenge II) and sarsen monument (Stonehenge III) were built in the centre of the original earth circle

megaliths. At the entrance to the enclosure stood two pairs of portal stones. The inner pair consisted of the fallen Slaughter Stone (Stone 95) and its missing partner (Stone E). The outer pair comprised the Heel Stone (Stone 96) and its partner, also lost, Stone 97. The socket of this last stone was discovered only in 1981 but it is surprising that, given its position in the design, its overriding importance in unravelling the mysteries of Stonehenge was not realised straight away. Probably towards 2800 BC a circle of sixteen or eighteen small unshaped sarsens was added to reinforce the magical power of the earth circle. Stones 91-94, the Station Stones, are survivors of this early megalithic structure and they were kept through many later changes of plan because they were well placed to act as horizon markers.

There are no large sarsen stones on the plain surrounding Stonehenge, so we have to infer that the portal stones, at least, were brought specially from the Marlborough Downs. The bringing of the four large portal stones from Overton Down near Avebury tells us much about the relationships between neighbouring communities in about 3000 BC. There were several small tribal territories separating Avebury from Stonehenge; transporting the stones those 38 kilometres necessitated the goodwill and co-operation of the communities in between. The operation could not have been attempted if these groups had been hostile to one another. The acquisition of the stones implies something else besides. The Stonehenge people either negotiated with the Avebury people for the consignment of megaliths or they were presented with them as a gift. We know that the Avebury people were every bit as obsessed with monumental architecture as the Stonehenge people and that gift-giving has always been common among archaic communities.

Although the great megalithic structures at Avebury were not built until much later, it is possible that there were some rough megaliths on the site as early as 3000 BC. It is not too fanciful to suppose that the Avebury people had a stone idol in position – perhaps the Obelisk – well before the stone rings were built. It seems more natural to suppose that the people of Avebury initiated the use of great sarsen stones, given that the nearby downs were and still are strewn with them, than to suppose that the Stonehenge people conceived of megalithic architecture without a model in an area bereft of suitable stones.

Stonehenge II was more extraordinary still. Once the Stonehenge people had adopted the practice of megalith-building in foreign stone, they developed it in a quite incredible way, importing 123 large stones of rhyolite and spotted dolerite, the famous bluestones, from Wales. It was in about 2250 BC that the bluestones were brought across from the Preseli Mountains in Pembrokeshire. For a time, some geologists thought it possible that the bluestones had been picked up by an ice sheet early in the Ice Age and dumped on Salisbury Plain as erratics, but the theory is now discredited. The most damning argument against it is that an ice sheet would have brought across a miscellaneous collection of bluestone and other rock fragments, not just the two-metre blocks that happened to be required for Stonehenge, and there is no sign of any stray fragments.

The inescapable alternative is that the bluestones were brought from Wales by neolithic man. The Preseli Mountains are the only place where the blue-green dolerite and rhyolite outcrop; the ancient quarries or rather collecting places have recently been identified at the eastern end of the mountains. From here, the 82 bluestone uprights, each weighing 4 tons, and the 40 lintels, were carried a distance of 217 kilometres as the crow flies. At first sight, it seems utterly impossible that a small-scale and archaic community could organise and carry through such a huge enterprise. Yet somehow it *was* done: the stones are there to prove it.

There were three alternative routes for the stone-gatherers to choose from. They all begin with a downhill trek 26 kilometres long from the Preseli Mountains to Milford Haven (Figure 33). From there, vessels of some kind embarked, possibly following the South Wales coast to the Severn Estuary, crossing to the English side to negotiate segments of the Bristol Avon, the Frome, the Wylye and the Hampshire Avon. This is the shortest route and the

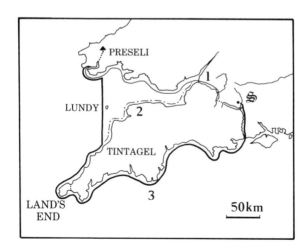

33 The bluestone routes from Wales

1 Shortest route, proposed by Richard Atkinson
2 A water route involving portage across the Penwith peninsula
3 The Land's End route

one favoured by Professor Richard Atkinson, the leading Stone-henge scholar, but it does include 39 kilometres of overland portage at three separate locations.

A second possible route begins in the same way, but continues along the north coasts of Somerset, Devon and Cornwall, crossing the neck of the Penwith peninsula to avoid a perilous rounding of Land's End. It then passes along the south coast to Christchurch Harbour and up the Hampshire Avon as far as Amesbury, just 3 kilometres from Stonehenge. The problem with this route is that sledges would have to be left in Penwith for re-use on the many journeys involved or else carried on board the vessels. Another problem is that the boats themselves would have to be carried or dragged overland, unless two separate flotillas were used. It does not seem a very practicable option.

The third route – the one that I am proposing – is a journey by water all the way. Under fine anticyclonic conditions in high summer, there is no reason why rounding Land's End should have been impossibly dangerous. Travelling in convoy would have reduced the danger still further. The length of the voyage could be shortened by sailing due south from Caldy Island, using the sun for navigation. Exactly halfway across the Bristol Channel, the west coast of Lundy was a perfect seamark, and a southward run from there brought a safe landfall at Bossiney, near Tintagel.

A sea voyage of this kind may seem over-ambitious, but the builders of Stonehenge II were clearly over-ambitious people. Certainly the hard technology of the age was able to cope with such a task. The most likely vessel for the bluestone enterprise is the composite boat; three 8 metre long dugouts, each with a 1·5 metre beam could be lashed together to make a substantial load-carrying raft. At sea the craft was propelled by paddles, on rivers by poling. For safety's sake, these voyages were probably sailed in convoy and we should visualise a flotilla of four composite boats setting off from Milford Haven at a time, each laden with a single bluestone. Since only one such voyage each summer would have been feasible, the organisation of the bluestone transfer must have extended over a period of fifty years.

Even more extraordinary than the transporting of the bluestones is what happened to them after they arrived at Amesbury. They were laboriously hauled over the downs, along the curving route that would later be followed by the Avenue, to be assembled at Stone-henge. The design of the bluestone circle was highly original. The stones were arranged in radial pairs, each pair carrying a radial lintel. In plan, the design looked like the rays of the sun and, in fact, a very similar symbol occurs on a much smaller scale in contemporary rock-art. At Newgrange, the Irish temple-tomb that celebrated the midwinter sunrise, there are several such sun symbols – one actually on the lintel of the roof-box that let in the winter solstice rays.

The addition of a stone circle to the earth circle reflects Stonehenge's frontier location. It was in the lowland zone that the earth circle had its beginnings: the soil was deep and the rock soft, so it was easy to dig a ditch and raise a bank. In the highlands, where the soil was thin and the rock hard, it was not so easy and a stone circle of megaliths acted as a substitute. The two traditions developed separately at first but in the later neolithic they cross-fertilised. Stonehenge is a classic case of an idea invented, exported, re-interpreted and then re-imported in its transformed state.

Towards the entrance, the bluestone circle was reinforced with additional stones to increase its magical strength and emphasise its orientation towards the midsummer sunrise. The entrance pillars made a double peristyle or colonnade. The rays of the newly risen sun on the summer solstice shone directly over Stones B and C, the re-arranged inner portal stones, passed along the bluestone colonnade, across the open space at the centre and lit up the Altar Stone on the far side of the circle. This once-revered god-stone now lies crushed and broken under other fallen stones. Stones just like it stand in places of honour in the neolithic shrines of Hagar Qim on Malta. Whether we think of them as phallic fertility symbols or as representatives of the sun-god himself, there can be no doubt that they are idols. The god-stone at Stonehenge is made of a sandstone that can only have come from Pembrokeshire, so it must have been collected along with the bluestones. In position, standing some 4 metres tall, it dominated the *sanctum sanctorum*.

Yet, startlingly original though the bluestone design was, work was halted when it was only a little more than half completed. The bluestone adventure was an extraordinary episode in the monument's history, with an appropriately extraordinary twist at its conclusion. The rejection of the bluestone design shows that the Stonehenge people had quite incredible resources. We might have thought that the gathering of 123 megaliths from Wales would itself overstretch a small archaic society. Not a bit of it. Far from exhausting themselves on the enterprise and basking in its triumphant conclusion, they extravagantly threw the design to the winds in favour of an even more grandiose scheme, using bigger stones.

Why was the bluestone project abandoned? Why were the stones brought from so far away in the first place? The bluestones, in spite of their evocative name, have no mechanical or aesthetic properties that could possibly justify the enormous trouble taken to bring them from Wales. We are left with only one alternative. The stones possessed (and perhaps still possess) invisible, meta-physical properties and we can assume that the same properties imbued their place of origin. Carn Meini was a magic mountain, the dwelling-place of the gods. Perhaps, by collecting fragments of it gathered from the hillsides and forging them into a magic ring in a distant land, the Stonehenge people were able to transport the gods themselves to Stonehenge. The magic circle then became a kind of celestial bird-cage, a spirit house, a haven for the divine powers of beneficence.

Can we advance the hypothesis that Overton Down, the source of the sarsen stones, was held in even greater awe, that it was an even more sacred site? It does not seem possible, looking at the landscape today; although there *may* have been some kind of sacred grove on the hillside, there is nothing now on the rather nondescript plateau to suggest that it might have been a holy place.

One feature of Overton Down that is of overriding significance is its proximity to Avebury. The sarsen collecting place was certainly in the territory of the Avebury people. I think it most likely that there was a mainly social or political motive for the changeover to sarsens. At an earlier phase in the monument's development, in around 3000 BC, the four portal stones were given to the people of Stonehenge by the people of Avebury, proving not only friendship between the two tribal groups but a particularly close friendship. In the succeeding centuries, doubtless many more gifts, mostly of a perishable nature, passed between the two and we should treat the seventy-five huge sarsens as the climactic gift from Avebury. What the Stonehenge people had given to Avebury we can only guess, but it was possibly an archaeologically invisible gift, such as a team of volunteers to assist in the building of Silbury, one of several great monuments raised by the Avebury people. Whether the Stonehengers were pleased or embarrassed by the gift of sarsens we shall never know, but they would have regarded it as binding: to decline a gift would have been a breach of etiquette. They had to accept the sarsens, even though the bluestones were sacred and acquired at such cost, in order to preserve the friendship bond with Avebury.

But first, how were the sarsens brought from Overton Down? Professor Atkinson has put forward the interesting argument that because the Kennet was fordable at Avebury but no further downstream the stone people must have brought the sarsens through the completed masterpiece of the triple stone ring before beginning their slow, ponderous journey south to Stonehenge. If that is so, once again we have an indication of a very close collaboration between the two communities. Some have suggested that the two cult centres were engaged in some kind of contest, but that hardly seems likely in view of the assistance given to Stonehenge by Avebury at two critical stages in its development. They were clearly engaged in a common endeavour in a spirit of collaboration. But these are matters for later discussion and we must return to the huge, supine stones on their stout wooden sledges, slowly creaking their way across Avebury's sacred precinct. The passage of the new Stonehenge sarsens through Avebury at the beginning of their long journey may have been the occasion of an important series of ceremonies. We can imagine the arch-priest or priestess of Avebury putting charms on the stones to sanctify them and ensure their safe arrival at Stonehenge. The Beckhampton Avenue leading away to the south-west and marking the first mile of the journey was very likely raised to celebrate the sending of the Stonehenge sarsens (Figure 29).

The route was determined by gradients, and the easiest route took the sarsen sledges by way of the A361, Redhorn Hill and the Ridgeway. Richard Atkinson estimates that it took 1500 people seven weeks to transport a single great stone. Even if that enormous labour force were employed for half of each year, it would still have taken eleven years to get all the sarsens to Stonehenge. Atkinson and most other writers have assumed that men were used for pulling, but we know that oxen were available. Although we think of oxen as slow, they are only 4 per cent slower than we are and in any case time was not a material consideration in the project. Because an ox is nine times stronger than a man, only 165 oxen would have been needed to drag the largest stone up Redhorn Hill. Assembling such a team of oxen would have been a large undertaking, but I think easier than calling up 1500 men. Some people would still have been needed to tend the stone and guide and encourage the oxen, but possibly as few as thirty.

A minor mystery has been made out of the penetration of the sarsens into the henge, as there is no sign of a temporary breach in the henge bank. In fact, it would have been easy to fill a stretch of the north-western Avenue ditch and drag the sarsens in through the main entrance. A temporary infilling will have left no archaeological trace. The inner portal stones were taken down at this time for re-siting, so there was ample space.

The sarsens were carefully shaped by one of three methods. Fine cracks made by pecking with stone tools could be fitted with wooden wedges: wetted, the wedges expanded and widened the cracks still further, finally breaking the stone in two. Alternatively, fires were lit along the line where the masons wanted the stone to break. Once the stone was hot, it was suddenly cooled by dowsing with water and cracked along the line by differential expansion and contraction. In addition, a row of men with stone hammers could strike the line in unison to exert an extra stress. By one or all of these methods, the blocks were brought to their present rectangular shapes.

The masons dressed the rough surface with large stone mauls, creating broad grooves 25 centimetres wide and 8 deep. They directed a second dressing at right angles to the first to remove the ridges. A third dressing was then applied, consisting of a careful working-over of the entire surface to remove all traces of bumps, grooves and ridges to produce a finely pocked 'orange-peel' surface. Finally, the masons dragged heavy sarsen grindstones backwards and forwards across the surface to smooth it off. The different faces of the sarsens were left at different stages. The backs or outward-facing surfaces were left fairly rough, whereas the sides were finished more carefully. The inner faces, as at Avebury, were given the best finish. The dressing of the sarsens alone would have provided ten masons with enough work to keep them fully occupied for fifteen years.

RAISING THE STONES

While the masons were putting the finishing touches to each stone and it was nearly ready to be raised, two or three other workmen began preparing a socket for it. The socket was made 30 centimetres larger than the stone all round, with three vertical sides and one sloping at 45 degrees; the back of the socket, opposite the entry ramp, was lined with stakes to stop the chalk being bruised by the rotating, grinding toe of the stone as it was raised. A small team of oxen harnessed to the stone dragged it forwards on rollers until its toe hung over the pit. Finally, hawsers slung round the stone's head were passed over shear-legs and harnessed to the twenty oxen or 180 men needed to haul the stone into a vertical position. The toe was deliberately made rounded or slightly pointed so that the final position could be adjusted with packing stones hammered in all round until the stone was exactly vertical.

One by one, over a period of many years, the huge sarsen uprights were raised. Then came what often appears to us the ultimate technological challenge – the achievement that never fails to impress the modern visitor to Stonehenge and must have struck awe into the hearts of neolithic men – the raising of the lintels. It is hard to imagine how the stones could have been raised to their present height with such primitive equipment. One suggestion is that an earth ramp was used to roll the lintels up to the level of the tops of the uprights, but there is no sign of the huge quarry that would be needed to supply that volume of material. It would in any case be a very energy-consuming method, as the ramp would have to be demolished and rebuilt for each lintel. An alternative theory holds that a timber ramp was used, but this would have to be supported in post-holes – a separate set for each lintel – and there is no sign of a maze of post-holes.

Plate 14 Stonehenge III. The tall stone on the right is Stone 57: with its fallen partner and a lintel it formed the central trilithon

34 Raising a lintel at Stonehenge; a reconstruction

A timber crib fits the archaeological evidence best and, when we look closely at the way the Stonehenge people would have used such a structure, we can see that in primitive engineering terms it was the ideal solution. The lintel was eased into place at ground level a metre from the uprights and parallel to its ultimate position. Seven men working a 4 metre long wooden lever raised one end of the lintel and a helper quickly slid a chock of squared timber under the raised end. The other end of the lintel was prised up in the same way and the operation was repeated until the lintel was 60 centimetres off the ground. A 6 metre square platform of squared timbers was built round and under the lintel, and the levering began again, this time from the platform. When the lintel had been lifted 60 centimetres above the platform, a second set of large squared timbers was inserted at right angles to the first. The process slowly continued until the crib was elevated into a tower, with the lintel raised to the same level as the tops of the uprights. At this stage the mortices in the lintel were prepared by direct measurement against the tenons on the adjacent uprights. When all was ready, the lintel was levered sideways until it was perched securely on the uprights.

Although the method may sound laborious, most of the work involved carrying and assembling relatively light timbers, albeit in large quantities. The engineers needed a mile of squared timber to build the crib, which was an enormous amount, but it was reusable and easy to dismantle once the lintel was in place. The extraordinary thing is that the raising of the Stonehenge lintels has always seemed to modern minds one of the most difficult undertakings for neolithic man, yet once the solution is seen it appears in itself to have been relatively little effort. We need not any longer envisage thousands or even hundreds of sweating savages with their muscles straining under an overseer's lash. A lot of work was involved, but in small amounts over long periods: the painstaking, piecemeal work of felling trees and squaring timbers, lifting and assembling those timbers into a crib, the careful insertion of levels and chocks, the careful positioning of a fulcrum close to the lintel, the judicious application of pressure to a lever by a mere half dozen people.

This, then, is the real nature of neolithic technology; the application of measured and modest amounts of energy over very long periods and only after long and careful planning. What seems impossible to achieve in a month is easy to achieve in a century. The equipment used was mostly rudimentary, but skilfully used. In our own times, we can compare Stonehenge with the transatlantic liner *Queen Mary*, which was built using only 5-ton cranes. Today, as in the neolithic, low technology can sometimes produce magnificent results.

Probably very large work forces were never involved in any of the great projects; the low population densities and cellular social organisation would have made it very difficult to assemble them. So we are left with startlingly ambitious projects that were undertaken by labour forces of perhaps only fifty people. The projects were sometimes planned in detail generations before they were to be completed. The greatest wonder of all is that those plans were held in the community's consciousness for such long periods and that people felt an overriding obligation to carry out plans devised by their ancestors.

Other writers have quite rightly made much of the triumph of engineering that Stonehenge represents, but it is also important to see it as a landmark in the development of symbolic gesture. The simple lowland earth circles were translated in the highland zone into stone circles marked out with upright slabs planted in the shallow soil. The stone circle idea was imported back into the lowland zone at a few prestigious sites and grafted onto an earth circle. At Stonehenge alone the stone circle idea was brought, literally and figuratively, full circle. At Stonehenge alone the circle was realised as a continuous girdle of solid stone: its magical strength was total. Rooted in the soil by its pillared uprights, it was raised heavenwards to symbolise the union of earth and sky, the world-disc offered up to the sky-god.

A BLUESTONE EPILOGUE

The sarsen structure succeeded in becoming all-the-world's image of a lost prehistoric heritage but, however successful, it is hard to believe that the bluestones were simply thrown aside for it. We know the stones were regarded as sacred and we also know they were later reincorporated into the design, so they must have been carefully preserved not far away from Stonehenge. It seems unlikely that the bluestones were merely dumped in a heap during the interval: they had after all been imported to act as a dwelling-place for gods.

Somewhere not far from Stonehenge, and still within its territory, the bluestones were built into a new monument that stood for perhaps two hundred years. The site of the temporary 'Bluestonehenge' has never been discovered, but then surprisingly little of the landscape near Stonehenge has actually been excavated, so it may be fairly close by without having been detected. Somewhere not far away, the sockets of the temporary monument lie hidden under the green turf. Perhaps those sockets will show us a small and congested design with the stones arranged in tight multiple rings; perhaps they will show us a great open ring with widely spaced uprights. Either way, the site will surely be uncovered one day.

Plate 15 The eastern sector of the sarsen circle at Stonehenge. Four of the bluestones can be seen in the centre

The exile of the bluestones did not last too long. In about 2000 BC they were brought back to Stonehenge. Every one of the original uprights was reincorporated. Twenty-two were arranged in a horseshoe setting inside the sarsen horseshoe. The remaining sixty were formed into a rough circle inside the sarsen circle, a kind of soprano parallel to the bass line of the sarsen structures. This harmonic addition was the climax of the Stonehenge design. The ancient earth circle and the Heel Stone remained from the initial design, the Station Stones from the first megalithic circle, the god-stone from the original bluestone circle, and now the bluestones and sarsens were joined together in a glorious midsummer marriage. The counterpoint of voices joined in an inaudible harmony still resonates across the plains, though we can now only dimly comprehend it.

CHAPTER 8

BY THE DEVIL'S FORCE

Then ignorance, with fabulous discourse,
Robbing fair art and cunning of their right,
Tells how those stones were by the devil's force,
From Africk brought, to Ireland in a night:
And thence to Britannie, by magick course,
From giant's hand redeem'd by Merlin's sleight . . .

SAMUEL DANYEL, 'Stonehenge: A Poem', 1624

The remarkable movements of bluestones and sarsens that seize our imagination were by no means isolated events. Many consignments of pottery and stone tools travelled long distances, not just from one territory to the next but across entire regions, and it is these transfers that give us the best proof that long-distance communication was a routine ingredient of life in the neolithic. Fragments of lava were somehow imported by the people living at the Sanctuary from the German Rhineland, probably for use as grain rubbers. We also know from the scatter of axe-heads that there was widespread communication among the regions of Britain: between Northumberland and Essex, Cornwall and East Yorkshire, Wales and Wessex. Maps such as Figure 22 show that rough-outs and finished tools found their way the length and breadth of the country. They do not show how the material was transferred, but some of the transfers can easily be explained in terms of overland routes. The distribution of type XIV axes into Lincolnshire and Wessex, for example, would be relatively straightforward along the ridge route of the Jurassic Way.

THE HIGH ROADS

There are problems in identifying ancient ridge routes. They were unmetalled and left no traces that archaeology can recognise. Nor were they fixed and well-defined like modern highways but shifted sideways to avoid eroded or waterlogged patches; we should really think of the roads as broad and ill-defined corridors of movement up to half a mile wide. We must be cautious in our claims and make sure there are sufficient concentrations of contemporary sites and artefacts along a ridge to justify calling it a neolithic ridgeway.

There are several major, long-distance ridgeways that stand up to the test. The Jurassic Way follows the limestone uplands diagonally across England from the Cotswolds to the Yorkshire Wolds or, more specifically, from Bath to Rudston, with the last stretch to the north of the Humber on chalk (Figure 35). Another route runs parallel to it but stays on the chalk outcrop. This starts in Wiltshire and Berkshire as the Ridgeway and continues along the Chilterns and East Anglian Heights as the Icknield Way; in effect it connects Avebury and Stonehenge with Grime's Graves and the Wash.

Leading eastwards from Stonehenge is a second major chalk high road, the Harroway, which on the North Downs of Surrey and Kent becomes the Pilgrims' Way. From Winchester a third chalk highway leads south-eastwards towards Butser Hill, where it becomes the South Downs Way and follows the crest of the chalk scarp to Beachy Head. It is easy to see how the convergence of four highways on Wiltshire may have contributed to the increasing importance of the Wessex heartland during the neolithic. Conversely, we can regard the extraordinary flowering of Wessex in the late neolithic as supportive evidence that the ridgeways functioned as important arteries of long-distance communication.

There were several shorter ridgeways, such as the Caistor High Street running 56 kilometres along the crest of the Lincoln Wolds and another High Street, in Cumbria, running 32 kilometres from the head of Windermere to Mayburgh. In Sussex there were short spurs leading from the South Downs Way to the causewayed enclosures of the Trundle and Whitehawk. In the lowland zone it is possible to identify nearly 1300 kilometres of highways. In the highland zone there are short stretches of ridgeway, often broken up by the ruggedness of the landscape. On Exmoor, for instance, there are four east–west ridgeways, averaging only 6 kilometres in length. The Chains Way leads from a neolithic village on Kentisbury Down to the Longstone ritual centre (Plate 38) and Chains Barrow. The second track runs from a cemetery on Bray Common to Two Barrows on Fyldon Common. After a gap of 4 kilometres, a third route connects Brightworthy Barrow and its stone setting on Withypool Common with Green Barrow, Old Barrow and Tarr Steps. The fourth route runs from Exford Common across Dunkery Beacon to Joany How.

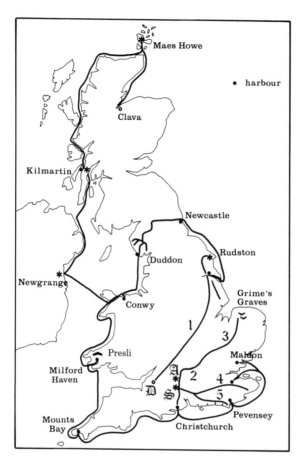

35 Communications.

1	Jurassic Way	5	South Downs Way
2	Ridgeway	A	Avebury
3	Icknield Way	S	Stonehenge
4	Harroway – Pilgrim's Way	D	Stanton Drew

Whether the ridgeways were used for long- or short-distance journeys is another question. The length of the major ridgeways is not in itself a proof that they were used for long journeys. The Exmoor high roads, with their short concentrations of barrows, stone settings and occupation sites separated by blank areas, suggest the opposite. People were, after all, relatively static. The main contacts with outsiders for the great majority of people were along the territory boundaries. This would suggest that the main use for the trackways, however long they were, would have been very local indeed, with people walking at most a few miles along

Plate 16 Tarr Steps. Some see this megalithic bridge as a medieval structure. It may well have been rebuilt several times following flood damage but it nevertheless lies on a neolithic route

them to meet their neighbours and exchange goods. Yet this does not preclude the use of the trackways for occasional longer expeditions, whether for trade or for social or political reasons or for religious pilgrimage. The two usages are quite compatible, although it is impossible to assess how many people were using the tracks as long-distance routes and how easy it may have been for them to negotiate the myriad territorial boundaries that the tracks presumably crossed. It is possible that the major highways were inter-territorial in much the same way that rivers are sometimes regarded as international thoroughfares. The concentration of neolithic and bronze age sites close to these routes makes that seem rather impracticable, but not impossible.

It is invariably easier to prove short-distance communication along the high roads. In Chapter 7, we located the Avebury-to-Stonehenge route used for transporting the sarsens. Since quite a wide corridor of open country was needed to transport the sarsens, we must suppose that the route was completely cleared at the outset and remained cleared for at least the decades needed to complete the operation. There must have been a social and political relationship between the peoples of the Avebury and Stonehenge territories that went beyond the transfer of the sarsen stones. It is reasonable to suppose that both during the project and afterwards the road was used for other kinds of communication. So we can add the Sarsen Road from Avebury to Stonehenge to our growing list of neolithic highways.

THE LOW ROADS

Not all the Sarsen Road is a ridgeway and this is a timely reminder that there were routes across low ground as well. On Mainland Orkney there was a lowland route connecting Skara Brae with the ceremonial centre on the isthmus between the Lochs of Stenness and Harray (Figure 36). After passing through the line of monuments that includes the Ring of Brodgar and the Standing Stones of Stenness, the road turned east along the southern shore of the Loch of Harray to reach the passage grave of Maes Howe.

It is likely that ceremonial centres on low ground in England were also served by lowland roads. People visiting earth circles in the Nene and Welland valleys would have followed the low gravel terraces along the valley sides. There is an increasing amount of evidence for the occupation of the lowlands, so we can expect to discover more and more lowland routeways. It seems clear, for instance, that a route along the River Nene's low terrace connected the causewayed enclosure at Briar Hill with Clifford Hill, the harvest hill beside the Nene at Houghton, 6 kilometres downstream.

In the Lake District, the central location of the axe factories and the scatter of stray rough-outs in the surrounding valleys suggests a radial pattern of tracks. This is confirmed by the stone circles, villages and knapping floors beside these routes (Figure 37). The axe factory high on Styhead with its Wagnerian setting stands at a natural crossroads: there are four routes down into nearby valley heads and it is still a busy nodal point for modern fell walkers. One route, up Aaron Slack and Windy Gap, passes between Great Gable and Green Gable before dropping into Ennerdale, the valley that leads eventually to Ehenside Tarn. Another, easier route drops sharply down to the south into the spectacular head of Wasdale, passing Wast Water to reach the settlement and stone circle near Seascale. Tracks from the Pike of Stickle factory led down Great Langdale to Windermere over into Little Langdale via Blea Tarn and then across to the Duddon valley; the sheltered Duddon estuary must have been one of the major exporting ports for the Langdale axes. Another track from Pike of Stickle led northwards over High Raise and along Langstrath to Borrowdale, the settlement at Portinscale and the stone circle at Castlerigg. This route continued east up the Greta valley, passing a village and two henges at Penrith before turning northwards to make for the Tyne gap.

It is fair to assume that most travellers on all roads would have gone on foot, as there is no positive evidence that oxen or horses were ridden. A chance find of a bit or bridle may yet alter the picture significantly, but at the moment it looks as if the

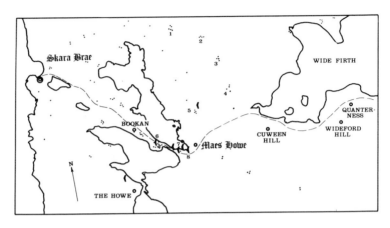

36 Mainland Orkney. The major chambered tombs are shown by circles. Each was the focus of a band or territory. It is probable that the barrow clusters (normally regarded as bronze age) also occupy neolithic foci.
   Examples of such barrow clusters are:

1 Knowes of Corrigall
2 Knowes of Trinnawin
3 Knowes of Trotty
4 Knowes of Setter
   Standing stones include:
5 Staney Hill

6 Ring of Brodgar
7 Stones of Stenness
8 Barnhouse Stone (marking
   the midwinter sunset as
   seen from the Maes Howe
   tomb chamber)

Stonehenge people went everywhere on foot. The strong and steady ox would normally have been used for arding and for pulling sleds and travois when bulk goods such as timber, stone, tools and pottery had to be transported. Waggons with solid disc wheels were available and may have been used to a very limited extent for carrying light loads along smooth and well-worn tracks, but over much of the country the terrain would have been too rough for the wheel.

TIMBER TRACKWAYS

In the unusual communication network developed in the Somerset Levels, nothing beyond walking would have been possible. The Levels began as a sea inlet, but the deposition of shingle bars along the line of the present coast sealed them off to form a freshwater reed swamp. During our period, the area of open water shrank to a few stagnant pools and channels while much of the swamp silted up to form raised bogs and fen woodlands of birch and alder. In this ambiguous environment – neither land nor water – it was difficult to use boats effectively and dangerous to attempt to walk through the bog, with its treacherous acid pools

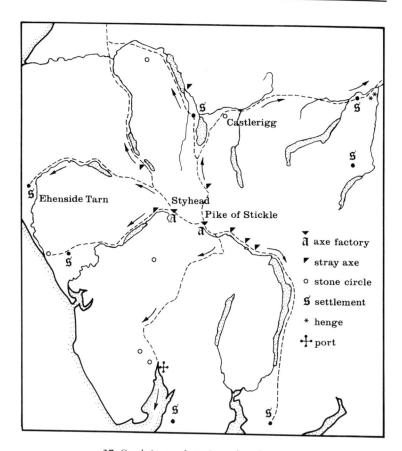

Castlerigg

Ehenside Tarn

Styhead
Pike of Stickle

▼ axe factory

▼ stray axe

○ stone circle

Ⓢ settlement

∗ henge

✝ port

37 Cumbria: axe factories and trackways

and half-hidden winding channels. People living on the higher ground solved the problem by building timber trackways to link the solid rock 'islands' together and join them to the ridge of the Polden Hills to the south (Figure 38).

The remains of the Sweet Track can be traced from the island of Westhay in the north to the hamlet at Shapwick in the Poldens. Built in 4000 BC, it is the oldest made road in Europe. The construction method shows that its builders were sensitive to the capabilities of different kinds of wood and were also engaged in forest management. They founded their track on straight coppiced lime rails of telegraph-pole size, laying them end to end and pinning them into place with pegs driven vertically into the peat bog. Where it was particularly wet, they piled turves onto the rails to raise the level of the track and keep the surface dry. The surface was made of split oak planks secured by wooden pins driven

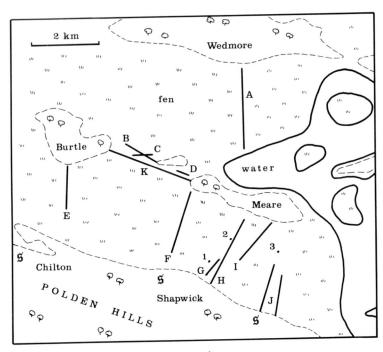

38 Timber trackways in the Somerset Levels

A Blakeway Track B Honeycat Track C Honeygore Track D Bell Track
E Chilton Track F Sweet Track G Shapwick Heath Track H Meare
Heath Track I Eclipse Track J Ashcott Track K Abbot's Way S neolithic
settlement. **Finds in the peat include: 1 Graig Lwyd axe 2 the Meare bow
3 the Ashcott bow**

down into the turf through specially made holes or notches. A
great deal of work and materials went into this project; 5
kilometres of split oak and 10,000 sharpened pegs were used to
make a walkway 1 metre wide and 2·4 kilometres long.

Nor was the Sweet Track an isolated project. Others were to
follow, such as the Abbot's Way built in 3000 BC to join the
islands of Westhay, Honeygar and Burtle. Abbot's Way was 3·2
kilometres long and used 20,000 metres of alderwood for the
transverse surface timbers, thousands of metres of birch stringers
for the longitudinal rails and some 50,000 birch pegs. The Walton
Track, which ran from Walton to Meare, was built about a
hundred years later and used a slightly different construction
method. Hurdles 3 metres long and 1 metre wide were
prefabricated off-site, presumably because of the unusually wet
conditions. The hurdles were woven out of hazel branches with
the edges and corners carefully bound with willow withies.

DUGOUTS, PLANK-BOATS AND SKIN-FRAME SHIPS

On open water, communication was much easier. The standard river boat was the dugout canoe hollowed out of a tree trunk up to 12 metres long. An analysis of trading links shows very high frequencies of type I axe-heads in west Cornwall, where they were produced, and along the River Avon in Wessex. River routes were clearly a major influence on the pattern of transport in three market areas: the Hampshire Avon, the Lower Thames and Essex, and the Humber estuary and lower Trent valley. The entire delivery voyage could in each case have been undertaken in a single vessel or flotilla. Alternatively it could have been done in stages with coastwise bulk shipments to river mouths and other natural harbours, where the goods were transferred to sleds or small river-going craft.

River boats were also used to ferry foot-passengers from bank to bank. The South Downs Way, for instance, is interrupted by four water gaps into which travellers had to descend to cross the rivers. The silt of the River Arun has yielded up the remains of two small dugouts and it is likely that each point where the ridgeway crossed a river was served by some sort of ferry. A similar service was needed where the Icknield Way reached the Thames and the Jurassic Way reached the Humber. In fact, at North Ferriby on the Humber, exactly where such a ferry would have been required, the remains of three plank boats, a winch, timber walkways and a laying-up platform have been discovered. They date from 1900 BC, just after the end of our period, but they indicate that by then a well-organised ferry service across the Humber was available. The sewn plank-boats of this early bronze age site show that attempts were being made to improve on the dugout, but these fairly large vessels (17 metres long overall, with a beam of 3 metres) were rather flimsy and probably restricted to the sheltered waters of rivers and estuaries. Although they had a substantial capacity for goods and passengers and the design was adhered to for at least a thousand years, they would not have been seaworthy.

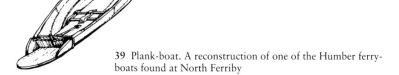

39 Plank-boat. A reconstruction of one of the Humber ferry-boats found at North Ferriby

Sea-going ships nonetheless did exist and they could have been made in two ways. The composite boat, made of three dugouts lashed together side by side to make a kind of trimaran, would have been quite stout enough to carry 7-ton bluestones from Milford Haven to Christchurch Harbour and then up the Avon to Amesbury. Probably for most cargoes, two-hull composites were adequate, especially since voyagers would rarely leave sight of land; quite modest craft would suffice for bay-hopping, however long the overall distance was.

The second type of sea-going ship was the skin-frame ship. The small coracles of present-day Welsh rivers show the general technique of construction, skilfully combining lightness and strength. The larger Irish curraghs have a similar construction. There are classical references to 'small boats formed of pliant twigs covered with the skins of oxen' spotted in the Irish Sea, and there is the Celtic legend of St Brendan who voyaged across the North Atlantic in a similar vessel. Tim Severin's reconstruction of St Brendan's skin-frame ship proved very successful in coping with the wave and weather conditions of the open ocean. The Bretons are known to have built a large skin-frame ship with a broad bottom and a high poop and prow, rather like the type featured in Swedish rock art of the neolithic and bronze age. The many vertical bars shown in such drawings are the light timber ribs showing through the taut hide and the double prow is a device to protect the skin from abrasion when beaching: the inner prow carried a figure-head.

A reconstruction skin-frame boat 7 metres long by 1·3 metres in the beam was made of alderwood branches and eight cow skins sewn together. It was very seaworthy and made three knots with a crew of six paddling. A curious effect of the double prow was that the waves tended to lift the lower keel to create a slight hydrofoil effect, enabling the skin boat to ride effortlessly and smoothly over the waves. The vessel remained stable and dry even with six people and a ton of cargo aboard. With planks fitted in the bottom of the boat to protect the skin from being damaged by hoof and horn, it was possible to transport livestock. So here, at last, is the method the pioneers used to introduce their animals from the European mainland. Here too is the most likely means of long-distance voyaging on the open sea.

The Swedish carvings show vessels that were a good deal larger than the reconstructed 7-metre boat. They were closer in size to the thirty-oar galleys that sailed the Mediterranean in the third millennium BC. Unlike the dugout, the dimensions of the skin-frame boat are not limited by the size of timber available and any number of cow hides can be sewn together. We can, in other words, visualise great vessels of perhaps 20 or even 30 metres in length plying majestically round the coastal waters of Britain.

40 Composite boat. A reconstruction of a sea-going vessel made from three dugout canoes. This one is about to embark from Milford Haven with a bluestone on board

There is no evidence that sails were used, but the rock carvings sometimes show a short mast with a blob at the top, which might represent a leafy branch mounted as an improvised sail. The Micmac Indians of Canada use this device to help propel their canoes; even a modest branch the height of a man can produce a significant amount of extra power.

But what evidence is there that sea routes were used in preference to land routes? Stuart Piggott felt in the 1950s that the sea route along the English Channel and North Sea was preferred to the Jurassic Way as a link between Wessex and Yorkshire. The bay-hopping coastal routes would get round the territorial boundary problems we envisaged for long-distance travel overland. Finally, and conclusively, there are concentrations of axes in the vicinity of natural harbours. If the bulk trade in axes was routed overland, we would find concentrations in areas of denser population, some of which would be well inland. But the focus on natural harbours proves that the axes were delivered or collected by sea. The importing ports, as closely as I can identify them, were Christchurch Harbour, Pevensey Bay in East Sussex, the estuaries of the Thames, Blackwater, Stour and Orwell, the Wash and the Humber (Figure 35). The thrust of the evidence, then, is towards coastwise trade over long distances for bulk goods, with transshipment at the importing harbours, followed by local distribution by sled or river boat.

But I am arguing this from the evidence of the stone axe-heads alone. There were other commodities to be transported besides axe-heads, as well as unladen traffic. The complete pattern was a complicated web composed of all the different kinds of communication discussed so far: both local and long-distance usage of ridge and lowland road routes, specialised wooden trackways in fenland areas, dugouts as ferries across rivers and composite boats and large skin-frame ships on the open sea. The overall picture is once again startingly evolved. Simple means were combined and developed to produce a result that surprises us with its elaborateness and ambition.

PART 3

THE CEREMONIAL
MONUMENTS

CHAPTER 9

EARTH CIRCLES AND EARTH LINES: THE RITUAL FUNCTION

Three summer days I roam'd, when 'twas my chance
To have before me on the downy Plain
Lines, circles, mounts, a mystery of shapes
Such as in many quarters yet survive,
With intricate profusion figuring o'er
The untill'd ground, the work, as some divine,
Of infant science, imitative forms
By which the Druids covertly express'd
Their knowledge of the heavens . . .
I saw the bearded Teachers with white wands
Uplifted, pointing to the starry sky
Alternately, and Plain below, while breath
Of music seemed to guide them, and the Waste
Was chear'd with stillness and a pleasant sound.

WILLIAM WORDSWORTH, *The Prelude*, 1805

The ceremonial monuments tell us about new aspects of the way the Stonehenge people lived but far more – and far more significantly – about what they thought of life. In this second half of the book, the emphasis shifts from the things they made and did to their thoughts, feelings, values and beliefs; from the material towards the non-material; from the secular towards the spiritual – although these distinctions and polarities would have puzzled them greatly.

The earth circles enable us to pass smoothly across from the secular world to that of the spirit, because they contain and blend elements of each. Some of the circles contained dwellings; some of them were thorough-going settlements. Durrington Walls incorporated some ceremonial features, such as the timber avenue and curved façade in front of one of the roundhouses, but it was not exclusively or even primarily a ritual centre. The large communal dwellings with their very secular middens show that the enclosure was a substantial proto-urban settlement. Other earth circles were

127

exclusively ceremonial centres. The various stone settings nested inside one another like Russian dolls at Avebury mark the monument out as a ceremonial centre, with no sign of the secular. Many of the smaller henges too were built as sanctuaries for religious purposes, functioning much as parish churches did in the medieval period. Variations in the design of earth circles seem to depend less on differences in religious belief than on slight local shifts of emphasis, as each community chose to highlight different elements in a single, commonly held system of beliefs.

Whether the number of rings in a causewayed enclosure held any particular significance for its builders is impossible to tell, but the circular or near-circular form chosen for nearly all the enclosures was certainly symbolic. The circle symbolised the sun on whose warmth everything depended, but it also represented the world-disc, the banks simulating the far horizon bounding the world of men and the enclosed *temenos* a microcosm of the world itself. This microcosm was fully within the priest-magician's power to control; he could gather and focus beneficent forces there; he could, conversely, send the gathered forces out like the fertilising rays of the sun itself into the surrounding fields, meadows and forests, calling the larger world into a fruitful submission.

Although the precise origin of earth circles is unknown, we can assume that they developed as a distinctively British offshoot of the enclosure tradition of the Linear Pottery Culture on mainland Europe. But the development of the sun symbol seems to have been a purely British obsession. Within the regions of Britain there were also preferences for particular sizes of monuments. The henges were small in Devon, Cornwall, the Thames valley and the Midlands, large in east Somerset and Wessex, and of mixed sizes in Yorkshire. They ranged from as little as 8 metres across at High Knowes in Northumberland to as much as 518 metres at Marden. In addition, the henges contained a large range of internal ritual features. Some had rings of stones; others had rings of posts, pits or deep shafts. Outside the henge entrance there were sometimes pairs of posts or stones to make a ceremonial gateway. Large-scale ceremonies involving entire communities could be performed in henges of 50 metres diameter or more. Such ceremonies would not have been possible in the very small circles, in which rituals of a more esoteric kind were probably performed by priest-magicians, and may not have been witnessed by the community as a whole. The ceremonial function of the circles varied considerably.

STONEHENGE AND THE MIDSUMMER SUNRISE

Time and again we are drawn back to Stonehenge as an inexhaustible source of information about the culture. This time it will illustrate for us the pre-eminence of the ritual function. The imposing single entrance of the initial design speaks of high ceremony and also of a concern that solar and lunar events should be marked. Two tall sarsen portal stones in holes 95 and E marked the entrance and the path followed by the rays of the midsummer sunrise. Just outside, arranged in six rows, were 53 stakes marking the most northerly positions of the midwinter moonrise through six lunar cycles. They prove that the Stonehenge people were observing the movements of the moon closely and continuously for a period of 112 years at least. The four large posts further out, set in the A holes, summarised the results of the empirical work with the smaller stakes, which were then removed. Beyond the A posts stood the two Heel Stones, forming a narrow, slot-like, outer gateway not for mortal visitors but for the midsummer sun. Inside the earth circle, the Stonehenge people dug out a ring of pits for votive offerings known as the Aubrey Holes (Figure 32).

The monument was then remodelled, using first the bluestones from Preseli and then, after a dramatic change of plan, the sarsen stones from Avebury. The central stone setting went through several further modifications, but the fundamental concept remained constant. The circles and horseshoes of standing stones were all built symmetrically round the principal axis of the monument, the line oriented on the rising of the midsummer sun.

Several ritual alterations were made to the entrance. The inner portal stones were taken down and re-erected in holes B and C on the sunrise axis. The northern Heel Stone was removed altogether, for a reason that has yet to be discovered, while its bereft partner was given the ritual protection of a circular ditch, apparently to protect it from sacrilege during the building of the Avenue. The Avenue consisted of two straight, parallel earth banks with external ditches making a 12-metre-wide processional way leading up to the entrance and giving forceful emphasis to the monument's main axis (Figure 41).

Stonehenge shares with some other henges significant astronomical orientations, and this feature has led many to see the monuments as primitive scientific observatories. As far as Stonehenge is concerned, the general orientation of the entrance towards the midsummer sunrise is suggestive. The more exact orientation implied by the inner portal stones, the axial stones B and C and the outer portal stones is even more compelling. But the first flash of the midsummer sunrise in 3000 BC was not only further north than it is today, it was actually almost two solar diameters further north than the position indicated by the two sets of portal stones. Those who try to advance the view that the Heel Stone itself pinpointed the exact date of the solstice are in grave difficulty, because the principal sight-line was not over the top of the Heel Stone but just to the north, between the Heel Stone and its missing partner. But even allowing for this, it is clear that the path between the two pairs of portal stones was never intended to align on the first flash of the midsummer sunrise, nor even on the half-disc.

The sight-line could have been used to fix the solstice indirectly, because the first flash of sunrise between the Heel Stones in 3000 BC occurred exactly thirteen days before and again exactly 13 days after the solstice. This method would have been as accurate in finding the solstice date as a direct observation. In one important way, it was a more reliable method. The gradual southward shift in the position of the sunrise would merely have reduced the number of days before and after the solstice when the first flash was visible between the Heel Stones. The Stonehenge observers could have gone on using this method right through the prehistoric period. But I do not believe that this was the principal purpose of the sight-line. The alignment's primary purpose was to celebrate and salute the full disc of the untrammelled sun, just as it floated free of the horizon on the summer solstice, which it did – right on the line – in 3000 BC. What was happening was not an astronomical observation but a ceremonial greeting of the midsummer sun, a celestial encounter with the highest religious and emotional content.

The fifty-three little stake-holes between the two pairs of portal stones nevertheless do represent astronomical observations – but of the moon, not the sun. The posts were markers for extreme northerly moonrise positions over a period of at least a century and, by recording results from many nineteen-year lunar cycles, they show a genuinely scientific approach. The larger and more permanent A posts summarised the results. The moon rose between the two right-hand posts (A3 and A4) a quarter of the way from the midpoint of the cycle to the major standstill, and between the two left-hand posts (A1 and A2) when the moon was halfway to the major standstill. This was accurate enough to tell where the moon was in its cycle, but not very precise. It seems that the A posts were erected so that the whole community could view the moonrise as part of a ceremony. In any case, the erection of Stone 97 blocked off the sight-line between A3 and A4. The midsummer sunrise ceremony had by then become more potent than the older moon rites.

The scientific work with the lighter stakes and A posts was thus done at an early stage, before the portal stones were in place. The stone monument celebrated cosmic events and seemed, by predicting, actually to control them. This powerful and brilliantly-conceived piece of theatre was only possible after a long period of observation. The wooden posts with their smooth sides and narrow points were ideal for accurate horizon marking and they were easy to move about quickly in a trial-and-error exercise.

The length of the timber 'prologue' stage at Stonehenge could until very recently only be guessed at, but the first radiocarbon dates for the car-park post-holes are astonishingly ancient. Three giant pine trunks soared up some 300 metres away from the central circle, acting as foresights for the north-western horizon. Their distance from the central precinct implies that great accuracy was sought; like the stake-holes they belong to the prologue phase. Post-hole B has a 'raw' date of 6140 bc, which cannot as yet be corrected but may correct to about 7100 BC in calendar years. Post-hole A is a thousand years older, 7180 bc, probably correcting to about 8100 BC. Archaeologists have been understandably reticent about these very remarkable dates, which speak of ceremonial and astronomical activity at Stonehenge even *before* the beginning of the neolithic.

The position of the posts suggests an orientation to the midsummer sunset and they belong to an era when the sun set well to the north of its present azimuth. The midsummer sun now sets at 310 degrees, but it has crept southwards at a rate of 0·02 degrees per century. In 8100 BC the sun would have set at 312·07 degrees, which is the exact bearing of Post A from the centre of the monument.

It seems scarcely credible that the preliminary work for the Stonehenge alignments began so early. Nevertheless, the evidence points to an origin for Stonehenge as a sun temple that stretches back into the remotest past. Long before the stones arrived, the magician performed his strange rituals in a wooden cult-house at the centre of the precinct and peered out at the twilit skyline through a ghostly maze of timber markers, painstakingly fixing the realms of sky and earth together in an everlasting moongate. In the slow course of time, the wandering sun and moon and the invisible forces of the underworld were to be harnessed inescapably to the will of man; seasons and crops and the fortunes of men would eventually and inexorably be brought under the magician's control.

By 3000 BC all the hard, raw, proto-scientific work in establishing the main lunar and solar orientations of the monument had been done. The clock was wound up. We can see now that the earth circle, the earth lines and all the various stone settings were fundamentally inessential to the pinpointing of sunrises and moonsets. As much could have been done with a simpler arrangement of posts and in the opening phase it was done in just that way. We should see the evolving stone monument of the middle and late neolithic not so much as an observatory but as a celestial temple, a ceremonial celebration of the heavens: as a temple to the strange, clock-like interaction between earth and sky, between the passage of the seasons and the fruition of crops, between the vagaries of the sun and moon and the destinies of men.

There is one rather unexpected link between the lunar and solar orientations. The stake-holes marking the most northerly winter moonrises show that, at the maximum, the moon rose well to the north of the midsummer sunrise position as marked by the monument's axis, but nine years after the maximum, halfway through the lunar cycle, the two positions coincided. The site was evidently designed as a stage on which the two polarities could be celebrated: midwinter moonrise ceremonies, at night and possibly by flickering lamplight, and midsummer sunrise ceremonies, at daybreak and by the light of the dawning sun. Perhaps in this coincidence of moon and sun lines there is a hint that every eighteen or nineteen years there was a special ceremony to celebrate the accord.

THE THORNBOROUGH AND PRIDDY CULT CENTRES

In certain areas, triplets or even larger numbers of henges were built, presumably to accommodate a whole series of different ceremonies. There is an 11-kilometre long line of monuments on the low plateau between the Ure and Swale near Ripon in Yorkshire. The three magnificent Thornborough Circles, each 244 metres in diameter, are equidistant, arranged in a straight line and with their entrances on the axis to north-west and south-east. The massive banks at Thornborough have both internal and external ditches 20 metres wide and 3 deep. The banks were built of large boulders coated with white gypsum crystals. It seems that this deliberate whitening of the bank was designed to make the monument look like the earth circles of the chalk country: a curious architectural back-reference to the chalklands. The passage grave of Newgrange was also whitened with a revetment of pearly white quartz blocks. The raw white chalk banks of the early causewayed enclosures gave rise to an association, conscious or unconscious, aesthetic or spiritual, between ceremonial monuments and the brilliance and purity of white rock. In landscapes that were predominantly green, white monuments were plainly visible from a mile or two away, shining out as territorial beacons all the way to the boundaries of the band territories.

The four Priddy Circles near Wells in Somerset are similar in purpose to the Thornborough Circles. They are spread along a north-south axis nearly a mile long. Each has an external ditch, while the banks were originally contained between timber palisades 4 metres apart, giving the enclosures the appearance of walled citadels. The three southern circles are similar in size with an overall diameter of 185 metres and equidistant, about 80 metres apart. They are very reminiscent of the Thornborough Circles and it is odd that there is a vast tract of countryside in between with no comparable triple earth rings. The nearest parallels are the original Avebury design, with its three stone rings, and the Knowlton Circles in Dorset. The northern Priddy Circle is slightly smaller than the southern three and further away, some 500 metres to the north. It looks like a later addition and I am reminded of the unfinished third stone circle at Avebury, which was also the northernmost structure in the sequence.

The recurring pattern of earth circle complexes can be explained in several ways. It could be argued that the circle was designed to contain the entire community and population growth may have necessitated the building of additional circles to accommodate everybody. This explanation is acceptable when the circles are small but it is hard to believe that the sequences of gigantic circles at Priddy, Thornborough and Knowlton were necessitated by simple population growth. The enormous size of the 'overspill' circles argues against it. It also looks as if the triplets of large circles were made as part of a single, coherent design and were constructed at much the same time. It is far more likely that the different sacred precincts were used for different ceremonial purposes. Possibly ceremonies to celebrate the various calendrical feast days were conducted in different precincts. Possibly there were several deities who were honoured separately; the henge complex could then be seen as a kind of Acropolis, with each circle as a temple dedicated to a different deity.

EARTH LINES

The earth circles were often associated in the later neolithic with pairs of earth lines known as cursūs. The conventional name is misleading, since it originates in William Stukeley's eighteenth-century fancy that the lines were racecourses on the model of the Roman circus. Stukeley's interpretation is almost certainly wrong but unfortunately the name cursus (pl. cursūs) has stuck.

The Stonehenge Greater Cursus, only 750 metres north of Stonehenge, runs for nearly 3 kilometres from east to west, 100 metres wide at the ends and swelling to 130 metres near the western end; this implies that it was made from east to west, as the final narrowing-off looks like the correction of a surveying error. The eastern end is marked by an earlier long barrow. In spite of its impressive dimensions, the official guide book dissuades us from visiting it on the grounds that it is not worth the trouble. I am reminded of Dr Johnson's remark that when you have seen one druid circle you have seen them all. The sad truth is that damage inflicted by the army and agriculture has reduced this

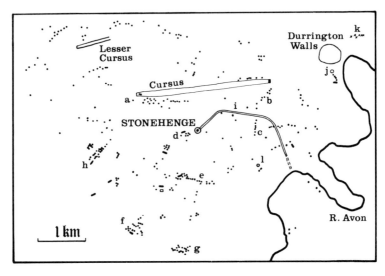

41 The Stonehenge area. Stonehenge became a metropolitan ritual centre. As a focus for barrow-building in the late neolithic and bronze age, it produced the densest concentration of burial monuments in Britain.
Barrow clusters: **a** Cursus group; **b** Old King Barrows; **c** New King Barrows; **d** Stonehenge Down group; **e** Normanton Down group; **f** Lake group; **g** Wilsford group; **h** Winterbourne Stoke group

Other features: **i** Stonehenge Avenue; **j** Woodhenge; **k** flint mines; **l1** – Coneybury Hill henge: the large pit outside this small henge may have held a stone marking the midwinter sunrise: another component in the Stonehenge complex

and most other earth lines to near-invisibility. The Stonehenge Lesser Cursus nearby is 365 metres long and 46 wide. Both features are surrounded by late neolithic and bronze age barrows, implying a role in funerary rituals.

The largest earth lines in Britain are those of the Dorset Cursus (Figure 42). It runs for 10.5 kilometres from Thickthorn Down to Pentridge, with an overall width of 92 metres, which it adheres to with a constancy that implies frequent measurement during the building. The Dorset Cursus was lengthened twice over: 2.4 kilometres from the well-preserved south-western beginning of the earth lines are two long barrows; the one set at right angles across the cursus was the original destination of the cursus and its end marker. About the same distance further to the east, at Wyke Down, there is clearly squared-off end bank with two more long barrows close by. The course of the earth lines was determined by the distribution of the long barrows. The inference is that the lines defined a sacred way for processions of some kind making visits to the long barrows. The great width of the cursus implies that large

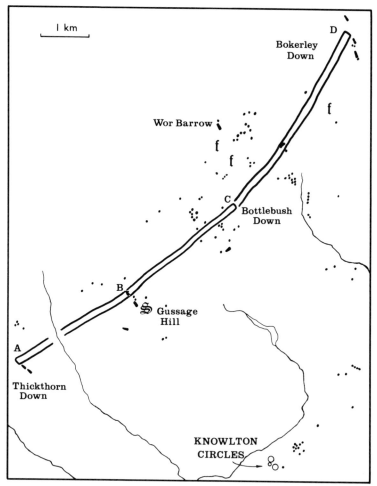

42 The Dorset Cursus. The monument was apparently built in three stages: A-B first, then B-C, then C-D, linking long barrows.   s – settlement; f – ancient field system

numbers of people were involved in the processions: probably the entire community.

An additional purpose for the Dorset Cursus has been suggested, relating the monument to lunar observations. The idea is that the levelled area just inside the Thickthorn Down terminal was an observation platform from which observers looked north-east towards a long barrow (Gussage St Michael III) on the skyline. In 2500 BC, when it is likely the cursus was laid out, the rising moon at its southernmost position would have appeared in the notch between the long barrow and the right-hand cursus bank. Several other lunar sightlines along the Dorset Cursus have been proposed. Although at first these ideas may seem somewhat exotic, we know from Stonehenge that there was an obsession with tracking the movements of the moon, so we may believe that lunar alignments could have been built into the Dorset Cursus. Even so, there was no need for anything more than isolated markers for these observations; what then was the purpose of the endless earthworks?

The excavation of the ditches and the raising of the banks meant moving the equivalent of half the volume of Silbury Hill, work that must have taken 1·3 million man-hours. Something more than skyline markers was in the hearts of its builders. We may believe that lunar alignments were included, but they were not the sole function. It is likely that the moon, as a night deity, was associated with death, so there is a link between the celestial observations – and the plangent invocations that doubtless accompanied them – and the visits to the long barrows.

The Dorset Cursus illustrates some major problems of interpretation that may never be resolved by excavation. Its enormous size is nevertheless perfectly in harmony with the other great monuments of the Wessex region, a land where projects were conceived on a gigantic scale.

We should also remember that there were many small cursūs, both in Wessex and elsewhere. At Milfield in Northumberland, we can see a close association between one of the smaller cursūs and a group of earth circles. The Milfield Avenue was designed to link together several little henges, passing close to two of them (Milfield South and Marleyknowe) and actually passing right through the centre of another (Coupland). It consists of roughly parallel ditches 15-30 metres apart and we know that it was built after the henges because it swerves to avoid Marleyknowe and narrows in order to pass through Coupland.

The earth lines at Maxey in Huntingdonshire lead down to a crossing place on the River Welland. The lines, 60 metres apart, are over 1.6 kilometres long with a slight bend in the middle, where a large earth circle 130 metres in diameter is superimposed on the earth lines. Dozens of smaller circles of various periods cluster round the large circle, about which we know very little, and it seems to have been the focus of the whole flurry of ceremonial activity at Maxey. The arrangement of earth lines passing through earth circles reminds me of the stone settings at Avebury where, in the final and complete design, a sinuous avenue of stones leads up to and then away from the Great Circle (Figure 29). It is the same general concept at Avebury realised in stone, and at Milfield and Maxey in earth.

Finally, the earth lines at the major cult centre of Rudston in Yorkshire deserve to be mentioned. Rudston is unusual in that it has three cursūs and they are clustered not round the henge, which is further to the north, but round the Rudston Monolith, giving us yet another variation on the pattern of earth circles and earth lines. The line and the circle, the fundamental forms of neolithic earth sculpture, may be reflections of two fundamental forms in primitive dance – the Indian-file processional dance and the Ring o' Roses round dance. Stonehenge itself has in the past been known as the Giants' Dance. The earthworks of the Stonehenge people owe their shape partly to an arcane symbolism that can be seen recurring at smaller scales, right down to the little cup-and-ring marks carved on rocks in northern Britain (see Chapter 15). Symbolic statement is certainly part of the answer, but the large-scale arrangements of circles and lines may well owe much to the simple choreography of ritual dances.

CHAPTER 10

THE OLD TEMPLES
OF THE GODS

This (island) is in the far North, and it is inhabited by people
called the Hyperboreans from their location beyond Boreas, the
North Wind. The story goes that Leto (Apollo's mother) was
born there. It is for this reason that Apollo is honoured above
all the gods. There are men who serve as priests of Apollo
because this god is worshipped every day with continuous
singing and is held in exceptional honour. There is also in the
island a precinct sacred to Apollo and suitably imposing, and a
notable spherical temple decorated with many offerings. There
is also a community sacred to this god, where most of the
inhabitants are trained to play the lyre and do so continuously
in the temple, worshipping the god with singing . . . Men called
Boreads are in charge of this city and over the sacred precinct.

Hecateus of Abdera *c*.350 BC, quoted by DIODORUS SICULUS
in *Histories*, 8 BC

THE ORIGINS OF THE STONE CIRCLES

If there is one distinctive and characteristic cipher of the
Stonehenge people, one artefact that distinguishes their culture
from all others, one single signature that identifies them, it is the
stone circle. The Stonehenge people were different from the people
who preceded them and from those who came after in many other
ways, but the one way that has caught the imagination of all is
this distinctive form of megalithic architecture. It is, in its simplest
form, a ring of stones planted upright in the ground, but among
the 700 surviving circles in Britain there are seemingly endless
variations on this simple theme.

The stone circles developed in the late neolithic, from about
3000 BC onwards, mainly in the higher areas of the north and
west, where the earth circles of the lowlands were reinterpreted in
stone. The reasons for the change in style are not hard to find. In
the thin soils and hard rocks of the highlands, quarry ditches were

difficult to dig. At the Ring of Brodgar in Orkney, a full-size quarry ditch was attempted in the hard sandstone, but it was usually considered more realistic, given the geological conditions, to dispense with the ditch altogether and mark out the 'bank' with a series of marker slabs, of which there were many available in the highlands. It is also clear that, by the time people started building stone circles, there was already a well-established tradition of building chambered tombs, so the skills for shaping and moving megaliths were already acquired.

The zones where henges and stone circles were built are not mutually exclusive. There is a 60-kilometre wide overlap zone running north–south through the centre of Britain. In this overlap zone, there is a tendency for both henges and stone circles to be unusually large. This has yet to be satisfactorily explained, but it looks as though the people living along the 'frontier' between the two cultural zones were fuelled by a frontier spirit: they seem to have been more dynamic and more daring.

Post-circles like Woodhenge were at the time of their discovery eagerly greeted as timber variants of stone circles, possibly as their direct lowland precursors. But we now see the multiple post-circles as roofed buildings, which none of the stone circles could ever have been. So the stone circles were not in any sense derived from timber circles, except in one very special case, which we will consider later; nor were the stone circles imported from the European mainland. In the past, too much of the British heritage has been attributed to importations from Europe: in the stone circles at least we have an incontrovertibly British innovation. This is not to say that stone circles do not exist in Europe. They do. There are several, for example, encircling passage graves at Los Millares in Spain, but they postdate the earlier British circles and the idea may well have been exported from Britain.

Aubrey Burl has made the most exhaustive analytical study of stone circles and is without doubt the leading authority on the subject. He believes that the earliest stone circles are to be found in the Lake District. These are plain rings of raised blocks arranged in approximately circular settings 30 metres across and enclosing an open, circular precinct. From the scanty dating available, it looked until recently as if the Newgrange Great Circle, 104 metres across, was emerging as the ancestor of stone circles in Britain. Even though few circles have been firmly dated, if the Newgrange circle was raised in 3300 BC, at the time when the passage grave was built, it would have been a strong contender; but it is now thought that the circle was raised significantly later than the passage grave.

Aubrey Burl thinks the Lake District circles are at least as old as the Stones of Stenness, radiocarbon-dated to 3040 BC, and probably older. Burl argues persuasively that the custom of building stone circles developed and spread with the developing trade in stone axes.

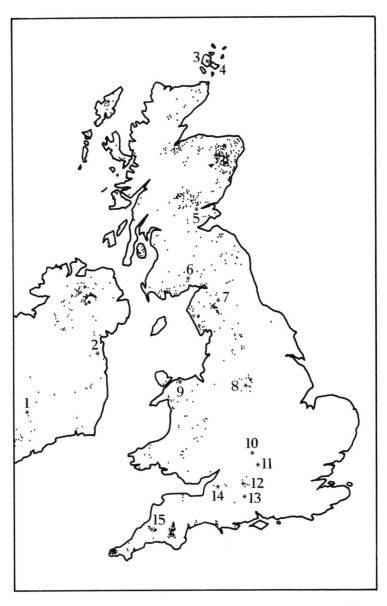

43 Stone circles. 1 Lios   2 Newgrange   3 Ring of Brodgar   4 Stones of
Stenness   5 Cairnpapple   6 Twelve Apostles   7 Long Meg and Her Daughters
8 Arbor Low   9 Druids' Circle   10 Rollright Stones   11 Devil's Quoits
12 Avebury   13 Stonehenge   14 Stanton Drew   15 Stripple Stones

The date of the Great Langdale axe factory, 3400 BC, implies that the circles were built as early as 3400-3200 BC. The almost completely destroyed Lochmaben Stone ring near Gretna Green yielded a radiocarbon date of 3275 BC when the Lochmaben Stone fell in 1982, so there is solid archaeological support for Burl's view. The Castlerigg circle, on the end of the ridge separating Borrowdale and St John's-in-the-Vale, stands close to a fork in the axe trade routes (Figure 37). It is a very fine monument, with two stately portal stones positioned rather unusually on the north side and a rectangular stone setting built on to the inside of the eastern perimeter. The significance of this east-facing sanctuary can only be guessed at, but it may be linked with the eastward orientation of many of the burial monuments of the lowland zone. The early Cumbrian circles are small compared with contemporary early henges in the region, with an average diameter of 37 metres compared with 73 metres for the henges. Transporting and raising the stones took more planning and effort than raising mere earth banks, so it is fair to suppose that the stone circles were comparable to the henges in terms of the manpower involved in building them.

The initial attraction to Cumbria was the well-drained and fertile lowland along the coast, the focus of early farming activity. Later, the valley floors of the mountainous core were brought into the economy for grazing and food-gathering and the higher slopes and cols were exploited for axe-manufacturing. The period of stone circle building in the Lake District is thought to be associated with the growth of the stone axe industry. The siting of stone circles at intervals along the axe-trade routes is very suggestive in this connection. It was probably the movement of people involved in the axe trade that led to the dissemination of the stone circle idea to other parts of Britain. Much of the trade went on by sea, so it was natural that many early stone circles were built on the seaways of the western coast of Britain, or not far from them.

Long Meg and Her Daughters, though not coastal, are a good example of a large circle belonging to this developmental, diffusion phase. The stone setting, 109 metres across, is situated on the road from the Lake District to the Tyne Gap, a route along which a great many of the Langdale axes were taken. There are traces of an earthen bank, showing an affinity with the Penrith henges 10 kilometres away to the south. There is a double portal to the south-west and Long Meg, a 3·7 metre high monolith, stands 18 metres outside this entrance; when viewed from the centre of the circle it marks the position of the midwinter sunset in the late neolithic.

The circles of the developmental phase tend to be large; there are fourteen over 61 metres in diameter. They also tend to have similar site characteristics. Almost all are low-lying, in valley floors, on river terraces or on low passes, usually beside water.

Long Meg stands on the edge of a broad sandstone terrace above the east bank of the Eden. Perhaps the finest and most extreme example of this type is the Ring of Brogdar, which stands only a metre or two above sea level on a narrow isthmus separating two large lochs (Figure 36). The nearness to water is a feature shared with the henges and it tends to reinforce the idea that the two types of monument were built with a common purpose, sharing a common symbolism.

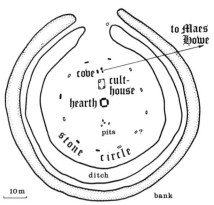

44 Stones of Stenness, Mainland Orkney. The so-called 'Dolmen' is here re-interpreted as a cove; its orientation towards Maes Howe implies a ritual link with the tomb. The circle contains an unusually complete suite of ritual furniture, telling us much about its function. Surviving stones are shown in solid black

The date when the Ring of Brodgar was constructed is not known for certain. It stands only a mile from the Stones of Stenness, which date to 3040 BC. Stenness is relatively small: its badly damaged stone circle seems to have had a diameter of only 30 metres even though it was surrounded by a 61 metre diameter earthwork. Brodgar is a larger and more spectacular project. Its stone circle has a diameter of 104 metres, very close to the size of Long Meg. The impressiveness of Brodgar is rooted in the careful selection and preparation of very regular, thin, straight-sided slabs of sandstone and the equally careful selection of the site, at the slightly raised centre of a broad and shallow basin. The combined effect of architectural purity and a sure sense of place is intensely dramatic.

The large scale of Brodgar, with its 142-metre diameter rock-cut ditch, itself representing over 80,000 man-hours of work, is such that it is likely to be later than Stenness. Given the dynamism of local cultural development seen in the Orcadian tombs (see Chapter 11), it is logical to regard Brodgar as the younger and

Plate 17 One of the Stenness stones, showing the fine quality of the neolithic mason's craft

more evolved of the two circles: it was probably built in about 2900 BC.

The rites performed at the stone circles were probably related to the nearby passage graves. The magnificent monumental tomb of Maes Howe is less than a mile away from Stenness. Just to the north of Brodgar, the Ring of Bookan marks the ruined foundations of what must once have been a passage grave rivalling Maes Howe in splendour. We therefore should treat the circles as the joint social and ceremonial centre-piece of a large complex of interrelated monuments.

This surge of architectural development was not confined to Orkney. Links have been sought among monuments by way of coincidences in their dimensions, but this is a will o' the wisp.

Plate 18 The Ring of Brodgar

Dimensions that appear very similar on maps drawn to a scale of 1:5000 turn out to be less so when smaller scales are used. Even so, it does seem odd that the Great Circle at Newgrange has a diameter identical to that of the Ring of Brodgar: odder still that the North and South Circles at Avebury also have that same diameter. The common dimension of 104 metres is the strongest evidence there is for the existence and widespread use of a uniform unit of measurement. Alexander Thom proposed that this unit (0·829 metres) be called the Megalithic Yard (MY) and that the circles we are discussing were deliberately designed with diameters of 125 MY. The problem, of course, is that for each of these four circles laid out in nicely rounded numbers of Megalithic Yards there are a hundred that are not. It may be that these four sites, which are admittedly very important centres on other counts, were laid out with the same diameters quite by chance. For the time being, we have to keep our minds open on the matter.

By the time we reach the building of Avebury, we have reached the culminating stage of the late neolithic. Extraordinarily, there are no radiocarbon dates yet for Avebury, but it is thought to have been built in 2600 or 2500 BC. Its plan incorporates two large stone circles later surrounded by a gigantic outer circle 332 metres across. This is by far the largest stone circle in the British Isles and when complete it consisted of about a hundred huge undressed stones. The largest were used to mark the main entrances to north and south. The colossal south entrance stones both survive (Plate

5), though only the Swindon Stone survives at the north entrance. This diamond-shaped megalith, weighing 60 tons, is balanced on one corner. Its partner was 'of a most enormous bulk' and from the measurements taken by William Stukeley at the time of its collapse in the eighteenth century it appears to have been the most enormous stone used in any British monument. Five metres tall, 3·5 metres broad and 2 metres thick, it must have weighed nearly 90 tons, almost twice the weight of the biggest trilithon pillar at Stonehenge.

The monument as a whole was certainly impressive enough to have been talked about on the other side of Europe and there is a possibility that the passage from Diodorus quoted as this chapter's epigraph contains references to Avebury as well as Stonehenge. Stonehenge, with its solar orientation, could be the imposing precinct sacred to Apollo and Avebury the notably spherical temple. 'Spherical' may be a reference to the monument's celestial connections, as classical writers used the word as a synonym for 'astronomical', or it may simply emphasise the multiplicity of circles incorporated in Avebury's design. Whether the music-saturated city of the Boreads who tended the sacred precinct can be identified with Durrington is impossible to say. Even Hecateus, whom Diodorus was quoting, lived more than a thousand years after the hey-day of Stonehenge – time enough for legend itself to become garbled.

Avebury is in every way the colossus of the British neolithic, but we should perhaps now turn to the ways in which it typifies the magic circle tradition. On Orkney, we saw the use of two stone circles in close proximity; at Thornborough, we saw the use of three henges arranged along a common axis. Avebury was initially laid out like this, with three stone circles in a row, but before the third was complete it was abandoned in favour of the more ambitious outer circle, ditch and bank. It was an unusual re-working of the triple-ring design. The commoner, three-in-a-row, layout was used at Stanton Drew in Somerset.

Stanton Drew illustrates several interesting features of site and design. The Great Circle, with its diameter of 113 metres, is the second largest in Britain. The situation, in a pass connecting the valleys of the Yeo and Bristol Avon, implies once more a regard for trade routes, although today the site is far from busy. Of all the English sites, Stanton Drew has more nearly than any other retained the appearance and atmosphere of a monument built in a neolithic woodland clearing. It has a beautiful protected site with tree-clad hill slopes forming a middle distance skyline on three sides and a more distant prospect on the fourth; the monument stands on a low terrace beside the water meadows of the River Chew.

One curiosity of the site is that because of a low ridge running east

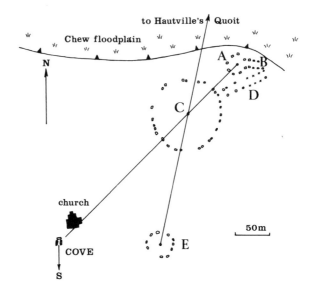

45 Stanton Drew.

A North-East Circle;   C Great Circle;
B Stone avenue leading to   D Wrecked stone avenue;
   water meadows;   E South-West Circle.
The straight lines show the monument's main alignments. Hautville's Quoit was a
standing stone that originally stood on the valley side 400 metres from the Great
Circle

from the Cove the Great and South-West Circles cannot be seen
from one another. The axis of the Great and North-East circles,
both of which have ruined avenues leading down into the water
meadows, can be followed to the Cove. This is a three-sided
building open to the sky and to the south and made of huge,
dressed slabs raised on the summit of the ridge. The Cove is one of
only five neolithic coves known to have been built: the others are
at Cairnpapple in West Lothian and Avebury, where there are
two. It now seems very likely indeed that the stone structure inside
the circle at Stenness, quite wrongly reconstructed in 1907 with an
extra stone to make a 'dolmen', was originally another cove. The
main slab of the Stenness cove, now recumbent, was originally
upright and oriented so that a magician seated inside the cove
with his back resting against it could just see the summit of Maes
Howe between the two portal stones.

   What special rites went on at these rare and remarkable shrines
we can only guess at. It cannot be a coincidence, though, that
three stones arranged in such a setting were the first stage in the
construction of a chambered tomb. Next came the roof slab, then
any transepts that might be required, then an entrance passage

Plate 19 Stanton Drew. Two short ruined stone avenues lead away from the stone circles to the Chew water meadows, in the left background

Plate 20 The Avebury Cove. The big slab on the right faces the midsummer sunrise. The Beckhampton Cove away to the south-west was oriented towards the midwinter sunrise. The tall stone on the left is the central stone's right flanker; the left flanker was a similarly tall and narrow stone and stood in the foreground

made of paired uprights and roof slabs; finally a mound of earth or stones was raised over the whole structure. I am not suggesting that the coves at Stanton Drew and Avebury are unfinished chambered tombs, but that they were intended to represent tombs: they were symbols of the tomb's heart. Recent excavations at Stenness provide us with a clear link between the cove and funerary ritual. The Stenness cove stands just 10 metres from the centre of the stone circle, where a large square hearth was found, containing pieces of cremated bone. Between the pyre-hearth and the cove, connecting them, as it were, stood a pair of standing stones and a small wooden shrine; pyre-hearth, standing stones, wooden shrine and cove were all arranged in a straight line leading directly to (or from) the henge's single entrance.

It looks as if the magician seated in the Stenness cove would have been plainly visible to others assembled in the stone circle, but the arrangement was different at Stanton Drew. Priests officiating in the substantially larger cove at Stanton Drew were invisible to people gathering in the Great and North-East Circles, but on emerging they became dramatically visible on the western or south-western skyline to those assembled in all three circles. Unfortunately, the medieval church has been built right beside the Cove and blocks its sight-line to the two northern circles, probably in a deliberate attempt to seal up whatever pagan power still resided in the monument.

The Stanton Drew complex contains a second axis. A line drawn through the centres of the South-Western and Great Circles and extrapolated to the north-north-east ran through a standing stone, Hauteville's Quoit, which once stood halfway up the valley side. There is no positive evidence of date, but Burl thinks the whole complex is a fairly late monument, built in about 2200 BC.

The stone rings of the neolithic were all laid out as true circles or attempts to approximate true circles. Whether the slight flattening of some of the circles, such as Long Meg and Castlerigg, was deliberate is very hard to tell. It was only after 2000 BC that other than circular shapes were consciously selected and we can take it that ellipses and egg shapes identify rings as later works. The monuments became smaller in the bronze age and progressively smaller stones were used in their construction – signs of degeneracy.

Most of the stone rings and stone rows in Scotland are late. It may be that population densities remained very low until the bronze age, when most of the monuments were raised. One exception is the group of highly individual monuments known as recumbent stone circles, which are concentrated in Aberdeenshire. The blocks of these perfect circles are carefully graded in height, the smallest to the north-east, the tallest to the south-west. The two tallest stones have a recumbent stone between them, like an altar or an entrance stone after the Newgrange model. These recumbent stone circles proliferated during the late neolithic and Burl explains this by increasing population density. In 2500 BC there were about fifteen rings; by 2300 BC the number had doubled; by 2100 it had quadrupled. This distinctive type of monument used and fused at the end of the neolithic several elements from earlier phases of circle building. The supine stone idea seems to have been imported from the Boyne valley in

Plate 21 Stones of Stenness. This structure, once known as 'The Dolmen', is another variant of the cove. The Stenness cove is aligned on Maes Howe, whose dark summit is visible in the distance

Ireland, while the ideas of grading the stones and having the entrance, albeit a blind one, to the south-west were taken over from the Clava tradition of chambered tombs clustered along the shores of the Moray firth.

Wales is a poor place for stone circles. There are only fifty rather small circles, all apparently of bronze age date. Southern and eastern Britain are also sparsely favoured, but there was a late neolithic flowering of the stone circle tradition along the north-south spinal boundary. This zone of creative exchange produced the rings at Avebury and Stonehenge; the rings at Balfarg, Devil's Quoits, Rollright and Arbor Low belong to a continuation of this phase into the early bronze age. But it would be a mistake to treat these frontier circles as a type or family: there are huge variations in form, technique and site history. The Great Circle at Avebury was completed at the same time, more or less, as the bank and ditch. At Stonehenge, the stone circle was added six hundred years after the bank and ditch and was not part of the original design at all.

THE SECRET MEANING OF STONEHENGE

The stone rings and horseshoes of each hectic revision of the Stonehenge design show original developments of the stone circle idea that require special explanation. Even the first circular stone setting on the site, the uncompleted (Stonehenge II) bluestone circle, was a highly original structure. In it, the stones were arranged in radial pairs, as at no other site, and it looks as if each pair was to have carried a radial lintel; the overall plan would have looked like the rays of the sun. The lintel idea was carried over into the next phase of construction – on a grander scale. Five great sarsen trilithons arranged in a horseshoe were surrounded by a sarsen circle with lintels running in a continuous ring. This was the ultimate climax of the stone circle idea, the solid girdle of rock a perfect symbol of completeness and security, and of the world-disc offered up to the heavens.

But what were the lintels for? Was there any other layer of hidden symbolism? Burl has suggested that the final arrangement at Stonehenge was a megalithic facsimile of a timber setting: many of the stones actually simulate carpentry techniques. This interpretation pre-supposes that the timber circles were roofless and that the posts were capped by lintels. But it is more likely that Stonehenge symbolised the internal structure of the great timber roundhouses, in much the same way that the coves symbolised the

46 Stonehenge III. A reconstruction of the completed sarsen and bluestone monument

essential, central parts of chambered tombs. If we view Stone-henge III in this way, the sarsen peristyle or ring represents the structural timbers of the outer wall of a roundhouse and the taller sarsen trilithons represent the stouter, taller timber rings with higher horizontal bearers designed to carry the radial rafters. We can see Stonehenge III as the structural essence of a roundhouse, its spiritual frame, or we can see it as a representation of a great roundhouse in decay. We know that the roundhouses were in use for long periods and allowed to collapse and decay in situ. If such buildings became associated with the deeds and aspirations of an-cestors, the wrecked and roofless timbers of an ancient tribal round-house must have stirred deep feelings in those who beheld them.

An awareness of the Stonehenge people's love of analogy, symbol and layered allusion is all that is needed, after all, to understand the final evocative design, the design towards which several generations groped their way driven by some unconscious and uncomprehended sense of collective identity. The final symbol, the cipher of the Stonehenge people, was the image of home: the nostalgic and sentimental image of the ancestral home not yet complete, not yet quite fallen into decay.

The present disintegrated state of the site is nevertheless not quite what its architects intended. Some stones have fallen in historic times; one of the trilithons, stones 57, 58 and their lintel, fell down on 3 January 1797. Some stones may have fallen as a result of natural settling and weathering, but it is not likely that the process began naturally. Many great stones at Avebury remain standing even though they are perched in holes only 40 centimetres deep. Stones of similar weight at Stonehenge have been uprooted from vertical-sided sockets up to 1·5 metres deep. We know about the large-scale vandalism at Avebury that went on through the medieval period and in later centuries too, bringing lasting disgrace on the village, but there is no record whatever of damage to Stonehenge during that period. It is likely that the Romans were responsible. We know that the Romans suppressed the druids with great violence because of their opposition to the Empire and that the druids' headquarters on Anglesey were destroyed. Normally the Romans tolerated native religions, but druidism was regarded as seditious and was put down with relentless ferocity. Although it is not known whether the druids ever used Stonehenge, it looks as if the Romans thought they were using it, perhaps remembering the druidical cult centre at Sarmizegetusa in Romania, where they felt obliged to smash down the stone pillars of a superficially similar-looking astrono-mical circle. Some of the leaning and fallen stones of Stonehenge can be raised, but some are irreparably broken. There can be little doubting that the slighting of Stonehenge by the Romans has made it the wreck we see today.

Although we are accustomed to seeing Stonehenge as a picturesque ruin, we must try to visualise it in its newly-finished condition if we are to understand its architecture and purpose fully. The same is true of Avebury and the other monuments. Another important feature to bear in mind is that, with the exception of the Stonehenge lintels, all the individual elements recur, in endlessly varying combinations, at site after site. The Stonehenge Avenue, for instance, has its equivalent at Avebury. Whilst the Stonehenge Avenue is made of parallel earthworks, the West Kennet Avenue is marked by stones (Plate 41), but both make a ceremonial approach to the circular enclosure. Even the D-shaped stone setting in the Avebury South Circle is a reference to the crescent-shaped forecourt of an invisible, never-to-be-built chambered tomb.

The underlying religious function of these concatenations of symbolic architectural forms is obvious. We should not think of the elements as being separate; the conceptual links surrounding them were supplied by the religious philosophy of the age, expressed in the form of myth, fable, song, dance and ritual. However hard it may be now to visualise these long-lost ephemeral elements, their scope at least can be gauged. The ring of votive pits at Stonehenge implies a dedication to earth, while the stones of the Ring of Brodgar, soaring heavenward, imply a dedication to sky. At many sites, one has a sense that the ring of stones fastens the two worlds together and makes a moongate through which we can step from world to world.

TO THE SUN, MOON AND STARS?

The sky orientation can be interpreted as primitive astronomy or as religious observance; the two ideas are very different in intention, but not incompatible. From 1900, and especially since the 1960s, the astronomical approach has been the focus of an enormous amount of research and speculation. Everyone is now aware, if misinformed, of the orientation of Stonehenge towards the midsummer sunrise; it is less well-known that many other celestial orientations have been proposed for Stonehenge and the other stone circles. Norman Lockyer was the first major advocate of this interpretation. In 1906, he proposed that the major axes of the monuments were aligned towards risings or settings of the sun, moon or stars on particular dates in the calendar. The problem is that the stone circles offer so many possible sight-lines that one of them at least is bound to have coincided with a celestial event. Taking the centre alone as the observation point, Stonehenge offers at least 111 sight-lines in addition to the generally acknowledged orientation of the main axis. If other places round the monument are allowed as observation points as well, as some Stonehenge enthusiasts assume, the number of possible sight-lines runs into thousands. Playing to his own rules, the archaeo-astronomer cannot lose.

Of the stars, ten were bright enough to be identified and observed easily by neolithic man: Aldebaran, Altair, Antares, Bellatrix, Capella, Pollux, Procyon, Rigel, Sirius and Spica. Observing these brilliant bodies would have presented no problem. The difficulty for us is that their rising and setting positions have shifted long distances. Capella, for example, moved 18 degrees along the horizon between 2500 and 1600 BC. Unless the exact date of a monument's construction is known, it is rash to attribute an axis or sight-line to a specific star.

With the slow-changing sun we are on surer ground. We also have the corroborative evidence of the long barrows, most of which are oriented to the eastern horizon: more exactly, they are oriented to various compass directions between north-east and south-east, the northern and southern limits of the sunrise. The long barrows were not used to make observations, but to offer obeisance or salutation to the sun; the rays of the rising sun were perhaps intended to rekindle the spirits of the dead as they shone onto the eastern façade. It would be sensible to assume that the general intention was similar in the stone circles, that the orientation was celebratory and magical rather than scientific,

Plate 22 The Ring of Brodgar. When seen from the centre of the circle, the stones on the south-western side seem to be horizon markers, but the site slopes in such a way that the stones on the north-eastern side fall well short of the horizon

unless there is some reason for believing that accuracy was sought at a particular circle. The worst excesses of the archaeo-astronomers seem now to be over. Gerald Hawkins's view of the Aubrey Holes as an eclipse predictor has fallen out of favour because it appears that the method would be inaccurate and useless. Even so, there is evidence at Stonehenge for complex observations over a very long period, of both sun and moon.

Orientations on star-rises may give clues to a monument's date and this is where Burl's estimated date of 1800 BC for the bronze age site of Callanish on Lewis comes from. Unfortunately the stars are, as we have seen, the least dependable of the heavenly bodies. One curiosity to emerge from all the work done on stellar orientations is that a great many monuments seem to have alignments relating to the star Rigel in about 2100 BC. Why there should have been this intense interest in Rigel is not at all clear, unless the explanation lies in the coincidence between Rigel's and the sun's rising and setting positions one-sixteenth of a year before and after the winter solstice. The observations of these two calendar points may have helped in fixing the date of the solstice. It may have been quite otherwise, with Rigel featuring in some myth now irretrievably lost but as important to its culture as the star of Bethlehem.

The recumbent stone circles seem to be oriented on significant southerly risings and settings of the sun, moon and Venus. Although it is tempting to see the people of this northerly region more closely touched by the duration of the winter darkness and so more aware of the celestial landmarks of winter, it is not really possible that the recumbent circles could be used for sightings. The general orientation, a little to the west of south, suggests to me the direction from which the sun shines during the warmest part of the day. As such, the orientation may be general rather than specific, an acknowledgment of and a plea for the sun's power.

STANDING STONES, DEATH RITES AND DANCING

If the stone rings offer an embarrassment of possible alignments, the isolated standing stones should be easier to interpret. Since they often stand near stone circles, they indicate very specific points on the horizon when the observer stands at a circle's centre. But it is not always so simple – witness the problems we had in interpreting the Stonehenge Heel Stone until the socket of its missing partner was discovered. One standing stone, the biggest in Britain, is large enough to be treated as a monument in its own right. The Rudston Monolith is a towering cylindrical pillar of gritstone 8 metres high, 26 tons in weight and was the focus of social and ritual activity in the Yorkshire Wolds in the late neolithic. It seems to have functioned virtually as an idol. When we see it in this way, as something approaching a pagan deity, we can understand why the medieval church was built beside it, in an attempt to neutralise or steal its primitive power.

The Longstone, above Challacombe on Exmoor, evidently played some role in late neolithic funerary rituals. The monolith stands amid a ridge-top cemetery with a rectangular mortuary enclosure nearby. Many of the little stone settings of the area are located close to the sources of streams in the basins of the West and East Lyn Rivers. The flat sides of Longstone seem to point towards a nearby spring and it be that it was a device, like the stone settings, to gather the spirits of the dead from their ridge-top tombs and send them down the streams to the sea (Plate 38).

The stone circles too are associated with death rites. The Ring of Brogdar and the Stones of Stenness are close by a cluster of chambered tombs. The Great Circle at Newgrange actually surrounds the passage grave. Coves, the symbolic tomb chambers, form focal points at both Avebury and Stanton Drew. There are larger issues attaching to these associations that will be discussed later, but the link certainly exists between the stone rings and neolithic beliefs concerning death and burial. This very specific association was only one of the circles' functions, though, as they also served as ceremonial centres for individual territories and thus also functioned as tribal identity symbols.

The Cumbrian stone circles are spaced fairly evenly, 8-10 miles apart, and this strongly implies a central place function for roughly circular territories of that sort of diameter. It would be very natural for each circle to become the social and ceremonial focus of its territory. The circular form implies that the people actually arranged themselves in a ring within the stone circle, either to squat on the ground while they watched priests performing rituals or to dance. The length of the circle's circumference may thus be linked to the number of people in the community that built and used it. Long Meg and Her Daughters could have accommodated up to 500 people, allowing each person 1 metre of space. Estimates of this kind lead us to suppose that there were 2000 people living in Cumbria. As this number could have been supported comfortably by the substantial areas of cultivable land in the region, the individual estimates of territorial populations and their relationship with circle size seem very acceptable.

This line of thought tends to confirm the view that the circle is not only a moongate joining heaven and earth but also the hub about which the wheel of neolithic society slowly revolved. The ancestry of the stone circle, rooted in the earthen, broken circles of the early neolithic, was an ancient one and its development was long and complicated. Many grave mistakes have been made in attributing simple, single purposes to these great, subtle and many-sided projects. They incorporate a bewildering matrix of symbols, beliefs and aspirations in their design, showing that they were used in a wide variety of ceremonial ways to express a holistic view of the universe, a view that saw no real division between man and nature, nor between earth and heaven.

CHAPTER 11

DIALOGUE WITH DEATH

Enjoy the beauty of this day and do not weary of it.
No one returns to tell how they dwell,
To say what things are needed,
To quieten our anxious hearts until the time comes
For us to approach the place where they vanished . . .
See! Not one has taken his things with him!
See! Not one who has gone has ever returned!

'Song of the Harpist at the Feast', Ancient Egyptian

In their burial monuments, the Stonehenge people achieved an architectural originality that rivalled and perhaps exceeded that of the stone circles. The tombs are certainly more explicit concerning their builders' attitudes to life and death: they speak of a brooding preoccupation that amounts to an obsession. The bodies of the dead often underwent two funeral rituals and even after the second ritual bones were sometimes fished out for further ceremonies. It would be easy to portray this sort of behaviour as morbid or even necrophiliac but, as we shall see, that interpretation would be wide of the mark. It was not so much the dead that interested the Stonehenge people as death itself, and we can see emerging an elaborate pattern of ceremonial activity based on a continuing interaction with the forces of life and death.

The monuments vary widely in their external form and internal structure, as we should expect over a period of twenty-three centuries of indigenous development, with different styles favoured in different regions at different times and the occasional 'cross-breeding' of regional styles. There are some parallels between developments in Britain and those on the European mainland, but no more than we might expect given a common fund of beliefs and funerary practices. The whole train of insular development, though, was launched by the introduction of two major European burial traditions. Right at the start of the early neolithic, in 4300 BC, as the farming economy was beginning to expand, the people of eastern Britain took over the earthen long barrow tradition from the countries of the North European Plain. At about the same time, the people of western Britain imported the idea of megalithic tomb building, which was then in its infancy in Brittany. But from then on, it is possible to interpret every development in terms of native innovation within the British Isles.

THE LONG BARROWS

The earthen long barrows were built in the lowland zone, where over two hundred have survived on the chalk hills. Originally there may have been three times that number, but a great many have been destroyed by farmers. The oldest dated long barrow, at Lambourn in Berkshire, was built in 4255 BC using stacks of turves, and all the barrows seem to have been raised, like this one, in open farmland. The main period for barrow building was 3800-2800 BC and the practice seems to have died out by 2500 BC. The barrows are between 20 and 550 metres long, but they are usually 30-90 metres: only four are over 150 metres long. The Maiden Castle Long Mound, the longest by far of all the long barrows, is a freak. Not only is it 550 metres long and bent in the middle: it actually overrides the earthworks of the early neolithic cause-wayed enclosure. No explanations have been offered for this odd structure, but it appears to be a hybrid between a long barrow and a cursus.

In plan, the mounds are parallel-sided with rounded ends or trapeze-shaped with squared-off ends. Burials, mortuary enclosures, mortuary houses, totem poles and other constructions are invariably concentrated under one end of the mound. The mound is unnecessarily long; if it was intended merely to cover the burials and other funerary deposits, a 10-metre mound would have sufficed. Another feature is the pair of quarry ditches running parallel to the barrow sides and often separated from them by a flat berm. The ditches are of the usual neolithic cross-sectional shape, steep-sided and flat-floored. The ditches supplied the material for the mound, but some have been delineated with such care that they were a design feature in their own right, an integral part of the monument.

The appearance of all the surviving long barrows is merely that of a low grassy mound with smoothly convexo-concave slopes, and perhaps two-thirds of them were always dump mounds of this type, but the appearance of the remaining one-third was originally very different. Fussell's Lodge in Wiltshire, for instance, had a revetment wall all round it made of stout vertical timbers. This would have given the finished mound the appearance of a large rectangular house 43 metres long and 12 metres wide with a

47 Burial monuments. Several of these types may formerly
have been more widespread

1 Orkney-Cromarty-
  Hebrides passage graves
2 Other round passage
  graves
3 Clava cairns
4 Earthen long barrows
5 Chamberless long cairns

6 Clyde chambered tombs
7 Portal dolmens
8 West Country chambered
  tombs
9 Cotswold-Severn
  chambered tombs
10 Medway chambered
  tombs

convex or slightly pitched roof made of living turf (Figure 48).
Underneath this was a smaller and even odder simulacrum of a
house. Directly behind the porch at the broader north-eastern end
of the mound lay buried the 9-metre long mortuary house. The
timbers of its low, pitched roof were supported by a ridge-pole
held aloft by three massive tree trunks. The large diameter of the

48 A long barrow in its original state. This reconstruction shows how the Fussell's Lodge long barrow once looked like a north European longhouse

trunks (1 metre) suggests that they may have continued skywards above the ridge roof as totem poles. The sloping timbers were covered with planks, a layer of flint nodules and a layer of turves. The little mortuary building with its strongly built roof may have continued in use as a charnel house for a long time before its door was closed, the timber wall was built and the great mound was raised over it, sealing it for ever.

The timbers of the revetment were larger at the broad end of the mound to make a more imposing wall. One of the massive end-posts of the mortuary house was incorporated as a focal centrepiece of the wall; the overall impression must have been close to the architectural concept of a façade. The trapeze shape of the mound added an element of false perspective, so that when viewed from anywhere along the façade the mound would have appeared to be much longer than it actually was. The convergence of the quarry ditches towards the south-west end of the barrow heightened this illusion.

The façade idea was developed further in the Lincolnshire and Yorkshire long barrows. The Giants' Hills long barrow at Skendleby in Lincolnshire, built in 3140 BC, had a façade made of vertical timbers in much the same way as Fussell's Lodge. It differs in that it was deliberately exaggerated by extending it a metre or two beyond the side walls of the barrow. The slightly crescentic shape also emphasises its role as a frontage, a cyclorama against which important rituals were to be seen; this development indicates and begins to define a forecourt area which at other sites became very important indeed. There was no entrance in the Giants' Hills façade and there seems to have been no intention of re-opening or re-entering the barrow once it was built – a common feature of the earthen long barrow.

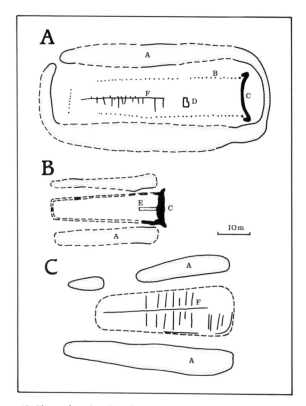

49 Plans of earthen long barrows

A Giant's Hills, Lincolnshire 3300-3000 BC.
B Willerby Wold, Yorkshire. 3700 BC
C Beckhampton Road, Wiltshire. 3300 BC.

Detailed features include
A quarry ditch; B revetment wall made of wooden posts;
C horned façade made of massive tree trunks set in a trench;
D mortuary house; E burnt mortuary house; F light fences
made of hurdles to assist in the phased construction of the
mound

Long barrows often had complex histories. Each site went
through an 'open' phase with a mortuary house, votive pits and
totem poles, sometimes with complex ox-hides hanging on them,
before the barrow was raised. At Kilham in the Yorkshire Wolds,
four phases of activity have been detected. First, a square
mortuary enclosure was fenced off. Then two parallel earth banks
were raised close together, with burials between them, in front of
the enclosure; a rectangular trench was dug round the whole site
and a continuous wall made of huge timbers raised in it. Later,
large quarry ditches were opened up along each side of the timber

stockade and the back half of the enclosure filled in with chalk; the 'forecourt' was filled shortly afterwards. The resulting barrow was not unlike Fussell's Lodge; a trapeze-shaped, timber-revetted mound 60 metres long and 10 broad. It was built at about the same time, too, in 4000 BC. The timber walls were set on fire and a short ceremonial avenue of timber posts was built leading up to the eastern end of the completed monument.

Not all mortuary buildings and enclosures were entombed inside long barrows. A trapeze-shaped enclosure 38 metres long and 21 metres wide on Normanton Down near Stonehenge had an east-facing entrance flanked by two timber walls. It is thought that the walls were designed to revet the bank terminals and stop the chalk rubble from obstructing the entrance. A similar near-rectangular enclosure can still be seen between the Longstone and Chapman Barrows on Exmoor. It has an external ditch and internal bank and an overall size of 36 metres by 14 metres, with its broad end towards the south-east.

Ploughing in some areas and the maintenance of sheep pasture in others have distorted the original distribution pattern. Even so, there must always have been an unusually high density of long barrows in Wessex, especially near the great henges, where densities are up to four times higher than the highest density in the Yorkshire Wolds. This may reflect high population density in Wessex, or higher levels of ritual activity, or both. Once again, the higher level of activity occurs in the overlap zones of earth and stone circles, perhaps another symptom of cultural stress.

Practically all the trapeze-shaped barrows are oriented to the north-east, south-east, or to some point in between: in fact one-third are oriented within a few degrees of east. Many of the parallel-sided barrows are also aligned west-east, so they too may have been intended to honour the rising sun. The sites of the long barrows were chosen with care. Those on hill-top or ridge-top sites turn out on close inspection to be false-crested: they are built on one side of the summit so as to appear on the skyline when viewed from the low ground on one side. This indirectly supports the view that they were built on the margins of farming territories, as has been argued for Sussex.

The little pitched-roof mortuary buildings may be a native invention, but it may prove to be an imported idea. Very similar tent-like mortuary houses have been found in Denmark, dating to at least as early as 4180 BC. The long barrow itself was derived originally from the communal longhouses of Poland and East Germany. These timber cabins were of about the same size and they were also wedge-shaped. The fact that many of the long barrows were built as simulacra of houses, even to the wooden walls and pitched roof, argues strongly for such an origin. The long barrows could not have been a British invention, as there were no domestic longhouses or comparable buildings on which the barrows could have been modelled. The parallels between barrow and longhouse cannot be inadvertent, but how could people living in the chalk hills of Wessex have come to build houses that imitated the shapes of Polish houses?

The answer lies in a burial tradition originating in Poland where, quite naturally, houses for the dead were built as replicas of houses for the living. The barrows in the cemetery at Sarnowo in Kujavia are 70 metres long, 10 metres wide and trapeze-shaped, with the broad end towards the north-east. This barrow cemetery is part of a widespread tradition that extended across the North German Plain, and we can find examples in Belgium and the Pas de Calais, only 80 kilometres away from the east Kent long barrows. The Polish barrow tradition certainly developed early enough to have been ancestral to the British tradition. There is no reason to suppose that any British barrow is older than 4300 BC: Barrow 8 at Sarnowo dates from 4450 BC. We can see the long barrows as part of a burial monument style that spread across the northern plains of Europe, finally arriving in Britain in 4300 BC. The longhouses that were built from Poland to the Netherlands were, however, *not* built in Britain, except at Balbridie. The sheer irrelevance in an insular, British context of the architectural references contained in the long barrow may help to explain the rather quirky and uninhibited development of the monument. It was, in its way, as exotic as the art deco cinema style that flourished in the London suburbs, totally unrestrained by local considerations and all the more exciting for its alien style.

THE CHAMBERED TOMBS

There is greater diversity and exoticism still in the megalithic tombs, of which some 250 survive in England and Wales and 350 in Scotland. Although a deliberate effort is required to spoil these monuments and it now seems incredible that anyone would wish to do so, many have been destroyed by farmers, as William Stukeley put it, 'for a little mean profit'. Probably there were originally twice as many.

The oldest, dating back to about 4300 BC, are the simplest. Three 1 metre square slabs set vertically in the ground, or even propped together on the surface, made a simple cupboard for the storage of bones, reminiscent of the shape of the much larger coves. A fourth slab set vertically on the fourth side turned this into a cist; a fifth slab set horizontally as a roof turned it into a dolmen. Probably the earliest megaliths were pure stone boxes of this type, but unsupported they would soon have fallen down and the idea of a supporting mound must have been developed very early on.

Among the Clyde cairns, the simple three- or four-slab chambers are likely to be the oldest. These box-tombs, about the same age as the earliest long barrows, were parallelled in the Orkneys and Hebrides by polygonal tombs, each roofed with a single capstone. The size of capstone that was considered manageable put a limit on the size of the chamber, so these early tombs were invariably tiny. The idea for these stone repositories may have come out of a very ancient, pre-neolithic tradition of cave burial. There are four neolithic cave burial sites in the Peak District. What could be more natural in areas where no suitable caves existed than building small artificial caves as substitutes? There was also a Mediterranean tradition of cutting tombs out of the living rock. Though common in the Mediterranean, this practice was unknown in Britain, except for one solitary monument in Orkney. The Dwarfie Stane on the island of Hoy is an isolated mass of sandstone 7 metres long; into it has been cut a short passage leading into the side of an oval chamber 3 metres long and 1 metre high. Outside lies a massive closing stone. This artificial cave is unique in Britain, but very much part of the European tradition. The lower chambers of the two-storey tombs of Taverso Tuick and Huntersquoy, also in Orkney, are partly rock-cut and the chamber plan is approximately the same as that of the Dwarfie Stone. It would appear that the imported idea of the rock-cut tomb was tried only once and found to be unsatisfactory. Perhaps the sandstone was too hard compared with the soft limestones of the Mediterranean, or else the alternative of using the natural flagstones that split so easily into fine building stones seemed more attractive. Either way, the rock-cut tomb idea was swiftly transformed in Orkney into a true megalithic style.

In Cornwall, the basic stone box idea was embellished with a pair of portal stones, creating a simple façade. The chamber is often higher at the portal end, so that the capstone is tilted. Often the uprights were not fixed in the ground. The chambers were built like card houses and have proved all too easy to dismantle: very few are now complete. Originally, they were held up by supporting circular mounds 10 metres across, although the big capstones were left showing for architectural effect (Figure 50A).

Zennor Quoit, like the other dolmens of this type, is situated above a hundred metres in the low hills of the Land's End peninsula, with fine views to distant hills, yet it cannot be seen except from the immediate vicinity. Unlike the long barrows, which were designed to be seen and to be impressive from nearby lowlands, the portal dolmens were secret places hidden from view. They seem to be located at the upper margin of cultivable land.

Plate 23 The Dwarfie Stane. This tiny rock-cut tomb has two side chambers. The blocking stone is in the foreground

There are more dolmens in Wales and south-west Scotland. In spite of the great distances separating these areas, the design of the dolmens is so uniform that we can be certain that the people who built them were in contact with each other by sea.

The next development was the addition of a megalithic passage, which became necessary when the low, horseshoe-shaped, supporting mound was enlarged into a higher, circular, covering mound; the access passage had to be walled and roofed to stop it becoming obstructed by mound material. The two small round cairns at Gleniron in Wigtownshire represent this early type of passage grave. The wrecked cairn at Broadsands, Paignton, is a variant of the type. It had a D-shaped chamber made of eleven small upright slabs 1 metre high. The gaps between were filled with drystone walling, which suggests a later date. The chamber was covered by a single capstone and access was by way of a narrow passage.

In the next phase of development, the passage grave chamber was enlarged. The size of the simple chamber was limited by the size of the capstone and the ways in which this fundamental problem was by-passed to give ever-larger chambers created an astonishing diversity of styles and forms. One solution was to plant extra upright slabs projecting into the chamber, dividing it into small, easily vaulted areas, yet giving a larger total floor area. Huntersquoy on Orkney illustrates the type of small stalled cairn produced by this method. Another solution was to arrange three

Plate 24 Trethevy Quoit

small chambers opening out of the central chamber; this quadrupled the floor space, but the capstone size remained the same. Two small cruciform passage graves of this type survive on the Calf of Eday in Orkney. A third solution, known as the Camster type and found in Caithness, had three chambers built end to end. The chambers were separated by stone jambs and the roof was built by a combination of capstones and corbelling, in which successive courses of small stones oversail towards the ceiling centre (Figure 51C). A corbelled vault is very fragile until it is anchored by a covering mound, so the introduction of this technique may have led to the development of larger and heavier mounds.

The passage grave idea was taken further near Inverness, at the northern end of the Great Glen, and along the southern shore of the Moray Firth. At Clava, which gives its name to the new type

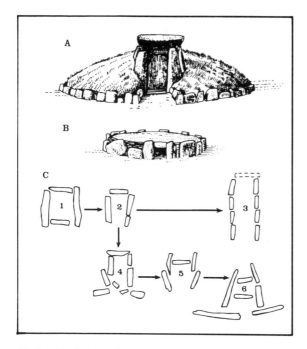

50 Cornish chambered tombs

A Reconstruction of Trethevy Quoit, a portal dolmen.
B Reconstruction of the Pennance entrance grave
C A possible evolutionary scheme for the chamber plan:
   1 Chun Quoit; 2 Breen entrance grave; 3 Tregeseal
   entrance grave; 4 Pawton Quoit; 5 Trethevy Quoit;
   6 Zennor Quoit

of tomb, the mounds were close enough together to form a true cemetery. Here the chamber walls were corbelled drystone vaults above a foundation course of earth-fast megalithic slabs arranged in polygonal plans. A new element was the circular kerb built as a revetment to the cairn. The kerb itself was supported on the outside by a lower mass of cairn material forming a wide step-like platform or rostrum from which the cairn proper seemed to rise: the effect is one of great dignity and tranquillity. A freestanding outer stone circle about 10 metres further out from the kerbstones created a ceremonial precinct round the monument. These relatively simple yet architecturally effective monuments are only found in a fairly small area near Inverness; it is rather surprising that these developments were not copied anywhere else in Britain.

The retaining ring of kerbstones and the freestanding stone circle were nevertheless used in the fully developed, climactic realisation of the passage grave idea at Newgrange in Ireland. It is

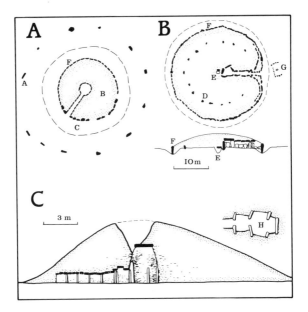

51 Round passage graves

A Plan of Balnuaran of Clava, one of the rare cemeteries of
  chambered tombs in Britain
B Plan and section of Bryn Celli Ddu
C Section and chamber plan of Camster Round, NE Scotland
  Detailed features include
A freestanding stone circle
B cairn of local river terrace cobbles
C revetment terrace
D buried stone circle
E ritual pit and decorated stone
F kerb stones
G ox burial
H central chamber

possible to see in the later monuments all kinds of back-references
to earlier designs. The ring of kerbstones alone was used in the
fine, large passage grave of Bryn Celli Ddu on Anglesey. Here, the
geometrical centre of the mound was marked by a ritual pit
surmounted by an elaborately decorated stone (Figure 72A): this
strange feature buried at the heart of the mound was concealed
behind the back wall of the polygonal chamber (Figure 51B).
   The people who built entrance graves at Land's End faithfully
copied the round, external form of the passage grave, but did not
put any substantial structure inside the mound, only small stone
cupboards entered directly from the edge of the mound. The
design is very uniform, with a coffin-shaped chamber. Entrance
graves on Scilly have traces of plaster on their walls and it may be

that many of the megalithic tombs of Britain were originally smoothed up with plaster. Perhaps some were painted, too, like their European counterparts. Only three of the Scilly tombs contained human bones; more typically they contained occupation debris and their location next to ancient fields implies that the deposits of fertile soil were votive offerings relating to a fertility cult. Even these relatively simple tombs functioned as rather more than mere graves. The precise origin of the entrance graves is obscure. The large number on Scilly suggests an origin there; although the area of Scilly is now very small, in the neolithic it was a single large island of some 180 square kilometres – some believe it was the lost land of Lyonesse, dimly remembered in Arthurian legend.

25 Drystone walling in the Unstan stalled cairn on Orkney. This is characteristic neolithic masonry, though here reconstructed, and often was used as an infill in megalithic architecture

We have to visualise many different threads of development under way in different regions of the highland zone, occasionally interweaving to form new hybrid styles. While the cruciform passage grave was evolving, for instance, the stalled cairn was evolving in an entirely different direction. The first stalled cairns were small: the three-compartment chamber of Bigland Round on Orkney was 4 metres long. From 3800 to 3000 BC, the idea was developed with ever-larger chambers and increasing numbers of compartments. The climax of this growth was the long stalled cairns of Midhowe, with its 23 metre long chamber (Figure 52), and Knowe of Ramsey, 27 metres long, with fourteen compartments. Needless to say, the production of a long narrow chamber distorted the shape of the covering mound: it too became long and narrow, but without implying any reference whatever to the long mound tradition of the lowland zone.

Plate 26 Unstan. The burial chamber of a stalled cairn. The side chambers were used for preliminary burial. The end compartment, separated by a low partition, was the final resting place for the skulls

At Midhowe, the chamber walls stand to a height of 2½ metres and enough remains exposed to give a powerful impression of the truly architectural conception of these monuments. The softly curving revetment wall, with its carefully stepped foundation courses and diagonally laid drystone, was intended to be seen as an architectural feature. Walking into the monument is a little like walking up the aisle of a miniature church, the straight central aisle flanked on each side by pillar-like slabs and culminating in a shrine-like end compartment at the western end. The stalls or bays on the north side of the chamber were fitted with low stone benches or shelves on which the bones of ancestors were laid out.

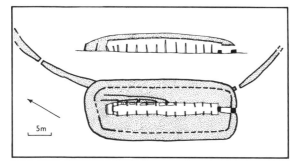

52 Midhowe. Section and plan of the most spectacular stalled cairn. The heavy black lines inside the cairn indicate secondary walling designed to retain the loose cairn material. The roof was probably made of long sandstone flags crossing the whole width of the chamber; the walls are preserved to a height of 2 metres and show no sign of oversailing

Plate 27 Midhowe. In the foreground is the entrance passage with its double blocking. The stalls of the long burial chamber can be seen beyond

It seems likely, by comparison with the more complete remains at Isbister on South Ronaldsay, that after a long time had passed the skulls alone were taken to the western end to be deposited in the shrine. When Midhowe was excavated in 1932-3, two isolated skulls remained in the end compartment.

The side walls of Midhowe's chamber rise to $2\frac{1}{2}$ metres without oversailing. If they began oversailing above this height, the ceiling must have been extremely high. The cairn is 13 metres wide, though, and with moderately steep sides a vault 5 metres high could have been covered. A corbelled vault could also have been stabilised by the addition of stone beams at about $2\frac{1}{2}$ metres – a technique used to dramatic effect at the Knowe of Lairo, just along the coast from Midhowe. But it is also possible that the chamber walls rose vertically to about 3 metres and were then spanned by very long horizontal slabs of flagstone. Either way, the complete monument must have been truly awe-inspiring and it is to be hoped that one day these questions will be satisfactorily answered and the tomb can be fully restored.

Midhowe is unusual in having a horned forecourt adjacent to its long north side. The curvature of the surviving hornworks implies that a huge area, perhaps a circle 70 metres across, was marked out for ceremonies. The diameter is, interestingly, very close to that of Maes Howe's circular, 'moated' precinct, implying that Midhowe had a comparable social and ceremonial importance.

At about the same time, and, remarkably, in the same place, the circular passage grave tradition was reaching its climax. The period 3300-3000 BC on Orkney saw the building of the series of great tombs that includes Quoyness, Cuween, Vinquoy and Wideford Hill. Architecturally, they were an extraordinary leap forward from any of the earlier design developments, both in construction methods and in aesthetic effect.

Plate 28 Wideford Hill chambered tomb. The cairn has weathered down so that we can see the concentric revetment walls

Quanterness has a round cairn over 3 metres high and 31 metres in diameter, covering a very symmetrical, drystone-built, rectangular chamber with six perfect rectangular side-chambers opening from it (Figure 53). The lower walls are vertical for a metre, then courses of large stones oversail at 11 degrees to the vertical, then courses of smaller stones oversail at 5 degrees to the vertical, until finally at a height of 3½ metres the walls are close enough to be bridged by a capstone. The chamber looks like a chimney. There were two circular revetment walls 8 and 10 metres out from the cairn's centre.

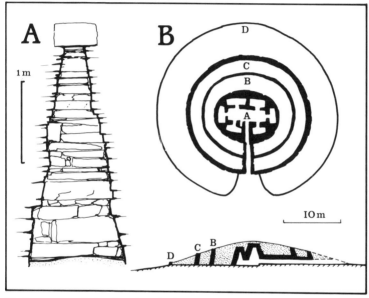

53 Quanterness. A chambered tomb of Maes Howe type on Mainland Orkney. A – Section through one of the side chambers, to show the corbelling of the drystone walls. B Plan and section of the whole tomb.

Detailed features include: A – burial chambers   B and C – revetment walls designed to retain the cairn material   D – kerb

This tomb has been backfilled and is not accessible to the public.

The small community that built Quanterness first quarried the site to make a level, circular platform. The internal plan of the monument was marked out with the axis of the main chamber carefully aligned due north-south; the very large blocks forming the lowest course of the chambers and passage were dragged into position. The main and side chamber walls were built to a height of about a metre, with stabilising drystone packing behind them. At this stage, the inner revetment wall was begun and the rubble infill between it and the central tomb-structure was used as a platform for masons working on the central structure. As the inner revetment wall reached a metre in height, and the tomb chambers 2 metres, the outer revetment wall was begun. The step-pyramid construction made work on the tomb chambers and in particular raising the lintels far easier. When the stepped scarcements were complete and the chambers securely roofed, the whole cairn was smoothed up to a rounded shape. Some have speculated that the stepped structure, now plainly visible in the degraded Wideford Hill cairn, was intended to be seen as an architectural feature. This would have given the cairns the appearance of small ziggurats, although tiny compared with their Sumerian contemporaries. But the layering of the infill between the revetment walls is deliberately sloped, and there is little doubt that the intention was to produce a smoothly rounded mound.

Plate 29 Maes Howe from the north

Maes Howe belongs to the same 'family' of tombs as Quanterness; it was the last in the sequence, built in 2900 or 2800 BC. Unquestionably one of the greatest monuments of ancient Europe, it has for a long time been regarded as an exotic, an early importation, the first in a degenerating series. But it is now seen as the culminating achievement of native tomb builders who had developed their skills over a period of a thousand years.

Its mound 35 metres across and 8 metres high, Maes Howe stands on an artificially levelled platform on top of a knoll (Figure 54). Whether we are to regard the whole platform, which is 76 metres across, as a sacred precinct is unclear: it is surrounded by a circular ditch, usually an indication that the enclosed area was a sanctuary. It may be merely that the ditch was required to keep the site dry; there are traces of a neolithic stone-built drain crossing the platform. The bank on the outer side of the ditch was

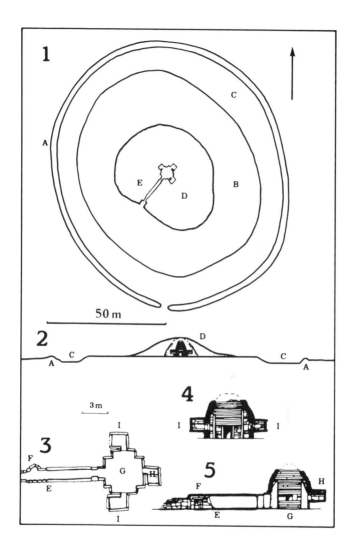

54 Maes Howe.

1 Plan of the entire monument, which is about the same size as the Avebury South Circle. 2 Section of the entire monument. 3 Plan of the entrance passage and burial chambers. 4 Cross section of chambers. 5 Longitudinal section of passage and chambers.

Detailed features include: A bank B artificially levelled and drained platform C shallow ditch (the monument is in effect a type of henge) D earthen mound E entrance passage F recess to take closing stone G central chamber H end chamber I side chamber once thought to be modern, but the radiocarbon date of AD 950 introduces the interesting possibility that the tomb was re-used in the tenth century for a Viking chief's burial and the bank was retouched because it had become weathered. Re-use of this kind would make sense of the claims made in twelfth-century runes in the chamber that treasure had been found there.

Plate 30 Maes Howe. The outer bank was part of the original neolithic design, later became weathered and was retouched in the tenth century. The broad shallow ditch can be seen to the right

The inner passage, oriented to the midwinter sunset, consists of three enormous slabs 7 metres long, each weighing over 3 tons. A technical problem was created and solved quite unnecessarily as, for all practical purposes, drystone or megalithic walling with much smaller stones would have been sufficient. It was a sheer display of technique. The passage opens into an unrivalled, cavernous central chamber, 4·6 metres square and 4·6 metres high. Three rectangular cells or side-chambers open above the level of the main chamber floor, each with its own massive closing stone. When sealed, they must have been difficult to detect. The impression, even with the closing stones pulled out, is quite unlike that given by any of the other, earlier, cruciform passage graves, which are of a more open design, yet do not seem so roomy. Even Newgrange does not convey this kind of spaciousness.

The masonry of the walls is almost cyclopean, with large flat slabs spanning nearly the whole width of the chamber. In the corners are huge angle buttresses forming squinches to the vaulting (Plate 31). The walls rise vertically for a metre or so, then

Plate 31 Maes Howe. One of the large, squinching buttresses in the central chamber

the courses oversail to form a beehive shape: originally at the apex there was a large capstone 4·6 metres above the floor. All the slabs were accurately levelled and plumbed. All in all, it is a superb piece of architecture, crafted by masons who took a pride and a pleasure in knowledge and highly-developed skills acquired over fifty generations. It would be hard to find any other monument in pre-medieval Britain that comes anywhere near Maes Howe in its handling of an architectural idea. Only Stonehenge itself is a rival. It is, as Stuart Piggott says, 'a superlative monument that by its originality of execution is lifted out of its class into a unique position'.

THE MARRIAGE OF TWO TRADITIONS

Even before this extraordinary climax to the passage grave tradition, a new phase of chambered tomb building had begun. Inevitably, the two early neolithic traditions of round megalithic tombs and earthen long barrows were married to produce a range of hybrid forms. The zone where the two traditions overlapped was the area where they combined earliest, from about 3800 BC onwards, to produce the Cotswold-Severn tombs. These are found in a fairly compact group centring on the head of the Severn estuary and spreading south-eastwards across the Cotswolds into Wessex and north-westwards into Wales. A typical example is a long, narrow, stone-revetted mound, trapeze-shaped, with convex 'horns' at the wider end and an entrance to the tomb chamber between the horns.

Wayland's Smithy in Berkshire began as a 17 metre long earthen barrow raised over a rectangular timber mortuary house containing the bones of about fourteen people. It clearly belongs to the eastern tradition of earthen long barrows. Then a much

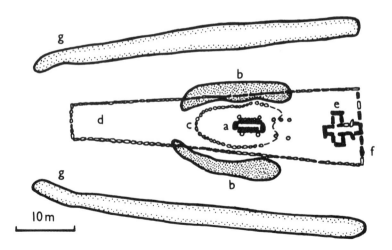

55 Wayland's Smithy, a Cotswold-Severn chambered tomb built in two phases:

a tent-shaped wooden mortuary house with sarsen stone floor and containing the remains of fourteen people
b quarry ditches for Phase I mound
c kerb of boulders for Phase 1 mound, raised as a long barrow in 3700 BC
d Phase 2 mound raised in 3500 BC

e cruciform chamber
f imposing façade of 3-metre-high sarsen stones
g Phase 2 quarry ditches

larger, chambered tomb belonging to the new, joint tradition was built completely engulfing the earlier monument. The new mound was trapeze-shaped, 55 metres long and 15 metres wide. It had no horns, but a slightly convex façade made of six great sarsen stones 3 metres high, three on each side of the entrance, made an imposing effect. The megalithic tradition extends to the interior, where a lintelled passage led to a cruciform arrangement of chambers borrowed from the passage graves (Figure 55).

Plate 32 The Devil's Den, a tomb chamber in Clatford Bottom near Avebury. The covering mound has been eroded away

The West Kennet long barrow near Avebury has a very similar external design, with an imposing flat megalithic façade, although this conceals internal differences (Figure 56). The five stones in the centre of the façade were added at the end of the tomb's use as a burial place: they were closing stones and they occupy an area that was originally a concave forecourt. Inside, the cruciform plan has been developed, with two pairs of transepts. The chambers nevertheless only occupy a small fraction of the enormous length of the barrow, which stretches away along the ridge top for 101 metres.

The trapeze shape of these easterly examples was directly borrowed from the eastern long barrows. In Wales, the tombs are horned. Some Cotswold-Severn tombs have blind entrances, where a fake blocked doorway was built between the horns. This may have had some ritual significance, but I think it was more a case of copying the external form as part of the general fashion, whilst maintaining local custom with regard to the internal arrangement of the chambers. It may also be that travellers to foreign territories would only be allowed to see the outward form of a monument:

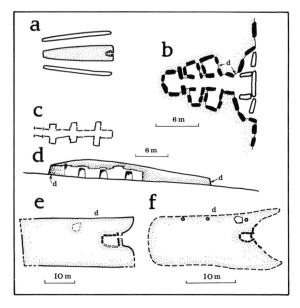

56 Cotswold-Severn chambered tombs
a West Kennet long barrow, Wiltshire: 100 metres long, it is
  one of Avebury's several large-scale monuments
b The chambers at West Kennet, used for disarticulated
  burials for up to a thousand years; the massive blocking
  stones filling up the crescentic façade were raised to mark
  the tomb's final closure
c Stoney Littleton, Somerset: chamber plan
d Stoney Littleton: longitudinal section
e Tinkinswood, Glamorgan: plan
f Pentre Ifan, Pembrokeshire: plan
Drystone walling (d) was used for revetment kerbs and
infilling. Of the seventy tombs that survive, half are being
damaged by modern ploughing; one (Heselton) has recently
been destroyed by archaeologists

the inner structure would remain a matter of guesswork.

Belas Knap in Gloucestershire illustrates this mismatching of
outer form and inner structure very well. The blind entrance
stands at the head of a funnel-shaped forecourt between two
bulbous horns in an impressive (and well-restored) façade 18
metres across. Meanwhile, four tiny chambers that are little more
than entrance graves were built into the sides and back of the
barrow.

The Clyde tombs form a distinct and separate group of
chambered long cairns centring on south-west Scotland. The main
focus is the Isle of Arran showing, like the Cotswold-Severn focus
on the Severn estuary, that the initial impetus resulted from
contact by sea – a crucial means of transmitting ideas. The Clyde

Plate 33 West Kennet long barrow. The façade and forecourt. The entrance to the burial chambers can be seen behind the very large blocking stones

cairns are usually wedge-shaped, 25 metres long and 15 wide. The passage and chamber are run together in a continuous gallery made of large stone slabs at the lower levels and drystone walling higher up. The gallery is subdivided by slabs set transversely and rising half a metre. It opens into the centre of a concave façade forming the backdrop to a perfectly semi-circular forecourt. The forecourt was the main focus of ceremonies and it was often paved or cobbled. Sometimes, as at Browndod, there was a standing stone at its centre.

A variation of this idea was the court cairn, in which a circular court was surrounded by a ring-cairn. The Clyde cairns were probably built over quite a long period and, although their precise origin is obscure, they are likely to be another marriage of the two older traditions. They were already being built in 3800 BC, so the style is unlikely to have been a straightforward export by Cotswold-Severn builders or even a grafting of the Cotswold-Severn style onto an indigenous proto-megalithic style. There were two apparently contradictory stylistic thrusts all over Britain: a centrifugal thrust, towards local individuation and divergence, and a centripetal tendency towards the re-use and re-amalgamation of a common fund of symbolic gestures. This second tendency is enough to explain the convergent evolution of the Clyde and Cotswold-Severn tombs.

Far away on Shetland, a third and very different hybrid emerged. The Shetland people took one significant architectural

Plate 34 Belas Knap, a Cotswold-Severn tomb in Gloucestershire. The horned forecourt climaxes in a false entrance. The careful restoration of 1928 gives a good idea of the tomb's original appearance

feature from the long barrow, the concave façade, and grafted it onto their existing round cairns. The result was a heel-shaped cairn. The curious kidney shape of the large Anglesey passage grave, Bryn yr Hen Bobl, was arrived at in the same way. Bryn yr Hen Bobl contains among many other extraordinary features a double porthole stone across its entrance. The porthole, a carefully drilled hole through a stone slab, was a symbolic doorway featured in a number of chambered tombs: it was another variant of the moongate idea. The entrance opens north-westwards onto a flaring V-shaped forecourt flanked by two rounded horns. To the south-west of the large kidney-shaped mound is a peculiar, long, narrow platform revetted with drystone walls and extending 85 metres out from the passage grave. It ends in a smaller round cairn. The plan may have been deliberately intended as a phallic symbol, which would certainly be consistent with the relationship between chambered tombs and beliefs concerning fertility.

The Medway tombs constitute the fourth hybrid group and, once again, they are geographically very distinct. In the sheltered vale between the greensand ridge and the North Downs, a small community of megalith builders raised half a dozen megalithic tombs. The Addington chambered long barrow, wrecked by the minor road running through it, was originally rectangular, 60 metres long and 10 wide, with a kerb of sarsen slabs and a stone chamber at the north-east end. Chestnuts, only a 100 metres away, had a D-shaped mound 19 metres across. Its roomy chamber, 3·5 metres long, 2·5 metres wide and 3 metres high, was made of two slab trilithons, like the entrance to a neolithic Maltese temple, and the façade consisted of two large sarsens on each side of the east-facing entrance. A chip of rose quartz implies contact by sea with the Channel Islands.

The tomb chamber alone survives of Kit's Coty, perhaps the best-known of the Medway sites. A drawing done by Stukeley in 1722 shows a long, low mound leading about 60 metres away to the west, with a recumbent stone, the General's Tomb, marking its far end. The General's Tomb was blown up in 1867 and the kerb stones have all been removed. The monument has been systematically wrecked by farmers.

The isolation of this group of chambered tombs in the midst of the earthen long barrow region seems peculiar. The tombs bear some similarity to the *dysse* tombs in Denmark and it has been suggested that the Medway megalithic style was derived from them. Long mounds of the *dysse* type developed in Jutland in the early neolithic and spread south across the North German Plain into north-east Holland. From the Low Countries the style could easily have been imported by sea to the Medway estuary. Yet it is unnecessary to postulate a foreign import when all the features of the Medway tombs are to be found in other parts of southern England. It would be more consistent with the processes we have observed so far to treat the Medway tombs as the chambered long cairn idea re-exported to, or re-interpreted by, the people of the eastern lowlands. The nearest comparable monuments are Cotswold-Severn tombs such as West Kennet and it may seem odd, if they are related, that the three intervening counties should be empty of megaliths. But if we propose a very normal human element, individual local communities exercising choice when confronted with new ideas – some accepting, some rejecting, the isolation of the Medway group seems less odd. If we also remember that many contacts were made by coastal voyages, the link between the natural harbour of the Medway estuary and the cluster of megaliths focussing on it becomes clear. Contact with the west is also confirmed by that chip of rose quartz.

EARTHEN ROUND BARROWS

A new complication in the already-complex evolution of the burial monuments was a second fashion for round barrows. The external form was a borrowing from the round passage grave tradition, but the internal arrangements and burial practices associated with the late round barrows mark them out as a new departure. They were especially common in Yorkshire, but there are isolated examples elsewhere in England and Scotland.

Some of the round barrows are very large and the best-known,

Duggleby Howe in the Yorkshire Wolds, is 38 metres in diameter. Its top was flattened to make a mill-stance, but it is still 6 metres high. At its centre, a pit 3 metres deep was dug into the old land surface and the intact body of a man was buried in it with a pottery bowl dating from before 3000 BC. In the pit-filling there were further burials, but without any grave goods. Later burials above and round the pit were covered by a mound 15 metres across. Then the mound was enlarged by the addition of a thick rubble layer containing over fifty cremation burials, so the second phase at Duggleby Howe marks a significant change in funerary customs.

BURIAL CUSTOMS

The feature that differentiates neolithic practices most emphatically from those of later cultures is the two-phase funerary rite. At Fussell's Lodge, in common with many other long barrows and chambered tombs, the mortuary building was a repository for skeletons that were already disarticulated. What was actually laid to rest in the tomb was a bundle of bones that had already undergone an earlier interment or exposure for at least two years. Fussell's Lodge contained bones from as many as fifty-seven people. Obviously a small farming community would take several years to produce so many corpses, unless there was war or famine and there is no other evidence that such disasters occurred.

A similar two-phase rite was practiced at Quanterness, where the remains of about 157 people had been separated into 12,600 fragments before burial. The bodies were exposed for two years before being gathered up for final burial and they must have been in an enclosure supervised with great care, since none of the bones had been gnawed by animals. After this excarnation, the bones were gathered and broken, to release whatever spirit remained. They were then scorched on a heather and brushwood fire outside the cairn, while at the same time celebrants either ate food or left it as a gift for the dead.

The tomb was periodically cleaned and it continued in use for a thousand years, from about 3420 until 2430 BC. Interestingly, the use of the tomb began, like that of Duggleby Howe, with the intact burial of a man. Although we should not regard either tomb as a mausoleum, in each case the idea of building a monument seems to have sprung from the death of a patriarch.

In certain areas, especially Yorkshire and Cumbria, cremation was practised. At one end of a long barrow, a cremation trench was incorporated into the design, presumably to improve the draught. After excarnation, the disarticulated skeletons were stacked along the trench with firewood. Some sort of fire was lit at the forecourt end of the trench and allowed to spread along it into the barrow. Often the bones at the inner end were unburnt, and it is evident that the whole process was an act of ritual, not an act of disposal.

A second important characteristic of the neolithic rite is collective, communal burial. There seems to have been no discrimination on grounds of age, sex or status: any member of the community could be buried in the endlessly re-usable chambered tombs. Quite what happened to those people of the lowland zone who were not buried in the long barrows is unknown, but the long barrows can only contain between 1 and 5 per cent of the community. Perhaps the rest were allowed to disintegrate in mortuary enclosures or, after excarnation, given a simple crouch burial. This emphasises once more that the long barrows were not designed primarily to dispose of the dead. They were not even primarily graves, but cenotaphs. They were not monuments to the dead, but to Death itself, and they should be seen as magic gateways through which life could be started anew and where the living and the dead could meet. The individual bones selected for burial in the barrows were simply a token of the community's commitment to the fertility cycle.

The chambered tombs could be entered and re-entered, filled, cleared and filled again. There was no limit to the number of souls they could hold. The rites practised at Quanterness show that there was a continually altering regard for the remains of the dead, but that even disarticulated, separated, broken and burnt pieces of bone were regarded with sufficient awe for those pieces to be enshrined in the tomb. At some time – how it was gauged can only be guessed at – the pieces of bone lost their magic potency. When this happened, they could be swept out of the tomb and across the forecourt to make way for new bones.

The entrances to the tombs were invariably made very small. Even the most ambitious monuments had constricted entrance passages and even more constricted doorways. The outermost section of the Maes Howe entrance passage has been discreetly enlarged for the modern visitor. You have to wriggle into the tall chamber of the Knowe of Lairo on your stomach. The smallest entrance I have seen is the south entrance to Taversoe Tuick on Rousay, which is only 0·4 metres square and helps to explain the folklore interpretation of the tombs as fairy dwellings: the entrance is just right for the little people. Why were the entrances made so small? It may be argued that the doorways of houses at Skara Brae are low-lintelled and the tomb doorways are modelled on those, but the Skara Brae lintels are not as low as those on the tombs. The answer may well lie once again in symbolic gesture. The doorway symbolises the junction of the two worlds, of the living and of the dead. We can pass from one world to the other,

Plate 35 The Knowe of Lairo, Rousay

but not without difficulty. There are physical, emotional and psychological difficulties surrounding birth, death and rebirth; it is only natural that these should be reflected in symbolic architecture.

Forecourt rituals involving fire, offerings of bowls, beads and food, often took place immediately outside this threshold between life and death. The forecourt at Cairnholy I in Galloway had a hearth close to the portal stones leading into the tomb. The ashes were covered with a clean spread of earth on which at least four later fires were lit. All this went on while the tomb was still in use. Later, a closing stone was set between the portals and a mass of masonry set against it to seal it for ever. At the base of the closing stone lay pottery, a jet bead and shells of edible molluscs – the final offering.

The Orcadians made similar offerings, but also added sacrifices of birds or animals that seem not to have been used for food. The offerings of dogs at two Orkney tombs could be explained in terms of the partnership that existed between man and dog in hunting; it is possible that dogs were honoured with excarnation like people and their bones were occasionally deposited in tombs in connection with some hunting rite. In view of the birds offered by other tribes, though, it seems more likely that each group adopted some element of the natural world as its totem or emblem: it might be an eagle, a seal, a dog, a skylark or even the sun. Another strange offering was made at Barclodiad y Gawres, a passage grave on Anglesey, where a boiled stew of whitings, eels, frogs, toads, snakes, mice, hares and shrews was

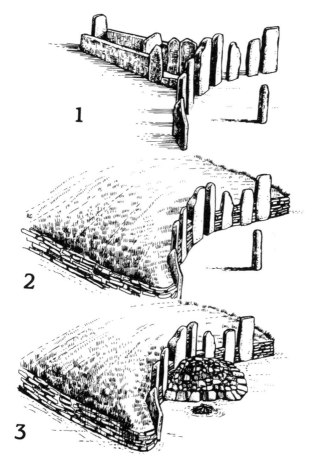

57 Cairnholy: the building sequence of a Clyde chambered tomb

1 The megaliths of the burial chamber and facade are raised
2 A drystone wall is raised as a kerb for a long covering cairn.
  The forecourt is used for rituals involving fires
3 After several centuries of use, the tomb is sealed up

poured out onto the central hearth. Small wonder. It is inconceivable that such a foul brew could have been intended for eating. Rather it provides us with a most ancient pedigree for the contents of the witches' cauldron: perhaps this piece of folklore is founded on a real piece of ancient magic.

Some of the complexity surrounding the funeral rituals can be seen in the sequence of events at the Nutbane long barrow in Hampshire. Archaeology reveals only the major events, the transformations of the site; the elaboration of detailed ritual that has left no trace must be left to the imagination. The first structure on the site was a small rectangular building 5 metres long and 4½ wide, with its long axis aligned west-east. Later this was replaced by a larger building 8 metres by 6, oriented crosswise over the site of the first. The second building was solidly built, with a ridge roof 5 metres high. The ceremonial use of the building was emphasised by the erection of a heavy timber wall or perhaps a colonnade of totem poles along each side. The forward edges of these 8 metre long colonnades made the outer corners of a concave façade 12 metres across (Figure 58).

58 Nutbane, a mortuary building dating to 3500 BC. The cult-house is flanked by totem poles and provides access to a small mortuary enclosure. The scene is probably representative of the first phase of use at many of the English long barrow sites

Behind the building and directly adjoining was a fenced mortuary enclosure, 6 metres square, used for excarnation – a reserved and ceremonial place, a taboo place that could be entered through the cult house. When the time was propitious, and no doubt accompanied by ceremonies, a small pitched-roof mortuary building was built inside the mortuary enclosure and the enclosure was filled with soil, covering the little wooden tent. Later, the cult house was set on fire. Even while the purifying flames were still leaping, work began on the great long mound; soil and chalk were thrown up, eventually burying the earth-filled enclosure, the smouldering and ruined cult house and the colonnade entirely.

We have to see the building and the destruction of all these structures as intimately related to ritual. The act of building and the act of burning, the act of making and the act of unmaking were themselves ritual acts. It is therefore misleading to look at the whole plan of a monument, with its ofen confusing array of pits, deposits, post-holes, mounds and revetments, in the same way that one might look at an architect's plan. Nevertheless, when we visit some of the monuments a powerful architectural impression comes across and at places such as Maes Howe we can be sure that the makers of the monuments felt them to be architecture too.

THE TRYSTING PLACES

The burial monuments are not mere graves. It is clear from the contents of long barrows that they were not designed as charnel houses. A few long barrows seem to have no human remains in them at all. They are dedicatory monuments, places where the dark forces of the universe could be confronted, propitiated, befriended: places where the polarities of life and death, decay and renewal, mysteriously joined and were converted into one another. They fulfilled, in other words, the role of churches or temples.

It may be that bits of broken bone were brought out into the forecourt from time to time and that oracles were received according to the way the bones fell. The long axes of some of the long barrows and entrance passages were aligned deliberately towards the sunrise or sunset in midsummer or midwinter: most commonly towards the equinox sunrise. But this does not mean the monuments were for astronomy. It means that the people who made them were nature-oriented and did not distinguish between their mental and spiritual and physical actions. Both funeral rites and agriculture were connected with the general idea of fecundity; celestial events were linked to the calendar and so too was the pattern of work on the land. The division between secular and spiritual, between magical and ecological, did not yet exist.

The chambered tombs acted as social foci in the highland zone. In the lowland zone, causewayed enclosures and henges met this need, but there was a dearth of enclosures of this type in the highlands. The forecourts of the chambered tombs thus take on new roles as meeting-places for discussion and for feasting, as well as for ceremonies. To some extent, the barrows of the lowland zone may have acquired a similar function for scattered farming groups. They have been described as trysting-places, and this rather diffuse, evocative term conveys well the sort of feeling that the monuments would have aroused.

In more concrete terms, the barrow or tomb may have come to be the 'central place' within a particular territory, however small. That is not to say that it needed to be geometrically central, but rather that it came, by associations, by magnetism, by permanence, to be socially and politically central in the group consciousness. In Wessex, the barrows were often close to that geometric centre too, close to the settlement, but in Sussex the barrows lay at the boundaries of territories (Figure 63). Either way, the barrow or cairn functioned as a major landmark, the enduring symbol of a people living in a half-tamed landscape, seeking to forge a covenant of continuity with their short-lived ancestors and with unknown generations to come.

PART 4

PEOPLE, POLITY AND PHILOSOPHY

CHAPTER 12

THE LAUGHING CHILDREN

Even such is Time, which takes in trust
Our Youth, our Joys, and all we have,
And payes us but with age and dust,
Who in the darke and silent grave,
When we have wandred all our wayes,
Shuts up the story of our dayes.

SIR WALTER RALEIGH, 'The Author's Epitaph', 1618

We laughed; our laughter betrayed scorn.
People on this earth should live in fear.
When men shake hands with time,
Time crushes them like tumblers
Into little pieces of glass.

ABU AL-ALA AL-MA'ARRI, 'Birds Through a Ceiling of
Alabaster', c.1020

Sir Michael Tippett showed a rare insight into the personality of the Avebury people in *The Midsummer Marriage*, where they appear as volatile and instinctual, profoundly attuned to the forces of nature and expressing their bond with nature in elaborate ritual dances. Tippett has them sing, 'We are the laughing children,' and this is the single most apt and potent image that I can find for people who were startlingly child-like in appearance, temperament and daring.

THE PHYSIQUE OF THE STONEHENGE PEOPLE

A typical, thirty-year-old Orkney man was 171 centimetres (5 feet 7 inches) tall and a typical woman was about 12 centimetres (5 inches) shorter. A height of around 170 centimetres was typical of the long barrow men of southern England too, though there were local variations. The Avebury folk were a little taller and the

Medway megalith builders were shorter than the average. They were lean and slender, with only moderate muscular strength. Often their bones seem too light and delicate to have coped with the megaliths – a reminder that thoughtful planning and a great deal of ingenuity were put into projects that involved manual labour. The Welsh appear to have been slightly more robust, but in general people were smaller and more delicate than they are today.

Their heads were narrow, giving them long, lean faces. Controversy has surrounded the shape of their heads ever since a classic nineteenth-century study of neolithic and bronze age skulls from Arran and Bute. A distinction was made between narrow skulls (dolichocephalic), in which the width of the braincase is less than 75 per cent of the length, giving a cephalic index of 75, and broad skulls (brachycephalic), in which the width is greater than 80 per cent of the length. A small sample of skulls was made to demonstrate that neolithic people had thin, long heads and bronze age people were more robust with broad, round heads and a higher cephalic index. Scottish and English skulls retrieved from neolithic tombs have an average index of 72 or 73. As more skulls are measured, though, it becomes clearer that head shape varied quite a lot throughout the neolithic, and that not everybody by any means had a long, narrow head.

Some of the Wessex skulls are quite child-like. The sexes were not sharply differentiated and the features were refined and dainty; their noses, for instance, were small and turned up. It

59 Skulls from Isbister. These two people lived in the Isbister community on Orkney some time between 3200 and 2400 BC. The stalled cairn in which they were found was in continual use for collective burial for 800 years

comes as something of a shock to realise that the people who conceived, built and used the great henge at Avebury were not only young people of slight and slender build, but were possessed of child-like faces. If in some way we were able to travel back over 4000 years and see the Avebury people performing their strange ceremonies in the stone circles and processing along the stone avenues, I think we would, initially at any rate, experience the strange sensation that we were watching children – children playing some elaborate and perhaps rather sinister game of make-believe.

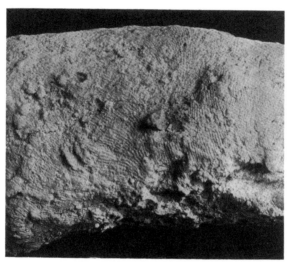

Plate 36 Neolithic hand-print. This antler-pick from Grime's Graves became coated with wet chalk mud during use. It now preserves the hand-print of one of the miners

We know quite a lot about their state of health, allowing of course for the fact that in dealing with the dead we are necessarily not dealing with people at their best. We can guess, though not be certain, that they were free of the stress-related diseases of the twentieth-century: that cancer and heart disease would be relatively uncommon. The great scourge of the neolithic was osteoarthritis; this painful and often disabling disease of the joints was endemic, appearing in quite young people. Some archaeologists have guessed that diet-deficiency illnesses were common, but there is not much evidence of anaemia or rickets. Some women in particular suffered from spina bifida. Other people suffered from polio, tetanus and sinusitis. Given the growth of livestock rearing in the late neolithic, a growth in animal-related diseases seems very likely: we should expect there to have been outbreaks of tuberculosis, brucellosis and anthrax in communities living close to cattle. The spread of diseases is likely to have been rapid too, since all the pottery utensils were unglazed and porous.

Dental problems included inflamed gums, pyorrhoea and abscesses. One poor old man at West Overton in Wiltshire had four teeth with chronic abscesses and must have been in constant pain at the end of his life. Aubrey Burl rather hastily put all these problems down to bad mouth hygiene, but the lack of dentistry would easily explain the relatively infrequent problems and the condition of most teeth was surprisingly good in the circumstances. It is generally reckoned that, through the neolithic as a whole, only 3 per cent of teeth had caries – a low proportion. In Orkney, a sample of nearly 900 teeth had remarkably few caries and gave a rate of less than 1 per cent. The Orkney teeth all had cracked enamel, though, which was possibly due to some local peculiarity of diet; cracked enamel seems not to have been a problem in southern England.

This litany of maladies conjures up a very wretched impression of life in the neolithic, but I have focussed on the nature of the ailments suffered by people at the ends of their lives and ignored the healthy. A tour of the wards of any modern hospital would give us an ugly list, possibly considerably longer, of the ailments of modern Britain. We can also be sure that ways were found of alleviating some of the illnesses. We know that primitive surgery was practised in the form of bone-setting and trephination. Broken arms and legs must have been an occupational hazard among flint miners, continually negotiating shafts up to 12 metres deep, and farmers, continually felling trees to clear new land. Fractured limbs were not a disaster, though, as they could be set successfully. Trephination was a more dubious practice and still goes on among some primitive groups today. It involves the careful removal of a disc of bone from the skull and was probably used as a cure for mental illness. Although unlikely to have been successful as a cure, unless shock cures, it was often technically successful as surgery, which is surprising in view of the equipment in use. The fact that many survived this traumatic operation implies that some form of narcotic drug was used as a painkiller or anaesthetic. No direct evidence of such a drug survives, but the inference is there and it does imply that there were ways of alleviating the more severe and distressing conditions our ancestors suffered.

They probably used placebos too. In contemporary simple societies, the administering of pharmacologically inert substances can give real relief, sometimes even curing conditions by auto-suggestion. Nor should we underestimate the curative and consoling effects of caring. A seriously ill Navajo Indian, for instance, became the focus of the entire group's continuous concern during a special ceremony lasting nine days and nights.

Even if the illness itself was not cured by this, the patient felt the love and concern of the group, which was a powerful reassurance, created a diversion and also gave the strength to cope with pain.

Infant mortality was high. Bones from barrow and tomb burials indicate that only 5 per cent of the population died in infancy and a further 5 per cent between the ages of one and four. These figures seem far too low and I suspect they are not representative. It may be that new-born babies, and perhaps children in their first year of life, were not accorded the usual funeral rites of excarnation followed by burial in the collective tomb but instead were simply buried informally. At Quanterness on Orkney, no infants under eight months old were buried, which seems to confirm this view.

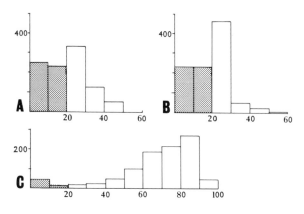

60 Life expectancy. Bar graphs showing age at death in three communities. Each column shows the estimated number of deaths per thousand per year in a ten-year age band

A Isbister, South Ronaldsay, Orkney   C Modern Britain

B Quanterness, Mainland Orkney

In neolithic Orkney, most people could expect to die before reaching the age of thirty. The population was therefore extremely young, with 40-50 per cent of the community below the age of twenty, compared with only 13 per cent today.

The crude death rate for the population as a whole was probably about 40 per 1000 per year, compared with only 14 for Western Europe today. If the death rate sounds very high, it is similar to that of many Third World countries. Even so, people lived short lives. Many men died by the age of 35; many women were dead by the age of 30. Burl estimates that 40 per cent of people died before they reached 20. At the same time, there were rare individuals who lived on to be 50, 60 or even 70; they must have seemed utterly exceptional and were very likely held in special regard. Of those surviving infancy, 60 per cent could expect to reach the age of 25, but only 30 per cent could expect to reach 40.

The Quanterness bones, thought to represent those of an entire community apart from infants, show the following age-distribution;

Age in years	Percentage of the population
0 – 2	6
3 – 12	16
13 – 19	23
20 – 29	47
30 – 39	5
40 – 50	2
over 50	1

People in Orkney in about 3200 BC had a life expectancy of only about 25 years. This very short life span is surprising, as it compares more closely with earlier mesolithic life spans than with contemporary life spans in other regions. Only 3 per cent of the Orkney people survived into the 40-60 age group, whereas 25 per cent of the population were living to that age in France. I expect that, although backed up by the recent results from the excavation at Isbister, Quanterness will turn out not to be typical of Britain as a whole and that, in the kinder south, 30-35 will prove to be the more usual life span.

Even in Orkney, though, some lived to be 50. The Cotswold tool-maker buried in the Heselton long barrow was about 55 and seemed to be in robust health. So, the average life expectancy may have been 30-40 years, but it was quite possible for individuals to live considerably longer. Aubrey Burl sees the people of neolithic Britain leading a wretched existence, stumbling forlornly from one crisis to the next and racked alternately by famine and disease. This view is really that of prehistorians fifty years ago. In terms of health, people were probably no worse off than they were in medieval Britain or in simple peasant farming communities existing today. Although they died young, they were not disease-ridden. A man of 40 would have been regarded as a very old man. A man of 50 would have been regarded as extraordinary; he would have to be more than twice that age today to excite the same wonder.

These old people must have been held in great respect, since they formed rare and precious links with the honoured past. They were, in effect, living exemplars of the revered tribal ancestors through whom the community established its claim to territory. It was the three-quarters of the population who were under the age of 20 (at Isbister and probably Orkney in general) who were the megalith builders, while their elders planned, advised, magicked and supervised. Some children as young as 6 developed osteo-arthritis in their spines, presumably as a result of carrying heavy loads. It comes as something of a shock to realise that the monuments were largely built by children.

CLOTHES AND ORNAMENTS

Only when we can establish what sort of clothes the Stonehenge people wore will we have a clear idea of what they actually looked like. Here we come up against one of the greatest problems we have so far encountered because, although clothes form part of the archaeologist's observational field, they are also perishable and virtually nothing has survived. We must hope that eventually the peat of the Somerset Levels will yield up the perfectly preserved remains of some hapless hunter and all his clothes and accoutrements. So far nothing of this kind has been discovered in Britain although there is a real possibility that shreds of cloth and a disintegrating fringed hood found a century ago and thought to be Celtic may actually have been bronze age or neolithic. Meanwhile, the best we can do is to look at the clothes that have survived in Denmark from the early bronze age, the period immediately following the neolithic. Then we can discuss the ways in which those clothes are likely to differ from those worn in Britain a few centuries earlier.

We could not do better than to start with the rather provocative outfit worn by a teenage girl from Egtved. She wore a miniskirt 65 centimetres long made from vertical woollen strands that were gathered at waist and hem in elaborate edgings; the waist edging was tied in a bow below her navel, with the loops hanging down in front. The skirt was slung low on her hips, so that her stomach was exposed. She also wore a short brown woollen tunic made in one piece, with gussets at the armpits and sleeves reaching just below her elbows. The neck line was high, wide and hemmed. On her stomach she wore a circular ornamental disc mounted on a woven belt with a large tassel on one end. The belt was 2 metres long and was wound round her slender waist several times.

The presence of flowers in her hair suggests that she was in summer dress and we would hope that she wore something warmer in winter. An older woman wore more substantial clothes in summer and winter. Her skirt was long, voluminous and reached the ground. It was loosely gathered at the waist by a long woven belt; the skirt was made of several pieces of woollen cloth sewn together with thick thread to make a large rectangle 1½ by 4 metres and must have been very warm. The tunic was more carefully made, with a high neck, sometimes embroidered. Both men and women probably wore cloaks in winter.

Women's hairstyles were as redundantly complex and varied as they are today. One style involved piling the hair up on the front of the head, increasing the height with a coif of false hair: the whole construction was held in place by a lozenge-meshed net made of black horse-hair and bound with interlacing cords. The horn combs women always carried with them, attached to their belts, show that they were fastidiously concerned about their appearance. Some women wore bonnets; these were elaborately made and obviously designed to draw attention.

The man's basic garment was a deceptively simple tunic that wrapped round the body from shoulder level down to knee or mid-calf. He fastened it round his waist with a leather belt and over each shoulder with a leather strap. The cut of the breast-line varied: it could be horizontal, or sloping down to one side, or tongued up to the throat. Over this tunic he wore a knee-length woollen cape that could be round, oval or kidney-shaped; it was fastened across his chest and the edge was flipped back at the neck and chest to form a collar and revers. The very striking effect of tunic and cape was enhanced by a jaunty round woollen cap, which could be either beehive- or fez-shaped. The caps, like the women's bonnets, were made with unusual care, with several layers of cloth to make them thick and cushiony, guaranteed to

61 Neolithic man and woman. A very tentative and speculative reconstruction. There is as yet no way of knowing how tidy or well-finished their garments were

keep their shape. The emphasis on bonnets and caps shows that they were the focus of attention. The cut of one's hat obviously said much about one's social status – or self-opinion – we cannot tell which. The man was clean-shaven and wore his hair long, combed back and parted in the middle; he too carried a comb.

Shoes varied almost as much as hairstyles. Some people wore well-made leather moccasins, while others wore simple foot wrappings made of a piece of cloth bound round the foot and tied round the ankles. There is some evidence that sandals were worn, and these may have developed as a type of binding for a cloth foot wrapping: certainly the addition of a sole would make the wrapping last longer and made walking on stony ground far more comfortable.

So much for Danish apparel in the bronze age. How far does it reflect what the Stonehenge people wore? In general, we can assume that change was slow and gradual in the prehistoric period. In general, too, we can assume that the same materials were available in the neolithic as in the bronze age. There has been a tendency to portray the neolithic as a period when barbarous, spear-waving savages scampered about in animal skins, with the quiet crafts of spinning, weaving and tailoring developing in the ensuing bronze age. Yet, at a great many neolithic settlements, perforated stones commonly 2 to 8 centimetres across have been found. Often they have been interpreted, in sympathy with the rather crass image of neolithic man already alluded to, as pendants. Some of the smaller ones, perforated at one end, probably are, but most would hang very clumsily or be too heavy. It would be more natural to interpret the smaller objects as spindle

62 Shaman. The magician was a key figure in the community

whorls and the larger ones as loom weights. Weaving could be done on a relatively simple loom built between two posts driven into the ground: the loom weights were used to keep the vertical warp-threads taut.

We should assume that both woollen cloth and linen were available as well as skin and leather. The major difference between neolithic and bronze age attire was in the proportions of materials used: in the neolithic a greater proportion of clothes was made out of skin and leather, with textiles coming in increasingly during the later neolithic. There is some evidence of this in the nature of the fastening devices that have survived. Large numbers of bone and antler pins were used, and they are ideally suited to fastening leather garments, though less suitable for fastening cloth. Many were used for fastening hair into buns. On Orkney, very elaborately carved pins were made. Some were so long (23 centimetres) that they were not just fasteners, but major decorative features. People were afraid of losing them, so little perforated lugs were incorporated into the design so that they could be tied on to the garment, whether cloak or tunic, with a leather thong.

Towards the end of the neolithic, gaiters with buttons came in and these imply trousers of some kind. We should perhaps visualise something looking like Jacobean breeches, probably for winter wear. Further support for the proposition that bronze age fashions were already in vogue in the neolithic comes from belt-fasteners. Some of them were made of bone, in the shape of a bottle opener; one end of the cloth or leather belt was permanently tied to the fastener through the smaller hole, while the other end was looped through the larger hole in a clove hitch. This very effective buckle was by no means the only type: 'sliders' made of bone or stone were also very common. The slider had a single, tapering slot through which both ends of the belt were pulled, presumably in opposite directions, Some fine examples of sliders made of polished jet have been found in Wales and lowland England.

In addition to these decorative garment-fastenings, there were many extra ornaments, such as stone pendants. There were also beads made of bone, antler, seeds and stone. The Stonehenge people appreciated the aesthetic quality of certain kinds of stone. The smooth, black shale from Kimmeridge in Dorset was in demand for beads over quite a large area extending west to Maiden Castle and Hembury. Rarer objects, like the boar's tusk pendant at Skara Brae, may have had a talismanic value or served to remind the wearer and his admirers of some great exploit. Certainly personal ornaments were of great importance. At Skara Brae, a little keeping-place containing a hoard of beads and pendants served as a vanity chest for one of the inhabitants. In a corner of the same house, Hut 7, there was a small whalebone basin containing red ochre.

This was used for facial decoration of some kind, perhaps for heightening the colour of the lips or for more extensive designs on the skin, cheeks and forehead. On mainland Europe, we know that face and body decoration using red ochre were widely practised. Many of the marble cups, bowls and pallettes of the Cyclades were used for containing and mixing the colour and some of the statues of the goddess were originally covered with red ochre stripes. At Skara Brae, several little pots containing cakes of red ochre were found, proving that people in Britain also decorated themselves with paint. The painting of face and body was widespread and it would be surprising if Britain remained unaffected. In view of the British climate, though, it is likely that clothing made body painting redundant and it may well be that the British went in for restraint with only a modest amount of decoration to the face.

CHAPTER 13

THE PEACEFUL CITADEL

Many nations have settled on other men's land,
Then fallen and likewise crumbled into the soil.
Rack your memory for lost ancestors:
It can only tell you they are gone.

ABU AL-ALA AL-MA'ARRI, 'Birds Through a Ceiling of Alabaster', *c.*1020

NEOLITHIC SOCIETY: THE CONTROVERSY

The nature of neolithic society is one of the most controversial matters of all. Of the wide-ranging views that have found their way into print, the prevailing one until the present century was that neolithic Britons were 'savage and barbarous, knowing no use of garments'. There was always a small, unorthodox minority who saw evidence of something higher. William Stukeley, for instance, in 1740 saw the elaborate monuments on Salisbury Plain as evidence of a stratified society with druids, arch-druids, kings, princes and nobles. The great numbers of arrows, axes and earthworks from the period were nevertheless generally interpreted as signs of warlike tendencies, and human sacrifice was taken for granted.

By 1935, Stuart Piggott was beginning to see in the archaeological evidence a more peaceful and idyllic scene. But others, such as Curwen, still saw everyday life in the neolithic as a brutal struggle for survival: his picture of the Whitehawk causewayed enclosure shows people living at the most primitive level, scratching a meagre and sordid existence in a shallow ditch. In 1940, Gordon Childe proposed a more complex society that remained largely at a subsistence level but was also involved to a small extent in trading; the many barrows were taken to indicate a deep commitment to religion.

In 1961, Richard Atkinson developed the idea that the monument-building on Salisbury Plain required an organised social hierarchy, with some sort of guiding authority. The fact that

204

the long barrows were found to contain only a small proportion of the total population, the élite, again argued for a stratified society. Later in the 1960s Alexander Thom altered the picture again by proposing a peaceful and intellectual society that spent much of its time on geometry, astronomy and surveying as a background to monumental architecture. In the 1970s, Aubrey Burl shifted the emphasis to ritual and superstition. The neolithic world became a twilit place of spirits and symbols where man nursed 'hopes of high talk with the departed dead', and where ritual counted for just as much as sound farming practice in the production of crops. But it is a fearful and deprived world that Burl depicts for us: 'in futility, it was religion that protected their minds.'

John Barnatt's view is less pessimistic. He concedes that people lived fairly short lives and that there was high infant mortality, but thinks that the neolithic way of life was no worse than the medieval: general living conditions changed surprisingly little over that long period. Neolithic people probably had leisure and, apart from occasional disasters such as floods or famines, the great stability of the culture would have provided security. Barnatt reminds us that people can make life very comfortable for themselves without leaving any significant archaeological remains.

Each of these responses to the neolithic is conditioned by and is to some extent a reaction to the previous response. In making a new synthesis, a new interpretation, we need to guard against the tendency to argue by disagreement; the tendency should nevertheless be reduced by our consciousness of the likelihood of bias. There is also a tendency which we will almost certainly not be able to escape, and that is to see the ancient society from the point of view of our own, whether in positive or negative terms. Jacquetta Hawkes once said that 'every age has the Stonehenge it deserves – or desires'. There is a sense in which each generation gets the neolithic society it needs or wants, too.

Inescapable though this sort of bias is, I think it is possible to reduce it to a lower level than ever before, because of the enormous volume of archaeological data now available. Provided the evidence is reviewed and synthesised piecemeal, without tendentiousness, we should be in a position to assemble the cumulative evidence for the nature of the society.

The focus of the culture – if we can identify it – will give us a very important element in the nature of the society. If, for example, the focus was the admiration of warrior-heroes, it would give us a good idea of the general type of subject-matter of songs and stories, it would imply the existence of a warlike, arrogant and self-regarding aristocracy, a tendency to seek quarrels with neighbouring territories in order to create opportunities for heroic action, and so on. The focus gives us the flavour of the society.

From the various major enterprises we have already seen and will yet see elaborated still further, it is clear that the neolithic culture was oriented to a cult or religion relating to fertility. Whether we look to agriculture, or earth and stone circles or chambered tombs and earthen barrows, the broad orientation is the same.

A STRATIFIED SOCIETY?

The burial monuments speak of an equalitarian society, yet several influential prehistorians have argued for a stratified society, so we need to review the arguments for stratification with care.

Euan MacKie recently put forward a theory in which small bands of specialist megalith builders travelled to various parts of Britain from the Mediterranean in order to convert the natives to their new religion. In this way, many separate cells of neolithic culture were launched, although each became hybridised with certain aspects of the indigenous culture. The missionary group, with its superior technology and scientific understanding, established itself as a secular as well as a religious élite, with special centres such as Skara Brae developed as monastic universities. Needless to say, the élite group did not soil its hands with farming: that was left to the peasants, who were apparently excluded from the great monuments but had their own causewayed enclosures. MacKie visualises the stratification developing from about 2900 BC, associated with Stonehenge I and Silbury Hill, and becoming more defined in about 2600 BC, the time when the superhenges were built.

A more moderate version of a neolithic stratified society has been suggested by Paul Ashbee. He argues that the very large later neolithic projects on Salisbury Plain required such large numbers of workers that a sophisticated social hierarchy must have developed. Durrington Walls, Stonehenge and the Cursus are seen as a regal aggregation comparable, though it is not clear how, with the palace complexes of Crete. The demands of a powerful aristocracy housed in the great Wessex henges stimulated the lower orders to ever-greater efforts, and a secular and theocratic hierarchy emerged. In other words, large-scale projects like the Dorset Cursus, which is estimated to have taken 9 million man-hours to construct, are offered as *de facto* evidence of powerful leadership, class division and an aristocratic élite.

'Oriental despot' theories were once very popular in explaining ancient cultural development. They were originally developed as a conscious or unconscious polemic against socialism. Such explanations contain the unspoken thrust that, because the great early civilisations were created by despotic, 'pyramidal' societies, modern civilisation also requires a pyramidal society to sustain and nourish it. In practice, of course, despotisms are usually short-lived; we have only to cite the careers of Mongolian Khans, Alexander, Napoleon, Hitler, Amin and Bokassa.

The élitist theories are unconvincing because, in the first place, there is no archaeological evidence of a distinct group of newcomers who might have brought a 'megalithic culture' with them. MacKie suggested that these culturally very different people came from one of the proto-urban civilisations developing in the Near East about 3000 BC, but there are no obviously distinct skeletal remains that might indicate an exotic origin. Nor is there any reason to suppose that Skara Brae was anything other than a villge inhabited by ordinary people: remains of several other stone villages have been discovered in Orkney and Shetland. There is no positive sign of a powerful despot and no sign of an aristocratic élite either.

Conversely, there are signs that the ritual enclosures, whether of earth or stone, held entire communities. It is only in the bronze age that the stone settings shrank to such a small size that only a handful of initiates could have entered. The neolithic circles were designed to include everyone, and that implies a democratic ideal. The big roundhouses in the superhenges were communal dwellings. The chambered tombs held the mortal remains of whole communities, for generation after generation, without any distinction of rank, at least in the early and middle neolithic. There were no royal mausolea. It was at one time assumed that Silbury Hill was the tomb of a great king, but excavation has shown that although the mound is authentically neolithic there is no burial in it. However much labour was involved, the large projects can be interpreted as products of a collective will; there is no need to presume that work was done to satisfy the capricious requirements of a despotic leadership.

THE QUESTION OF LEADERSHIP

How, then, was this equalitarian society organised? Many relatively simple societies have a headman or bigman. Chieftains only emerge as societies become more complex and there is a sharper need for leadership, although even then that role may be more symbolic of group identity than political. The headman is the oldest and simplest type of leader. Unobtrusively and without any apparent authority, he holds the tribe together. It is possible that early neolithic groups had no leader at all: the simplest societies are pure democracies. The African Nuba, for instance, have elders, distinguished by their clothes, who make decisions for the group by committee; the younger men between 13 and 30, who traditionally go naked and are further distinguished by elaborate body painting, are excluded from the decision-making. On balance, I think nominal leadership by a headman is more likely; the very substantial material achievements of the culture seem to require some kind of chairman, foreman and spokesman to facilitate organisation. It is perhaps worth reflecting that although great publicity has been given to the exercise of kingship among the Inca, Maya, Toltec and Aztec communities, *all* the other aboriginal societies of the Americas have been democratic in nature. It is quite possible that, in neolithic Europe too, democracy was the norm.

Studies of burials in Yorkshire show that until about 3500 BC there was a simple equalitarian society. There was no difference in the way that men, women and adolescents were treated in death: only young children were treated as inferior. After that date there was increasing differentiation until, by the late neolithic, 2500-2000 BC, a simple four-tier society had evolved, with the four 'layers' consisting from the bottom upwards of children, women and adolescents, men and bigmen. It seems very likely that this was the pattern in other parts of Britain too.

The character and role of the bigman can be constructed to some extent by looking at an analogous figure, the village leader of Papua New Guinea. He qualifies for his position by his personality, not by any hereditary right; he is confident, original, a man of ambition and initiative, with conspicuous leadership qualities. He has no special rights or privileges, but he is expected to lead discussions and act as a spokesman for the group.

A conspicuous feature of New Guinea tribal societies is the exchange of gifts and the bigman is invariably at the focus of this giving and receiving. At the *moka*, a large-scale ceremonial gathering at which pigs and other gifts are often exchanged, the bigman acts as host and master of ceremonies. He makes a long speech: 'Whoever you are, from whatever tribe or clan, all you men of different ancestors, hear me. . . . The ceremonial axes of stone, the carved spears, the women's headnets, their capacious netbags, the pig ropes, the wooden spades, where are they all? . . . Now these gifts I make to you. Take it all. Whatever you do with it is your affair. Eat my gifts and go.'

By means of such gestures, the bigman voices the will of the group and holds it together in an otherwise ungoverned society. Apart from the bigmen, there seem to have been no significant vertical divisions in neolithic Britain other than that between men and women. There may conceivably have been horizontal divisions by occupation, and we should consider these. It may be thought that without an overseer the whole concept of occupation or work is irrelevant: that people would not have worked at all. In practice, communal work without authority is quite effective, as a man from the north coast of New Guinea has explained; 'A man who toils by himself goes along as he pleases: he works slowly and pauses every time he feels like it. But when two men work together, each tries to do the most. One man thinks to himself, "My back aches and I feel like resting, but my friend there is going on: I must go on too, or I shall feel ashamed." The other man thinks to himself, "My arms are tired and my back is breaking, but I must not be the first to pause." Each man strives to do the most, and the garden is finished quickly.'

A CLASSLESS SOCIETY?

Although we cannot be certain, it looks as if mining was not a full-time occupation; the seasonal mining and knapping activities of the mesolithic period probably continued into the neolithic. Traders were probably not a special class, although the geographical, political and ethnographic expertise involved means that the same people were involved each time. If trading adventures were annual or biennial, a small party could be released from the agricultural routine to go on the expedition. It is easy to imagine potters and carpenters doing their specialised work on a part-time basis, when the need arose. Masons and engineers would be required less frequently still, so we cannot really suppose that they were full-time professionals unless they were rootless nomads, which is unlikely for social reasons; a greater uniformity of style and quality would also have emerged from the archaeological record had this been the case. In general, it appears that most of the specialists participated in the common activities of cultivation, livestock-tending and hunting, fitting in their specialist services as and when the demand arose.

I tend to think that the shaman or priest might have performed only his specialist work, but anthropologists have noted that shamans too are often only part-time. It is only when societies emerge well above the subsistence level, with substantial and regular food surpluses, that ritual specialists such as priests, diviners and curers and technical specialists such as traders, potters and flint knappers become full-time. On that basis, it looks more likely that full-time specialists in the modern sense emerged only after the neolithic.

It seems extraordinary to us that such achievements could result from activities that we would regard as hobbies, but that is only because we take such a self-limiting view of our talents and skills. In archaic societies, people often develop specialisms out of pride; often the activity is passed on through families as a kind of personal tradition; often it is regarded as an hereditary calling. The work is done out of joy in being able to do it, pleasure in being able to serve others, and satisfaction at recalling a link with revered ancestors. We can see the natural coherence of a society not divided by classes, not divided by occupation. People were able to realise their individual identities at the same time as serving the group and fulfilling family honour.

THE POLITICAL GEOGRAPHY OF BRITAIN

People have often visualised Stonehenge as a centre for an area far larger than the immediate clan territory. It is tempting to see either Stonehenge or Avebury as a sort of national capital, but there is no evidence that this was so. Indeed, there is no evidence that there was a nation at all; the idea would probably have been incomprehensible to the Stonehenge people, except perhaps in a very limited sense that we will explore later, and then only at the end of the neolithic. Britain was composed of myriads of separate, small-scale, modular societies, each one entirely self-governing. Britain was therefore not governed, did not exist as a country, but only as a unit of purely physical geography. The small-scale cellular structure seems to have spread across the length and breadth of Britain. Decentralisation was total, with all decision-making taken right down at the local commune level.

We can infer cellular or segmentary societies where the evidence shows a pattern of similarly functioning sites such as settlements dispersed and relatively evenly spaced. This implies mutual repulsion and a division of the spaces separating the focal sites into cells or territories round the foci. It is also necessary for the sites to be equal: there should be no detectable hierarchy that might imply regional capitals, for instance. This rather abstract description is best illustrated by example. Figure 63 shows part of East Sussex as it was in the neolithic. The twenty known settlements, including causewayed enclosures and open stances, were marked in and the modal (i.e. commonest) distance between nearest neighbours was calculated at 2·25 kilometres. If each settlement, home to as many as fifty people, stood at the centre of its territory, we can assume territories with an average radius of 1·13 kilometres. The result, as the map shows, is that the long barrows tend to be on or very close to the boundaries of the territories. This significant fact tends to confirm the validity of the technique as well as showing that the barrows were, amongst other things, boundary markers and may have been taboo places, not to be visited too often. Interestingly, Falmer Pond is on a boundary as well; I had already wondered whether the ring of 170 sarsens round the pond might represent the wrecked site of some megalithic structure.

The pattern in Sussex was probably typical of large areas of lowland England, with dispersed farming groups creating an overall

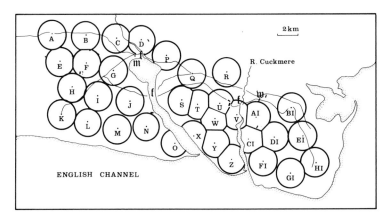

63 Commune or band territories in East Sussex. The coastline is reconstructed to its position in 3000 BC; the Ouse and Cuckmere floodplains are thus shown as sea inlets and Pevensey Levels as a large natural harbour. Tracks are shown as thin black lines.

M Lewes Mount, a harvest hill	**F** possible ferry;
	W Wilmington Giant

Occupation sites (? indicates no positive evidence)

A Ditchling Beacon ?	R Selmeston
B Plumpton Plain ?	S Blackcap ?
C Offham	T Lord's Burgh ?
D Malling	U Bostal ?
E Stanmer ?	V Frog Firle
F Balmer ?	W Hobbs Hawth
G Kingston	X Bishopstone
H Falmer Hill	Y Seaford ?
I Bullock Hill ?	Z South Hill
J Breaky Bottom	A1 Fore Down
K Whitehawk	B1 Combe Hill
L Ovingdean	C1 West Dean ?
M Saltdean ?	D1 Friston ?
N Hoddern Farm	E1 Pea Down
O Castle Hill	F1 Crowlink
P Glynde ?	G1 Belle Tout
Q Firle	H1 Bullock Down

population density of about 1½ per square kilometre. Meetings at the causewayed enclosures could imply some higher level of organisation, but clans (i.e. kinship groups) would be sufficient to explain them. In the Great Ouse valley in the East Midlands, there were eighteen territories each of about 5 square kilometres, while the even distribution of barrow clusters round Stonehenge shows that the territories there were on average 5·1 square kilometres. The East Sussex territories were about 4·1 square kilometres. The generally convergent results from these widely spaced sample studies imply an unexpected degree of uniformity in the lowland zone, with a continuous pattern of small cells, each about 2·4 kilometres across. The extreme dispersion this implies was related entirely to the small size of the communities and the needs of agriculture. Dispersion is the most efficient settlement pattern for farming, as it enables people to live in the centre of their lands and shortens their walk to the fields.

Counteracting this centrifugal force was a centralising tendency. There was a natural social impulse, to want to meet people other than the immediate group. There may have been a need to collaborate in the building of some of the larger monuments, although I think this need has been exaggerated. An elaborately designed and ambitious project like the Quanterness tomb could have been brought to fruition by as few as twenty people. Only the largest projects and the manhandling of the largest megaliths of the later neolithic monuments would have required the co-operation of two, three or four neighbouring cells. Most of the chambered tombs and earthen long barrows could have been – and almost certainly were – built unaided by the people of a single cell. Big projects, like Maes Howe, required ten times the total amount of labour, though this does not necessarily mean that ten previously separate cells were involved.

Some prehistorians have graded monumental projects according to the total number of man-hours invested in them. Isbister, a medium-sized chambered tomb on South Ronaldsay, represents an investment of some 12,000 man-hours, whilst Maes Howe represents 39,000. The stones and ditch of the Ring of Brodgar represents 200,000 hours of work. Too often we have assumed that these figures represent the numbers of workers involved in the projects or the size of the territory they commanded, but a more decisive indicator of the size of the labour force is the largest single unit of work involved. For instance, an earthen long barrow may have required 5000 man-hours to complete it, yet because of the tasks involved one well-motivated and persevering person could have built it single-handed, working 5 hours a day, 50 days a year for 20 years. It would have been a lifetime's work, but the single largest unit of work was nevertheless manageable by a single person. So, unless we know that a project was completed very quickly (and radiocarbon dates are not yet accurate enough to tell us this), we need only postulate the smallest possible labour force for, say, raising a Stonehenge lintel or a Maes Howe entrance passage slab. In fact all the evidence points to the monuments having been raised over rather long periods spanning several generations, so this 'minimalist' approach is likely to be closer to the reality than the Hollywood-style 'cast of thousands' popularly envisaged.

The small tribal groups of perhaps 50-100 people were self-organising and self-sufficient. Their ancestry and their ties with their lands gave them a strong sense of identity and this was probably often expressed in totems of various kinds. Some of the long barrow tribes of southern England seem to have identified with bulls. On Orkney, there were groups apparently identifying with red deer, dogs, sea-eagles and song-birds. It is not inconceivable that the Quanterness people actually called themselves 'Skylarks', whilst the Isbister people were 'Eagles' and the Cuween and Burray people were 'Dogs', dressing themselves up to look like their totem animals for dancing and rituals. Such totems are usually linked with a belief in the transmigration of souls from man to animal (and back) after death. In New Britain, a relationship of this kind exists between a tribal community and sharks. The belief even survived into historic times in Orkney, where there is a saying: 'I am a man on the land and a selkie in the sea.' The selkies, or seals, were very likely the totem animal of more than one neolithic tribe.

But the small tribal groups with their strange totemic preoccupations were not entirely turned in on themselves. The people of each group could meet their neighbours at the common frontier to exchange goods, ideas, news and gossip. In this way it was possible for all these things to spread gradually from cell to cell across the region, eventually covering huge distances. Each cell tended to evolve in sympathy with its neighbours, or remain in stasis with its neighbours. Those cells sharing ideas in common formed a tradition block. Innovations could appear anywhere in the cellular structure and spread outwards from their various starting-points. Some cells, exerting their right of choice, did not adopt innovations, so some traditions overlapped while others did not. The political structure and the processes affecting it explain perfectly the rich variety of cultural traits displayed by the thousands of individual cells, all drawing eclectically on a more or less common fund of ideas, resources and techniques.

Cultural provinces are apparently implied by distribution maps of the axe trade, pottery styles and burial monuments, but when these maps are superimposed on one another neither the boundaries nor the core areas coincide. Instead, it seems that these different traditions were received and accepted or rejected quite separately at the local level. The effect, when viewed geographically, appears rather disorganised to the modern eye.

The neolithic was a period of minimal government, so how then do we explain the Wessex superhenges? Are they to be regarded as the ceremonial centres of unusually resourceful and enterprising groups of the same small size as the Sussex territories? Alternatively, we may see the superhenges as late neolithic expressions of tribal identity, whilst the barrows and barrow clusters were expressions of local group identity. The dating of the superhenges fits in well with this idea, and we saw in Yorkshire that social stratification peaked at the same time, implying a countrywide evolution with an increase in the status of men and a tendency, probably for feasts and ceremonies only, to aggregate into larger units. Some writers like to see this resulting from the initiative of powerful chieftains, but the gatherings could as easily have resulted from a communal wish for increasing collectivism in ceremonial and decision-making.

Figure 64 shows the large henges as metropolitan centres for tribal territories in Wessex. Avebury, Durrington, Knowlton and Mount Pleasant each have an associated cluster of long and round barrows, showing that the heartland of each tribal territory was already being established in the middle neolithic and that the late neolithic development was a crystallisation of a process long under way. Territorial boundaries are likely to have followed easily recognisable landforms in the no-man's-land separating each heartland from the next. The boundary between Knowlton and Durrington territories would have been easy to recognise if it followed the Nadder valley from Tisbury to Wilton and then the Wylye valley to Salisbury. The boundary between the Knowlton and Mount Pleasant tribes is harder to identify because the no-man's-land, the area of low barrow density, is very wide. A frontier along the Stour valley would seem likely, as this would have made the Mount Pleasant, Knowlton and Durrington chalk territories roughly the same size. It is possible that the Frome valley was another boundary. Although there is no other evidence for the hypothesis, it would put Mount Pleasant right on the edge of a South Dorset Downs territory and could explain the insecurity that led to the building of the massive stockade there right at the end of our period.

Marden is peculiar in being so close to Avebury and in not being the focus of barrow-building. Its position suggests that it functioned as a metropolitan centre for a tribe occupying the Vale of Pewsey and probably, for the sake of a mixture of soils, the northern edge of Salisbury Plain. The low-lying vale was probably still uncleared forest in the early neolithic, which would explain the low frequency of long barrows. Stanton Drew acted as a similar, non-chalk centre for a tribe farming the low ground between the Mendips and the Bristol Avon. Priddy, less certainly, may have served Mendip and the Somerset Levels.

The tribal territories, or 'nations' in the North American Indian sense, were about 1000 square kilometres in area in Wessex, if we assume they extended off the chalk and onto the surrounding clay lowlands. Colin Renfrew has suggested that Maes Howe and the complex of monuments associated with it functioned as a kind of cathedral centre for the whole of Mainland Orkney, an area of about 800 square kilometres.

By the end of the neolithic, a number of pan-British ceremonial

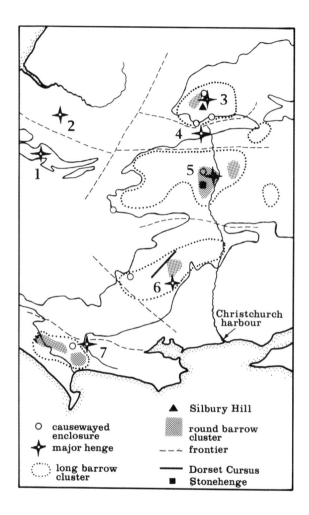

64 Wessex superhenge territories. In the later neolithic, larger territories based on tribal confederations seem to have developed. Each had its own major secular and ceremonial centre, a large henge or stone circle

1 Priddy Circles   5 Durrington Walls
2 Stanton Drew   6 Knowlton Circles
3 Avebury   7 Mount Pleasant
4 Marden

The empty space between territories 6 and 7 is curious. The South Dorset Downs may have been shared between 6 and 7, or their territorial marker monuments may have been destroyed by farming centres had emerged (Figure 35). As yet it is unclear how far people travelled to wonder and worship at these great centres but, apart from Stonehenge and Avebury, they are surprisingly evenly spaced;

Maes Howe–	Kilmartin	400 kilometres
Newgrange –	Rudston	410 kilometres
Kilmartin –	Rudston	400 kilometres
Rudston –	Stonehenge	350 kilometres
Newgrange –	Avebury	400 kilometres
Stonehenge –	Carnac	425 kilometres

I include Carnac in the list because the megalithic culture of Brittany was much more closely linked with that of Britain than with the rest of mainland Europe. Evidence of even spacing on this very large scale seems to suggest an extrardinarily high degree of geographical awareness and contains a hint – no more – of tribal confederacies of the order of 400 kilometres across. But the even spacing of such a small number of sites may also be coincidental and it must be left as an open question unless some corroboration can be found.

The pan-British centres were probably recognised as great places or places of power well outside their own territories, giving them the status, identity and recognition that their builders wanted for them. The number of different pottery styles found at the pan-British centres gives some evidence of this status. Four barrows in the Stonehenge area each contained three different types of pottery. The Avebury area has four barrows with three and one with four types of pottery. The norm for Wessex barrows is just one type of pottery, so the pottery confirms what the dense barrow clusters and the scale of the monuments are telling us – that these were metropolitan centres with contacts way beyond their local boundaries.

We can also recognise natural features that were held in special regard as places of power. One was Carn Meini, the sacred mountain in Pembrokeshire that provided the bluestones for Stonehenge. The dolerite that was quarried from the slopes of Carn Meini is a dull-looking stone and it is difficult to think of any mechanical or aesthetic quality it possesses that would justify the endlessly repeated journeys made by the Stonehenge people to procure 123 blocks of it. The stones possessed invisible, magical properties and the same quality imbued their place of origin; Carn Meini was a magic mountain and perhaps the dwelling-place of gods. The summit is awe-inspiring: an amazing coronet with pinnacles dominating the landscape for tens of kilometres around, visible on clear days from North Wales and even, it is said, from Ireland.

The superb natural harbour of Milford Haven just to the south became a focus for seafarers and there is archaeological evidence that numerous bays and inlets were used as harbours, including Mount's Bay, Conwy, Christchurch, Pevensey, Maldon and the Humber. Trade routes by land and sea focussed on these places. We can thus detect quite a number of foci – the ceremonial centres, the settlements, the harbours, the magic places.

A LAND WITHOUT WAR

At the boundaries, friendly relations were maintained with the people of neighbouring communities. The system of territorial markers, probably originally far more elaborate than the few relics we see now, ensured that no one could enter a neighbouring territory without being fully aware of it. Whether the encounters were formal or informal, circumspect or open, is impossible to tell. There are very few signs of defensive structures and even fewer of hostile action. The causewayed enclosure at Orsett in Essex was 'defended' by two deep, steep-sided ditches and a high palisade. The defensive palisade at Mount Pleasant may reflect one of two things. It could relate to the site's proximity to the River Frome, which I suggested earlier may have been a territorial boundary. It could also, with its construction date of 2100 BC, relate to the changing social and cultural conditions at the transition to the bronze age, a period of greater instability and tribal rivalry.

Flights of arrows at Crickley Hill in Gloucestershire and Carn Brea in Cornwall have been interpreted as evidence of the attack and defence of settlements, but these may have been isolated incidents. Otherwise, the evidence points to a very long and uninterrupted period of peace, never since attained anywhere in Europe. This requires explanation, if we are to avoid the accusation that this is an unrealistically idyllic picture, contradictory to the nature of man.

Peace and friendship were probably maintained as they are in many present-day societies by ritual feasts to which neighbouring groups are invited and by exchanges of gifts. Something along the lines of the potlatch of the North American Indians was probably a common event. A potlatch is a large-scale ceremonial feast at which gifts are given to members of another tribe; a stimulus to generosity in this activity is that the benefactors' status depends on the lavishness of the gifts. In Polynesia there are similar gift-exchanges and in aboriginal Samoa large quantities of mats, cloth, canoes and pigs were handed over at a marriage or funeral. Some of the exchange goods were made specially as gifts with no utilitarian value, such as mats that were far too large for use. The

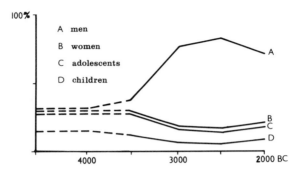

65 Status-split. Grave-goods in Yorkshire show that the status of men and women changed in the middle of the neolithic. The status of men reached a peak round the time when the superhenges were being built

gift in return could be identical. This non-utilitarian aspect may help us to understand the otherwise rather peculiar exchanges of stone and flint axes between highland and lowland peoples in neolithic Britain. Although differing mechanical qualities have been attributed to axes made of different materials and the exchange *can* be explained in these practical terms, the differences seem marginal. The exchange is better understood primarily in terms of mutual gift-giving, with the utility of the goods taking a secondary importance.

We can uncover mechanisms by which friendly relations might be maintained, but they do not explain the predisposition to peace that pervaded the neolithic. This predisposition is best explained by the notions of stasis and a common ideology. Stasis is the normal state of traditional societies, both today and in the past and it is worth emphasising, in the attempt to shed bias as far as possible, that the twentieth century has been a time of quite unprecedented social, technical and cultural change. There has been nothing like it in the history of the human race. It is *our* condition that is abnormal.

A society can be kept static by the exertion of laws, customs and moral and religious precepts. In practice, in the sort of archaic society I envisage, these four controls would have been inseparably interlocked. The small cellular communities were united by an ideology – a shared universe of ultimate values and a common orientation towards goals and the techniques for attaining them. A common fund of fixed and deep-seated beliefs and aspirations is all that is required to explain stasis and peace. The ideology meant that problems were invariably perceived in a particular way and that the action needed to solve them would also be perceived in a particular way. This magnetisation of the Stonehenge people meant that perceptions were clearly focussed and it was easy for them to agree on a course of action. In present-day Britain we have a much larger community, elaborately organised, with a hierarchy of decision-making strata. Yet, because there is no shared belief system nor ideology, there is no agreement on the direction that economic and social development should take, no agreement on premises and, most disastrously, no consistent corporate action. In contrast to this depressing lack of effective action by disunited millions, we can see how shared beliefs and perceptions allowed consensus and dramatically effective action among the Stonehenge people.

Konrad Lorenz argued that the high levels of aggression displayed by modern man are partly the result of the large society in which he lives. Modern man has too many acquaintances, too many low-level social contacts for him to cope with all of them in a friendly way; his capacity for friendship is overtaxed. In the lower density, smaller scale of neolithic society, people were not overtaxed in this way. Each person would know the thirty or forty other people in their group very well indeed and possibly as many again scattered in neighbouring communities and territories further afield. The situation was slightly more complex than this, but we could summarise it as follows.

First, there was a fairly low population density, so that friction with neighbours, whether individuals or groups, over land or any other resource was unlikely to occur. The low density also meant that social encounters were infrequent and highly valued. Second, there were opportunities for the orderly and controlled release of aggression in hunting, slaughtering livestock for food and for occasional sacrifices. Third, because of the nature of the ideology (see Chapter 14) there was a displacement of any latent aggression between the individual and the group into the collective drama being enacted between the group and the cosmos. Fourth, by analogy with other archaic societies, we can assume that every individual had to pass through several initiation rites. The rites of passage put into an orderly and harmless form the need of each person to struggle for identity. The old identity and the new were clearly defined and there was a formalised, stepped passage from rank to rank.

The intimacy that the Stonehenge people enjoyed with other members of their band meant that all relationships were personal. The subtlety of those numerous close relationships was probably expressed in a wide range of terms. In New Guinea, it is quite common to have twenty terms denoting different types of relationship. Often there are styles of relationship in an archaic society that have no equivalent in modern societies, such as the institutionalised friendship. This is a formally pledged comrade-ship between two men, involving each other in an obligation to help the other in every way he can.

It is likely, especially in the late neolithic when social contacts were multiplying, that fraternities developed too. The Plains Indians evolved numerous fraternities, each based on an experience or interest shared by its members, such as supernatural experience societies, feasting societies, dance societies and military societies. The Cheyenne had lots of these clubs, including women's craft guilds. I am not suggesting that anything on this scale evolved, but it may be that admission to particular roundhouses at Durrington, for example, depended on membership of some kind of fraternity. In a small society with finely worked-up networks of relationships and skilfully evolved methods of earthing dangerous identity crises, there would be no misfits. The family and the clan provided a continuous background pressure to conform. It can scarcely be regarded as an authority-system, since lawless behaviour would not occur to anyone except the mentally ill as an alternative to conformity; life outside the group would have been impossible and unthinkable.

The common ideology meant that children, now frequently so unruly, were easily disciplined. With adult solidarity and unity of teaching objectives, there was very broadly based supervision and any adult would correct misbehaviour. A child would receive a similar response and similar correction from the whole adult community. In present-day archaic societies, children are usually treated very gently when they misbehave and are guided towards acceptable behaviour by enthusiastic encouragement. Among the Koita people of New Guinea, this type of treatment leads to the children responding well to a request from any adult, and they usually grow up kind and considerate.

With the intricate inner workings of the small-scale society in view, we can now begin to see how the larger groupings emerging in the late neolithic may have led to disaster. If the Durrington-Stonehenge tribal territory had a population of 8000 as has been suggested, there would have been too many people for them all to have known one another as individuals. This may have been the way in which the popular idea of 'tribal behaviour' began. So we have a way of explaining the transformation of British society at the onset of the bronze age without conjuring up waves of foreign invaders bringing a new culture with them. All the changes could have occurred as a result of developmental processes within neolithic society. However gradual and imperceptible the sinister process of germination, the Stonehenge people carried within them the seeds of their society's destruction; the laughing children grew the sterner faces of bronze age warriors.

CHAPTER 14

THE GREAT MYSTERY

The holy man goes apart to a lone tipi and fasts and prays, or
goes into the hills in solitude. When he returns to men, he
teaches them and tells them what the Great Mystery has bidden
him to tell. He counsels, he heals and he makes holy charms to
protect the people from evil. Great is his power and greatly is he
revered; his place in the tipi is an honoured one.

Chief Piece-of-Flat-Iron of the Sioux Indians

The thoughts and beliefs of the Stonehenge people are unquestionably the most impenetrable of all the mysteries that this book
will touch upon. Some prehistorians claim that nothing can be
known of the beliefs of a long-dead people without writing.
Although no documents, creeds or philosophical utterances
survive, it is possible to see in the monuments and inscriptions
assertions of a committed and deep-seated belief. A quest for a
great lost faith must be worth attempting, even if, in the end, the
most potent secrets are kept from us. I believe that, by assembling
what seem to be the most ancient European mythic traditions and
testing whether they mesh together to make a coherent religious
philosophy consistent with the archaeological evidence, it will be
possible to reach closer than ever before to the deepest aspirations
of the builders of Stonehenge.

BELOW THE HOLLOW EARTH

The stasis and great stability of their society tell us that it was
gripped by a pervasive ideology, and we know that great emphasis
was placed on monument-building, ceremony and death. On these
broad foundations, we may be able to reconstruct at least the
lower courses of the philosophical edifice. The elaborate rituals
and buildings associated with burial speak of an obsessive
preoccupation with death. Anxiety about death is fundamental to

the human condition, permeating societies of all periods and levels of civilisation. An ancient Egyptian poet wrote, 'O Atum, what does this mean, that I must go into the desert? It has no water, it has no air, it is very deep, very dark, boundless. . . .'

The continual re-handling of the bones and repeated visits to the tombs nevertheless show that the Stonehenge people did not regard death as final. In fact the death cult was intimately linked with a fertility cult. Folklore and legend surviving in Wales and Ireland represent a fragile tradition of heroic nature-gods and -goddesses dwelling in the chambered tombs or in the earth itself, with the tombs as gateways to the underworld. There is a growing tendency among scholars to regard the folk-tales as originating in the bronze age or neolithic, even if in the meantime they have become extremely garbled. At the heart of many of these bizarre tales is a regeneration cycle, a story of growth, death, other-worldly journey and rebirth. The endlessly regenerate earth passes from spring to summer to winter and back again. Out of death, optimism springs. As Pindar wrote, 'Happy is he who, having seen these rites, goes below the hollow earth; for he knows the end of life and he knows its god-sent beginning.'

That such a cycle should be neolithic in origin is entirely natural when we think back to the fundamental economic enterprise of the culture. The definitive characteristic of the neolithic is that it sought for the first time to domesticate animals and plants. This arrangement and control of the forces of nature was a gigantic step away from the nature-dependent palaeolithic and the enormous efforts the Stonehenge people put into ritual and monument-building testify to their awareness that they were meddling in the affairs of the gods. Neolithic man knew that his action in supplanting the forest with his own vegetation was hubris and did all he could to propitiate and enlist the sympathy of the gods.

The rituals and the ploughing and sowing were essentially geared to similar ends. In an undifferentiated society, religion and foraging are not regarded as separate endeavours, and the neolithic farmers recognised at an early stage that a *gestalt* approach was needed. It was not sufficient to will the appearance of grain and meat. The seasons had to follow one another in the right order and man had to plough, sow and reap at the right times. Nature was seen probably for the first time as an intricate and complex organism, with each part dependent on the others, while the production of food was seen as a symbiosis of man and nature. Man dies and turns into earth. The earth in its turn shapes itself into new life. The cycle of fertility repeats endlessly. Man could, in the context of primitive agriculture, see his own death in relation to soil fertility and could offer up his own body as a token of commitment to the common project.

He may have believed in the immortality of the individual soul, and there are certain post-mortem rituals that imply that he did, but the principal emphasis was on collective survival of death. Individual bones would not be re-animated, but the tribe and its welfare would. One of the old names for Newgrange was Brug Oengusa, the bru or mansion of Oengus, the Youthful Hero who was the son of the Daghda, the principal god of the Celtic pantheon. The Daghda and his people, the Tuatha De (People of the Goddess), were supposed by the Celts to have inhabited Ireland in the remote past and retreated into the fairy mounds, the chambered tombs, before the Celts arrived. It is entirely consistent with the ideas we are ascribing to the neolithic that the long-departed Tuatha De, in all probability the neolithic people of Ireland, are at one and the same time entombed in the fairy mounds and living on from age to age. In one Celtic romance, the body of Diarmaid, Grainne's lover, is taken to the Bru of Oengus. The three hundred strong household of Oengus is addressed by Oengus himself:

'Horsemen of the fairy mound without defilement,
Let Diarmaid of the fine shape be lifted up by you
To the Bru, sweet, full of hosts, and everlasting.'

But that rest with the hosts in the fairy mound was not undisturbed. Skulls and long bones were removed for rituals in the forecourts or in distant earth and stone circles. Skulls were regarded as cages for the spirits and were used to carry spirit power to places that required sanctification. They were sometimes smashed to pieces, probably to release the spirit power where it was needed. The long bones were sometimes perforated, apparently to make whistles or flutes. In archaic societies today it is often thought that objects made from human bones can induce sleep or trance, and this may give us another ingredient in the stone circle ceremonies.

The sandstone discs found at Avebury, Windmill Hill and West Kennet seem to forge a link between the ceremonial enclosures and the tombs in the Marlborough Downs, and they are found in tombs, barrows and pyre-ashes in other parts of Britain. The purpose of the discs is not known − perhaps they are sun symbols − but they clearly link the burial customs and the ceremonies of the stone and earth circles in a single cult.

The megalithic coves associated with some of the stone circles make an obvious reference across to the burial monuments, too. The three great slabs are arranged in exactly the same way as the first stones of a tomb chamber, though on a larger scale. The symbolic tomb resonates with multiple symbolism: it is the cave of the dead, the mother's womb, the tomb, birth, death, rebirth, the

Plate 37 Watersmeet. It has been suggested that the spirits of
the dead buried in the ridge-top barrows on Exmoor may
have been guided to springs by stone settings. Once delivered
to the streams, the spirits were released into the sea

fulcrum of the regeneration cycle. Interpreted like this, it is easy to
see why the Avebury Cove is at the centre of the design, at the
centre of the Avebury mystery, within a circle within a circle.

MANA, MYTH AND MAGIC

With such ideas and the seasonal regeneration cycle in our minds,
we are very close to a neolithic myth. At one time, there was a
tendency to believe that non-literate, prehistoric societies must
have been animistic. Anthropological studies show that quite

elaborate myths are possible and even a belief in relatively abstract and distant high gods may have prevailed. Animism, the belief that individual organisms have souls that may survive death, is common in non-literate societies, but it is only one stratum of the neolithic belief-system, in which animatism operated as well. Animatism is the belief in an impersonal and pervasive force, called *mana* in Melanesia, animating the universe in general, including objects that to western eyes are inanimate. In fact, the distinction between animate and inanimate did not exist. This explains the curious sensation that many 'modern' people experience in stone circles, where the stones were probably treated as surrogates in the ritual dances; even when the mortals had gone back exhausted to their homes or sailed off on trading adventures, even when the dancers rested in their tombs in a thousand pieces, the stones continued the ceremonies for all eternity.

Animatism transformed the world into an awesome place, where every stone and river was permeated with the living spirit, and must therefore be treated with care. It was a belief that enabled each person to participate in a very concrete way in the supernatural world. Once again, the distinction that we now make between nature and supernature would not have existed in the neolithic mind.

A distinction is often made between religion and magic. The religious man sees himself as subordinate to the will of supernatural beings, whereas the magician sees himself as controlling supernature. The magician adopts a proto-scientific approach, following prescribed procedures to the letter in order to achieve predicted results. We may wonder why the fallacy of magic went undetected, but the neolithic magician must have cannily concerned himself with fundamental and realisable goals like the sequence of the seasons and the changes in sunrise and sunset positions. In other words, the magic of the neolithic had success built into it. Although we may now see significant differences between magic and religion, it is probably unwise to read such distinctions into the practices of the neolithic. The edges between magic and religion were probably as blurred as those between nature and supernature, between sacred and secular, so we need not worry too much about whether we use 'priest' or 'magician' to describe the master of ceremonies at Stonehenge.

Much more important is the myth the master sought to re-enact. The myth is a pedigree of a people's filiation and a charter of its religion's validity, so it is vital that we explore the contents of neolithic mythology.

Plate 38 The Longstone, Challacombe, Exmoor. This ridge-top monolith is the focal point for a ritual centre that includes a rectangular mortuary enclosure and a barrow cluster

THE EARTH-GODDESS

We have a very clear picture of the Earth Mother. A statuette of her, 11 centimetres high, was found at Grime's Graves on a pedestal of chalk blocks beside a gallery entrance at the bottom of shaft 15. A chalk phallus rested beside the goddess, together with some chalk balls. In front of this fertility group was an altar of mined flints arranged in a triangle, with a chalk cup at the base of the triangle opposite the goddess, and antler-picks on top of the flints. The gallery was unproductive and the ritual objects assembled at its entrance were a direct appeal to the chthonic power for more flints. The fat and fertile goddess was thus closely associated with the earth and everything it produced – from crops to minerals (Figure 66).

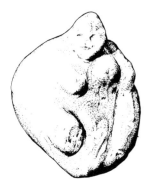

66 The Grime's Graves goddess

The fact that the second funerary rite involved committing the bones of the dead to the earth probably means that the earth-goddess was also in a sense the death-goddess too, receiving the dead back into her womb for eventual rebirth. Predominantly, though, she must have been the mother, the provider of food, the giver of agricultural produce, like Demeter, a corn-goddess. Images of her would have been decorated with corn crowns and corn-stalk insignia, and she would have been regarded as living out in the fields. An early analogue can be seen in Isis, the thousand-named. As sister and wife of Osiris, she was known as the Creatrix of green things, the Green goddess, the Lady of Bread, the Lady of Abundance and the Star of the Sea (because of her association with Sirius). We can imagine that titles very similar to these, perhaps even these same titles, were used in praise of the little goddess at Grime's Graves.

The ritual pits that are such a feature of many neolithic rites were probably made for offerings to the chthonic earth-goddess. The so-called 'god-dolly' carved out of ashwood and found head downward under the Bell Track in the Somerset Levels has been interpreted as a hermaphrodite. Although it may have been intended to incorporate the sexual characteristics of both god and goddess, I think on balance that the alleged phallus is supposed to be the leg of a seated goddess. So here too the assistance of the earth-goddess was asked for, in this case to hold firm the new trackway where an earlier construction had weakened and sunk into the mire.

The fat, green, productive side of the earth-goddess must also have had its winter aspect. The dark side of the goddess is seen in

67 The Bell Track goddess. This seated goddess carved from
a piece of ashwood has lost her right leg

the Black Demeter enshrined in the cave of Phigalia in Arcadia. In
winter, the earth-goddess retreated underground, leaving the
surface of the earth to wither and die. The Black Demeter was
portrayed with a horse's head and woman's body in a long black
robe and was intended as an image of the bare, wintry earth
stripped of its green mantle. The use of a totemic animal to
represent the deity is something we shall have to consider again
later. If animals were used to represent gods, as seems very likely,
it becomes even more difficult to interpret remains that include
animal bones, especially when the deposit is of a ritual nature.

The annual decline or disappearance of the earth-goddess
during the winter required explanation, and this is where the
narrative element of the myth has its origin. In the Tammuz myth,
originating in Syria, the narrative involved the death of the hero
Tammuz and his descent into the underworld. The grief-stricken
Ishtar or Astarte, his divine mistress and a contemporary of the
British neolithic earth-goddess, journeyed through the underworld
to look for him, so she too disappeared from the world of men.
During their absence, life in the upper world went into decline and
the queen of the underworld, Eresh-Kigal, was persuaded to allow
them to return so that nature could be revived. The story varied
endlessly in the ancient myths, with Astarte becoming Persephone
and Venus, but it remained essentially an explanation of the
cyclical decline and revival of the landscape. Most importantly, it
invariably involved a second deity, frequently neglected in studies
of the neolithic.

THE SKY-GOD

And the azurous hung hills are his world-wielding shoulder
Majestic – as a stallion stalwart, very-violet-sweet! –
These things, these things were here but the beholder
Wanting; . . .

GERALD MANLEY HOPKINS, 'Hurrahing in Harvest'

We know from the earliest literate and graphicate societies of the Mediterranean coastlands that a resurrected vegetation-god was just as important as the earth-goddess. We also know that the god was a sun-hero, in effect an aspect or functionary of the sun-god or sky-god. At the very early period we are dealing with, it seems likely that there was little differentiation among these ideas, and that sun-god, sky-god, sun-hero and year-god were all one and the same. Tammuz is one of the earliest names we find for the sun-hero, but Adonis is a transformation of the same idea. Adonis, the youthful hero who was loved by both Aphrodite and Persephone, was obliged by Zeus to divide his time equally between the two goddesses of love and death, who are really the two aspects of the earth-goddess again. Adonis was associated with the growth of cereal crops and can be regarded as a barley-god, indicating his origin among neolithic cultivators.

The eventual fate of the barley-god when the harvest was over was death. Burns wrote of John Barleycorn,

> They wasted o'er a scorching flame
> The marrow of his bones;
> But a miller us'd him worst of all,
> For he crushed him between two stones.

A harvest rite re-enacting the death of Tammuz, Adonis or the barley-god was a widespread element in European folklore until modern times. Adonis perishes under the reaper's sickles, or is trodden under the hooves of oxen on the threshing floor. The harvest rite is, and always was, a strange mixture of violence and voluptuousness, presumably resulting from the happy associations of the harvest with feasting side by side with the necessary death of the presiding barley-god. The Adonis cult hovered sensuously between pain and pleasure. Adonis and Dionysus and John Barleycorn all presided over harvests and the production of intoxicating drink, whether beer or wine; the pain and pleasure included the ambivalence of drunkenness.

In Northern England, the last corn to be threshed was threshed on a man's back; onlookers would say, 'The Old Man is being beaten to death.' In Austria, the man who threshed the last of the corn was ritually throttled with a straw garland; after the simulated strangling, he was tied up and thrown in a river. There were many similar harvest-murders all over Europe until the turn of the century and they may well have been a toned-down version of rituals that originally ended in real human sacrifices, like the English bog-burials of the iron age, in which the victims were tied up, stunned, strangled and thrown into swamps. In Devon, in the nineteenth century when the harvest was done, the party of reapers stood in a circle on high ground overlooking the fields and holding their sickles aloft. One reaper standing in the middle held up some ears of corn tied with flowers. The party greeted this symbolic harvest with the thrice-repeated chant, 'Arnack, arnack, arnack! We have 'un, we have 'un, we have 'un!'

John Barleycorn, as he is known in Britain, was often buried in the form of a corn idol during the ploughing that followed the harvest, as at Haxey in Lincolnshire:

> They ploughed, they sowed, they harrowed him in,
> Throwed clods upon his head,
> And three men made a solemn vow,
> John Barleycorn was dead.

The long ancestry of the corn dolly, made afresh every year to be destroyed every year, can be traced back through thousands of years to the neolithic myth of the earth-goddess who was annually impregnated by her mercurial consort, the sky-god or sun-god, who then declined in power in readiness for the next fertility cycle. The names change from region to region and from age to age, but there is a continuous and coherent tradition of a seasonal appearance made by an impregnating male deity.

The autumn aspect of the year-god was sometimes represented as a ruminative decline. The 'Thinker' statuettes of Romania are contemporary with the British neolithic and show the god sitting with his head in his hands, contemplative, defeated, his physical power ebbing. But the decline of the corn-god was not always thought of as an exact parallel to the solar year. Instead it was sometimes dramatised into a murderous sudden death, often involving mutilation. Osiris was a corn-god, the son of sky and earth, just as the neolithic crops were the fruit of the union of the sky-god and earth-goddess. Osiris' remains were mangled and mutilated and it is thought that mortal kings may later have been murdered and dismembered in emulation. Romulus was dismembered by senators and buried in pieces. Pentheus king of Thebes and Lycurgus king of the Edonians were also torn to pieces, one by maenads and one by horses. The Thracian Orpheus was torn limb from limb by Bacchanals, whilst on Crete Dionysus was cut to pieces by the Titans. The dismemberment of the fertility-god may have been psychologically necessary in some communities to explain the extensiveness of the fertilisation.

If we think in terms of the year-god, then he must die at the winter solstice. There are traces of this idea in the brief appearances of the aged, but still benevolent, Father Christmas on 25 December and Old Father Time on New Year's Eve. But he must also be reborn. A spell for the revival of the year-god from the ancient Egyptian Coffin Texts tells us of the poignancy of the interregnum:

'Ah, Helpless Sleeping One!
Behold I have found you lying on your side,
The great Listless One.
Come, let us lift up his great head and rejoin his bones:
Let us reassemble his limbs and put an end to his woe.
May the moisture begin to rise for this Spirit!
Osiris, live!
Let the great Listless One arise!'

The most conspicuous mythic survival of the rebirth is the celebration of the birth of Christ very close to the winter solstice; in this respect he can be seen as yet another manifestation of the year-god. It was unsatisfactory for the Church to celebrate the birth and death of Christ simultaneously, so the Crucifixion is commemorated close to the time of year when it is thought to have happened, round about the spring equinox. In fact, in the early days of the Christian Church the Crucifixion was fixed in Rome, Gaul and Phrygia at the equinox itself, with the Resurrection celebrated two days later, on 23 March in the modern calendar; this use of the equinox may have been a reference back to the cult of Attis, whose death was also celebrated at the equinox. The astrological year still begins with Aries, the equinoctial sign.

The beginning of summer naturally marked the beginning of the year-god's period of power, his accession to the cosmic throne. The May Day celebrations that still survive as unvarnished pagan rites in Britain are a reference to this mythic event. The arrival of the summer-bringing god is marked by the appearance of various simulacra, usually men dressed up in leaves and known variously as the Green Man, Jack-in-Green, the Tree, Little Leaf Man, May King or Green George.

As the sun rose higher in the sky, so the year-god's power increased, reaching a peak on the summer solstice. This day was always a feast day when the high-summer aspect of the god, fiercely powerful and virile, was portrayed. Unfortunately all the midsummer giants except one have gone, but in the medieval period the parading of these unconscious images of the ancient

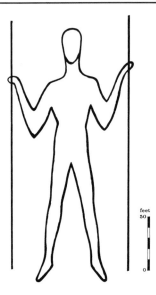

68 The Wilmington Giant restored. This representation of a prehistoric fertility god was carved on the north-facing slope of Windover Hill in Sussex. It has not been firmly dated

sun-god was common in northern Europe. Dunkirk's Papa Reuss was 15 metres high with a long blue robe striped with golden rays. London, Chester, Coventry, Burford and Salisbury are all known to have had their own giant processions on Midsummer Day.

The orientation of Stonehenge to the midsummer sunrise is a proof of the ancestry of these celebrations, and it is just possible that an effigy of some kind was raised at Stonehenge too. The orientation of the culture to sun and sky indicated by the earth and stone circles suggests a special relationship. It may even mean there was a totemic identification with the sun: that the people of neolithic Britain actually thought of themselves as being in some sense Children of the Sun or Sky. I have developed elsewhere the idea that the Wilmington Giant in Sussex is an icon of the god in his high-summer aspect, arriving through a dipylon gate to ripen the crops and ensure the harvest.

To summarise, the neolithic myth of a sky-god closely identified with the sun followed the annual pattern of solar strength and weakness. The annual reappearance of the sky-god in his high-summer aspect was vital for the ripening of the crops, but it was important also to try to explain the god's decline during the autumn and winter. The narrative approach made it possible for the all-powerful god to be overcome by treachery, but it was sometimes felt necessary psychologically for the god to will his own destruction, to surrender to sacrifice. There are elements of this type of acquiescence in the deaths of both Odin and Christ. In the story of Samson, himself an ancient sun-hero, his name deriving from the Hebrew *Shemesh* (sun), suicide is the strong man's way of surrendering his power, but it is interesting that he is first weakened by the treachery of Delilah, who cuts off his sun-ray hair, the symbol of his strength.

A narrative poem from ancient Sumer lists some of the many roles and qualities of the high god, Enki:

'My father, the king of the universe, brought me into existence.
I am the fecund seed engendered by the great wild ox,
I am the great storm that goes forth, I am the lord of the land,
I am the gugal of the chieftains, the father of all the lands,
I am the big brother of the gods, who brings full prosperity,
I am the record keeper of heaven and earth,
I am he who directs justice with the king An,
I am he who decrees the fates with Enlil on the mountain of wisdom.

We have no comparable writings from the Stonehenge people, but the later myths of regeneration contain many elements that clearly had their beginnings in a neolithic agricultural society. The sky-god, or guardian-god as I have called him elsewhere, is the most general manifestation that can be detected, but the same deity had other aspects as year-god, sun-god, corn-god or barley-god. During the passage of the seasons, the god went through several additional transformations, including the Divine Child, the Youthful Hero, the Green Man, the Midsummer Giant, the Sickle-god, the Thinker and Old Father Time. For at least the first four of these calendar transformations, Dionysus seems the closest anthropomorphic parallel to the neolithic god that can be found in later literate societies. His elemental wildness, fierce virility and very early association with an ecstatic cult mark him out as a likely candidate, especially since he was a barley-god and thus closely linked with cereal cultivation. The image of Dionysus was often a mere upright post, draped in a cloak and leafy branches. Perhaps we should reconsider our interpretation of isolated standing stones . . .

The qualities of Dionysus were typified by the bull and he was often worshipped in this form. One statuette shows him draped in a bull's hide with the head, horns and hooves hanging down behind him. This can be linked across to the otherwise inexplicable 'head-and-hooves' burials found in some neolithic barrows in Britain. They may represent bull-effigies of the neolithic god himself – proto-Dionysus. In this connection, it is relevant that Osiris, another corn-god, was also identified with bulls. At Memphis, real bulls were revered as surrogate gods representing Osiris. In sculpture of the Roman period, the sun-hero Mithras is shown kneeling on the back of the solar bull, plunging a knife into the beast's side. This division of the god into two aspects of the one self was a way of getting round the problem of power waning yet continuing. Significantly, cornstalks often sprout from the bull's tail or from the wound itself. At Chambéry in France, when the last stroke was given at threshing, the farm workers used to say, 'The ox is killed,' as if they too regarded the corn-god as an ox.

The ancient rites of Tammuz are among the earliest surviving versions of the myth. The death of Tammuz was marked annually by a special ritual of lamentation. Flutes made sad music over an effigy of the dead god while a lament was chanted, a lament put into the mind of the bereaved Ishtar:

'Her lament is for a great river, where no willows grow,
Her lament is for a field, where corn and herbs grow not,
Her lament is for a pool, where fishes flourish not,
Her lament is for a thicket of reeds, where no reeds grow,
Her lament is for the depth of a garden of trees, where honey and wine flow not,
Her lament is for a palace, where length of life is no more.'

Similar laments would have been attributed to the bereft neolothic goddess, when the time came for the sky-god's departure. The benign earth-goddess slept through the winter, a passive, latent power, after she was abandoned by her energetic but ephemeral consort, proto-Dionysus. Each summer she was roused from her slumber and remarried to the returning god, who then supervised the growth of crops, governed the harvest and bade farewell to his people and his bride. The divine marriage itself may have been celebrated by a people preoccupied with ceremonial. In the great September mysteries at Eleusis, the marriage of the sky-god Zeus and the corn-goddess Demeter was acted out by the high priest and priestess of Demeter, although the love-making was only a pretence. They went into an inner sanctuary, and then the priest emerged waving an ear of corn, symbolising the fruit of the divine marriage.

THE FIRE RITUAL

Fire festivals too are deeply ingrained in the European tradition and, although it is not possible to prove a neolithic origin, they are totally consistent with the worship of a sun-god and with the most powerful type of sympathetic magic. In modern times, they have been commonest at the spring equinox and summer solstice, but they also occur at midwinter, May Day, Hallowe'en and Twelfth Night Eve. Midsummer Fires in Germany were accompanied by singing and dancing, while people wearing chaplets of mugwort and vervain looked at the fire through bunches of larkspur to keep their eyes healthy. In Glamorgan, blazing wheels were sent rolling down hills simulating the sun's movement through the sky. Hallowe'en and Beltane (Celtic May Day) fires were once very common in the southern parts of the Scottish Highlands. In England, the Hallowe'en fire festival has been transposed into November the Fifth: the burning of straw effigies in feast-fires goes back many centuries before the unfortunate Guy Fawkes. The midwinter fire feast seems to survive only as the Yule log.

The fires were sun-charms, sympathetic magic of the most direct and artless kind, willing the sun to continue in his expected round. They are exactly the kind of magic that we would expect of the neolithic magician. The fires were also purificatory; we know they were a major feature of the ceremonies on the forecourts of the chambered tombs, not for the incineration of bones but for ritual scorching. Like so many of the ritual activities of the Stonehenge people, the fires had more than one layer of meaning.

SACRIFICE TO THE UNDYING SUN

Some of the burials, too, have more than one meaning. Try as we might to put the idea from our minds, the sinister possibility that some of them show signs of human sacrifice has to be considered. The most frequently cited evidence comes from the eastern end of the Long Mound at Maiden Castle in Dorset, where Mortimer Wheeler found the remains of three young people; he described with his habitual relish how they had been hewn limb from limb. For a long time it was assumed they were neolithic sacrificial victims, but only two of them were neolithic, two seven-year-old children whose bodies probably became disarticulated after death. The third skeleton – the one that really had been butchered – was that of a young Anglo-Saxon boy who died in AD 635. The man buried in the ditch at Wor Barrow in Dorset is also referred to occasionally as evidence of neolithic violence, but the leaf arrowhead between his ribs could as easily be the result of a hunting accident. We should only suppose it was murder if we already knew the culture to be violent, which is not the case.

At Whitehawk, the remains of a child of seven were found curled up in a deep post-hole, accompanied by a slab with rough incisions carved across it. This, like the child burial at the centre of Woodhenge (a three-year-old with a broken skull), looks very much like a foundation sacrifice. We must be prepared to interpret these two burials as child sacrifices. It is just possible, of course, that the raising of the totem pole at Whitehawk and the start of building work at Woodhenge were delayed until a suitable dedicatory corpse was available. No ritual murder need have been involved. But I think it probably was.

Some of the skulls in Wessex burials have been violently split in two. There is continuing discussion among archaeologists as to whether these terrible wounds were inflicted before death, actually causing death, or resulted from some later accident such as the collapse of the burial chamber. Again, we cannot be sure, though I tend to think the skulls were deliberately broken, like axes and other artefacts, after excarnation and before final burial. Only rarely do we have real evidence of human sacrifice and, as at Whitehawk and Woodhenge, it is usually evidence of child sacrifice. The Zoroastrians sacrificed to their sun god, too, and their words may help us to understand why the Stonehenge people were prepared to go to such extremes:

'When the sun rises, then the earth, made by Ahura, becomes clean. Should the sun not rise, then the Daevas would destroy all things nor would the heavenly Yazatas find any way of repelling them. He who offers up a sacrifice to the undying, shining, swift-horsed sun – to withstand the darkness, to withstand the Daevas born of darkness – offers it up to Ahura Mazda, and offers it up to his own soul. I will sacrifice to Mithra, the lord of wide pastures, who has a thousand ears and ten thousand eyes. I will sacrifice to that friendship, the best of all friendships, that prevails between the sun and the moon.'

THE HARVEST HILLS

The Stonehenge people were intoxicated with their vision of the universe and their own place in it. To the modern materialist, the scale and durability of their monuments may appear to prove that they were excessively entangled in the numinous, but the remarkable ceremonial designs they crafted out of rock and earth were intended to be more than mere stages where the community's relationship with the cosmos could be dramatised. They were intended as actual expressions of that relationship and as machines for sustaining it. These monuments to the cyclic passage of time and the link between time and the fortunes of men have long outlasted the time-obsessed culture that created them. That they have endured beyond all but the most distorted and fragile folk-memories is not, I think, just a sad miscalculation. The monuments were designed to stand for all eternity, in a way that no later monument of man has ever been.

Stonehenge man thought of time as a continuum and of the

story of the human race as a continuum too. He probably had no concept of history in the modern sense at all, was unaware of the preceding mesolithic and unaware that the succeeding metal and machine ages were to come. He thought in terms of a changeless and perpetual calendar, with the people and their relationship with nature continuing unaltered until the ends of time. Tomorrow would always be substantially the same as yesterday. We have not this security and can no longer measure our tomorrows by the yardstick of what happened yesterday – or even today.

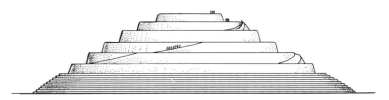

69 Silbury Hill. This profile shows the tiered construction method. The lowest, stepped, tier was cut out of the living rock

One of the largest and most spectacular of neolithic statements about time and man's dependence on its cyclicity is Silbury Hill. The completed monument was a truncated, tiered cone, 40 metres high and 159 metres in diameter, raised in a series of stepped, circular shapes. The lowest stage was cut down into the living rock, but the six concentric rostra raised above it, each 5 metres high, were built of chalk blocks (Figure 69). The method of construction may have been adopted to ensure slope stability or to make construction work easier: compare the similar techniques used at Quanterness. But the shape of the seven-tiered chalk ziggurat may also have been some arcane symbol; the concentric circle is a motif that recurs in rock carvings and earth circles. The ziggurat shape itself was at the same moment, i.e. in 2800 BC, being invented in Sumer. The lower terraces were filled with fine chalk rubble and turfed to give a smooth surface; only the uppermost ledge is now visible and that may be the result of weathering.

At the heart of Silbury is a small conical mound of clay 5 metres across and 1 metre high, raised during the last week of July or the first week of August, to judge from the entombed plant and insect remains. This links up with the tradition, surviving until recent times in Scotland, of building harvest hills to celebrate the first-fruits festival in the first week in August. Although the first-fruits feast was late being incorporated in the Church calendar as Lammastide, it was well established under the pagan Celts as Lugnasad. Folklore often associates neolithic tombs and stone circles with this pagan feast day, which makes me think it may

Plate 39 Silbury Hill. The slope in the right foreground was artificially steepened in the neolithic, during the excavation of the deep 'moat' to the left. Rock for the mound was quarried from this moat, which in places is 10 metres deep

have been a major neolithic festival. This would be quite understandable at a time when the outcome of the harvest was very uncertain.

We can imagine the first fruits of the harvest being laid out as offerings on the flat summit of Silbury, where sky-god and earth-goddess might be deemed to marry. The Creek Indians of North America held a first-fruits festival or busk as the main ceremony of their ritual calendar. As soon as the first ears of corn had ripened, the shaman made an altar of white clay over a hearth, then raised an arbour of green branches over it. After elaborate preparations that included a two-day fast, the feasting began.

We should expect that monuments similar to Silbury were built for the same purpose elsewhere. Silbury is conspicuous because of its enormous size; just like other Wessex monuments it is spectacularly exaggerated. Other regions were content with modest stone circles: Wessex had Avebury and Stonehenge. Other regions had earth circles of a modest size: Wessex had super-henges. It was the same with harvest hills, which were built elsewhere but on a much smaller scale. Merlin's Mount at Marlborough is 18 metres high and 90 metres across and, like Silbury, stands in water meadows beside the River Kennet. Its precise original shape is not known, as it was 'landscaped' in 1650 to make it part of a formal garden.

Other harvest hills include the Mount at Lewes and Clifford Hill near Northampton, the first standing on the floor of the Ouse

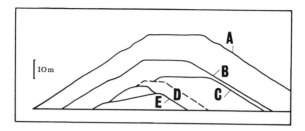

70 Harvest hills. Profiles to show relative sizes.

A Silbury Hill B Clifford Hill C Merlin's Mount at
Marlborough D Hatfield Barrow (destroyed) E Lewes
Mount

valley beside what was a tidal lagoon in the neolithic (Figure 70), the second rising up beside the River Nene. There seems always to be an association with life-giving water. The Mount is 13 metres high and 52 metres across, just one-third the size of Silbury. Clifford Hill is 26 metres high and 115 metres across, just two-thirds the size of Silbury. The traditional explanation for Clifford Hill is that it is an unfinished Norman motte, but the Roman coins found on its summit show that both the hill and its summit form, a circular platform, date back at least to the Roman period. It was common for people in Roman times to drop coins on ancient sacred sites to appease local gods.

Rather larger than the Mount, but now unfortunately destroyed, was Hatfield Barrow, a harvest hill 60 metres in diameter and at least 11 metres high, standing in the Marden superhenge beside the River Avon. It was excavated to destruction in 1818 by Colt-Hoare and Cunnington, who were confused to find not a trace of a burial; Colt-Hoare concluded that the mound was a 'Hill Altar or a *locus consecratus*'.

Doubtless there are many more harvest hills that have gone unrecognised. If they were any smaller in diameter than the Lewes Mount, for instance, they might be mistaken for large round barrows. Silbury should be seen as the head of a family of harvest hills, though unique in its colossal size. It contains 354,000 cubic metres of chalk, covers over 2 hectares of land and is the largest man-made prehistoric mound in Europe.

Pyramid construction in Egypt at about the same time went on regardless of the funerary needs of the pharaohs: it was to a great extent an end in itself. Bringing together a very large labour force from all over Upper and Lower Egypt, it helped to develop a feeling of national unity, as well as ensuring that unemployed hands were not engaging in antisocial activities. Similar socio-political needs probably underlay the building of Solomon's Temple. For this too a large unskilled labour force was drawn together in a symbolic act of national unification in the building of

Plate 40 The Ring of Brodgar. The Salt Knowe, the very large mound in the background, has not been opened. It may be a harvest hill or it may contain a burial chamber

a great religious symbol. Instead of the work force toiling in servitude, it may have been drafted more in the spirit of National Service; although compulsion was involved, the supervision would not have been unduly severe. Perhaps Silbury too was an intensive labour project, the 21 million man-hours needed to complete it designed to bring together neighbouring groups into a closer social fusion. It is a possibility. There can be no doubt that social unification would have been reinforced by such a project but, at the same time, Silbury is only one of a suite of great monuments in the Avebury region, and it is very much in the Avebury tradition. On the whole, the religious explanation is the more consistent.

THE JOURNEY TO THE WORLD'S EDGE

Like most archaic societies, the Stonehenge people would have had important rites of passage. These ceremonies mark the passage of individual people from infancy to childhood, childhood to adolescence, adolescence to adulthood and perhaps ranks of seniority in adulthood. At each of these turning-points, the individual is obliged to separate himself from his earlier sub-culture and exist for a time at the margin of the society. This state without status often produces, because of its negation or even privation, an intense self-awareness. The liminal or marginal state is followed by re-integration as the initiand re-enters his society at a different level.

In societies where the rites are numerous and carefully structured, people are subject to profound emotional experiences that assist in the development of ideas of selfhood. These ideas may be less individual than modern, western ideas of individuality because they are to a great extent given by the community; but conversely modern, western ideas of individuality would probably seem selfish, anarchic and irresponsible to the Stonehenge people. For it is probably the case that in neolithic Britain individuation occurred largely in rites of passage, where it would not disrupt or subvert the social structure.

On top of this, neolithic communities underwent collective rites of passage related to the solar year. In the *I Ching*, the solstices are seen as boundaries, moments of enormous tension when the earthly kingdom needs to be safeguarded and even sealed off until movement back in the opposite direction is under way. This feeling of cosmic crisis pervaded neolithic society on certain calendrical feasts, especially the solstices. We can imagine people gathering in the earth and stone circles and forecourts as the moment of crisis approached.

The magic circles thus take on another function as liminal refuges for whole communities during solstitial crises. In this respect, it is useful to apply to the circles the idea of intense statelessness that was seen in the individual rites of passage. The boundary, whatever it is, is a place that is not a place, in a time that is not a time. Entering the magic circles, particularly on the solstices, people stepped out of normal geography, out of normal time, into a condition of intense collective awareness. These were moments when the great occult wisdom of the community was realised and the deep knowledge of the basic structure of their culture came home to people.

The liminal stage of the initiation ceremony invariably involved deprivation of selfhood, the denial of the individual ego. By analogy, the seasonal initiations of the Stonehenge people into the solar cycle must have had a damping effect on group and individual aggression drives. More importantly from the point of view of establishing the pervasive values of these extraordinary people, the regular and repeated journey to the world's edge must have given them a unique sense of destiny. Certain individual rites, such as the puberty or funeral rites, have a special flavour of individual destiny; even in a modern secular society, the funeral rite has this flavour because of its utter inevitability. To the Stonehenge people, the collective rites associated with the solar calendar must have had the same flavour of destiny. They were continually occupied with integrating and re-integrating into the largest scales of the natural order. It was not just that they walked with the gods: they participated in and sought to resolve the periodic crises of the universe.

CHAPTER 15

THE SPEAKING STONES

The long unmeasured pulse of time moves everything.
There is nothing hidden that it cannot bring to light.

SOPHOCLES, *Ajax*

Most of the artwork that has survived lacks the formality of design, the obviously premeditated composition and the finesse of execution to be seen in the contemporary work of much of mainland Europe. This apparent deficiency may seem strange, because the technology available was similar, but the primary intention was not artistic in the modern sense at all but symbolic and religious instead. We tend to think of patterns on cups as decorative purely and simply, but the marks on neolithic cups may well have had some other intention. They may have been applied talismanically to ensure that the vessels lasted well or even to ensure that they should yield good food and drink. So if we apply a purely aesthetic judgment, we may be missing the point. With some artefacts, the ritual function is very obvious indeed. Neither realism nor beauty of technique is evident in the earth-goddess figurines from Somerset and Grime's Graves.

The best-preserved of the great monuments, by contrast, do show a recognisable aesthetic drive and a desire to move the onlooker by means of subtle and dramatic architectural effects. The artistic drive was channelled into these very large-scale earth sculptures rather than into smaller artefacts. At Avebury I have always had a powerful feeling that the whole landscape has been laid out as a piece of landscape architecture (Figure 29), with stone avenues framing Silbury and leading away from the focal stone circles towards lesser shrines and settlements, the whole setpiece in its shallow amphitheatre with great barrows punctuating the smooth skyline.

On a smaller scale, there are numerous architectural devices that we can recognise at Avebury. From outside, the stone circles are concealed by the bank and the twist in the Kennet Avenue

Plate 41 The Kennet Avenue. The section excavated and restored by Alexander Keiller. The Ridgeway and the Sanctuary are on the skyline to the left

prevents the visitor from seeing the colossal portal stones flanking the South Entrance until the very last moment; there is a transparent attempt here to heighten the drama by surprising the visitor with sudden large effects. The entrance causeways were excavated slightly to make the banks on each side seem even higher and more impressive. The ditches are also much deeper next to the entrances for the same reason. A similar desire to excite and impress was noted earlier in the design of some of the long barrows. The tapering, trapeze shape was intended to give a *trompe l'oeil* effect to a visitor approaching the façade of the monument. The deliberately created false perspective made the barrows appear considerably longer than they actually were.

A similar effect was achieved in the drystone vaults of some of the Orkney tombs. The chamber walls at Quanterness taper gradually inwards to a capstone at about $3\frac{1}{2}$ metres. Looking up from below there is an illusion of much greater height. The illusion is even more spectacular at the Knowe of Lairo on Rousay, where the ceiling is actually 4 metres above the floor, but appears to be 5 or more. The remoteness of the ceiling is accentuated by the narrowness of the chamber and the stone beams or flying buttresses that divide off the roof space just above head height.

The entasis in the sarsen uprights at Stonehenge has often been mentioned as an illustration of architectural refinement. This slightly convex swelling of the sides of each stone increased the

Plate 42 Two stones of the Kennet Avenue, showing the pairing of shapes

effect of bulk, solidity and permanence. It became a regular feature of the much later classical period, when every column was entastic. The stone avenues may be seen as rather informal forerunners of the colonnade, an idea that was fully developed much later by the Romans at Palmyra. The walls of the horned forecourts, whether stone-built or timber, created a kind of theatrical cyclorama against which ritual dramas or dances could be seen.

At most sites the builders showed an instinctive appreciation of the quality and potential of the available materials, which were exploited in very different ways. At Avebury, the richly gnarled and characterful surfaces of the sarsens were often left in their natural state and made an integral part of the quality of the whole monument. Each stone is left as an individual, an original, each wrinkled and writhing skin seemingly containing a separate utterance from the earth-goddess herself (Plate 11). At Maes Howe, the fissile quality of the sandstone was exploited in an entirely different way to produce enormous slabs and flags with very smooth surfaces. The effect there is startlingly modern, with immaculately coursed masonry, only the spectacular corner buttresses and the vast slabs of the entrance passage betraying the same neolithic obsession with the colossal that we see at Avebury (Plate 31). Everywhere, though, we can see that the Stonehenge people appreciated the aesthetic possibilities of the various types of rock.

There are many surviving examples of small, portable works of art. In Orkney and on the Scottish mainland, stone objects as big as a fist were carved into symmetrical patterns, often with elaborate spikes or rounded knobs projecting from them. Some were fluted, others carved with intricate spirals (Figure 71B). By contrast with most of the remaining artwork in Britain, these stone balls show a dedication to a preconceived design that was apparently worked out very carefully in advance of the carving. They are also symmetrical about at least one axis, a rare feature in small-scale art of this period. Whether these were regarded as objects of beauty or something else is open to speculation. In view of what we are learning about the culture, it seems unlikely that they were just ornaments, and much more likely that they had some magical value or were made as prestigious gifts, conferring status on their owners.

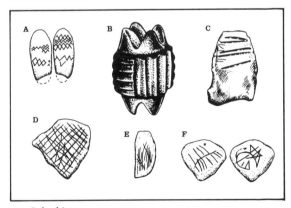

71 Cult objects

A Schist plaque, Ronaldsway
B Stone object, Skara Brae
C Chalk talisman, Combe Hill
D Chalk talisman, Whitehawk
E Chalk talisman, Thickthorn
F Chalk talisman, Windmill Hill

Elsewhere in Britain, the place of the stone balls was taken by flat plaques or tablets with carvings on one or both sides. One of the finest, found at Ronaldsway on the Isle of Man, is a flat, oval schist plaque with zigzags scratched on both sides (Figure 71A). In one pattern, the zigzags are done in parallel rows; in the others they are staggered so that they form lozenges. Both chevrons and lozenges appear repeatedly in neolithic art and their possible meaning will be discussed later. Significant in this respect is the similarity between the Ronaldsway plaque and Iberian plaques. The main difference is that the Iberian plaques have a stylised representation of the face of the earth-goddess on the upper part, whereas the Ronaldsway example does not. It may be that the Ronaldsway plaque, in spite of this omission, is also intended to symbolise the earth-goddess. The chevron pattern appears again on a finely scratched plaque from Graig Lywd. Here the zigzags are developed into a horizontal zone bounded by two straight lines; the 'upper' half of the plaque is more informally decorated with at least two separate hatched areas.

The chalk tablets of southern England are often scribed with sub-parallel lines, like the one from Thickthorn and the two I recently discovered at the centre of the Combe Hill causewayed enclosure and on the bank of the Sussex Ouse (Figure 71C). Another design, found at Harrow Hill and Whitehawk, is the criss-cross, two sets of sub-parallel lines intersecting at right angles. A curious detail found on some tablets is a semicircular notch cut into the edge with rays drawn from it. One of the most thought-provoking is a tablet found at Windmill Hill with a variant of the criss-cross on one side and a unique curvilinear design on the other (Figure 71F).

I became convinced early on that these enigmatic statements are nearer writing than decoration, not least because a limited range of ciphers recurs repeatedly. The chevron may be a simple water symbol relating to fertility, or it may derive from basketry patterns. The multiple chevron from Graig Lwyd is reminiscent of a pottery pattern found as far afield as Orkney and Durrington Walls; on the pottery it looks like an imitation of basketwork. Why this should have been thought worth inscribing on the Graig Lwyd plaque is not clear, unless it is the textile pattern of the earth-goddess's skirt.

Some think the sub-parallel lines may symbolise streaming rain. The Whitehawk tablet, I believe, holds the key to this particular family of ideographs. The criss-cross pattern is very similar to the pattern of furrows made in the ground by cross-arding; we therefore have to treat it as a type of sympathetic magic, a statement of intent or a ritual re-run of the act of arding. The ard-furrowed stone would have acquired magic potency and as such would have been a most useful portable charm. Once we see the

Whitehawk tablet in this way, the similar pattern carved in the flint mine on Harrow Hill explains itself to us as a very similar prayer to the Grime's Graves goddess: an attempt to make the rock itself productive.

The triangles and lozenges were probably intended to symbolise the fields that provided the grain. Pottery designs sometimes combine lozenge and point, the point symbolishing the seed sown in the field. Doubtless the tablets were used as more general good luck charms and were applied in many different situations. We can imagine people carrying the charms on hazardous sea voyages, on visits to neighbouring territories and on hunting expeditions as well as when working in the fields, as an aid to all-round productivity and well-being.

Much of the artwork was fixed, engraved on the living rock or on the great stones of megalithic monuments. One of the most extraordinary and elaborate of these is the meander design carved in the passage grave Bryn Celli Ddu on Anglesey. The apparently

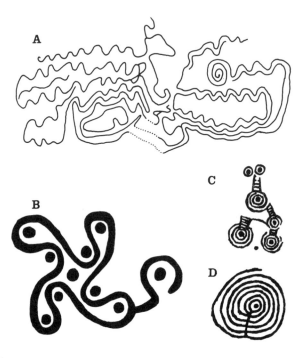

72 Neolithic symbols.

A Meander carved on stone in Bryn Celli Ddu passage grave;
B Swastika stone, Woodhouse Crag; C Cup-and-ring and
ladder symbols, Panorama Stone, Ilkley Moor; D Spiral cup-
and-ring symbol. Cauldside Burn, Kirkcudbright

endless wanderings of the line end in a spiral, another of the great symbols of the neolithic (Figure 72A). The finest spiral in Britain is the 5½-turn spiral enclosing a cup-and-ring at Cauldside Burn, Kirkcudbright (Figure 72D).

The meander may once again symbolise water or some mythic river. It may symbolise the snake, itself a symbol of vitality and periodic rejuvenation and therefore a very appropriate totemic beast for the Stonehenge people. Or it may be more abstract, a symbol of a labyrinthine spiritual journey. The association with the spiral tends to confirm this last interpretation. The spiral is a multiple symbol of reflection preparatory to action, of detachment preparatory to commitment, of dissociation preparatory to initiation, of sleeping and waking, of dying and being reborn. The triple spiral at the centre of the Newgrange passage grave, where the dead were rekindled by the rays of the midwinter sun, and the belly-spirals on the goddess statuettes of eastern Europe indicate that the spiral links together the polarities of life and death. It is thus the most powerful and abstract of the neolithic ideograms.

73 The Westray Stone

The Westray Stone, discovered on the island of Westray in 1981, is a major work of neolithic art, as well as an important development of symbolic utterance (Figure 73). The metre-long stone was originally the lintel of a passage grave, now wrecked. It bears halves of two sets of concentric circles, three pairs of double spirals, and thirteen cups integrated into the design as focal points. At the centre, in a spandrel left by the circles and spirals, is a nest of three lozenges. The symbolic vocabulary is very reminiscent of that of the great kerbstone of Newgrange in Ireland, but the double spirals are arranged in such a way as to suggest pairs of eyes. Perhaps they are the all-seeing eyes of the all-knowing earth goddess.

Some of the cups-and-rings seem to be related to the spiral idea. The symbol consists of a small pit or cup surrounded by one or more concentric circles. Usually there is a 'tail' leading into the cup, crossing the circles. Often a rock is covered with a whole swarm of cups-and-rings. The largest single collection is at Achnabreck, close to the Kilmartin pan-British ceremonial centre. A regional variation is found on Ilkley Moor in Yorkshire. All round the moorland edge, on flat gritstone outcrops projecting out over the steep valley slopes, are clusters of cup-and-ring carvings with ladders instead of tails (Figure 72C). The Swastika Stone, also on Ilkley Moore, bears an even more extraordinary variation on the theme, nine cups arranged in a cross, with a single serpentine line snaking around them. A tenth cup, perhaps an afterthought, is included by means of a sickle-shaped 'ring'.

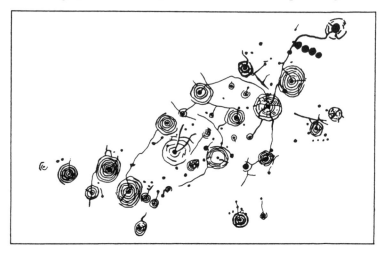

74 Cup-and-ring symbols at Achnabreck

The cup-and-ring carvings are concentrated in central Scotland, with two clusters at Kilmartin and Edinburgh, and Ilkley Moor as a very conspicuous separate concentration. Very similar carvings are found in Portugal, Spain and Switzerland: just occasionally they are discovered in southern Britain, such as the Carne Down barrows on the Dorset Ridgeway. There is a tradition in Welsh folklore that, if only we could understand the carvings, we would gain access to the arts and sciences of the whole world. They were evidently a reductive symbol of some great truth, to be recited again and again so obsessively across the rock surface. At Newgrange, the symbol was incorporated into a formal design as part of the monument, but in Britain it was simply repeated, apparently, over natural rock surfaces. The discovery of a cup-and-ring on the *back* of one of the Newgrange stones confirms that the symbol was already part of the metaphysical currency of the neolithic by 3300 BC.

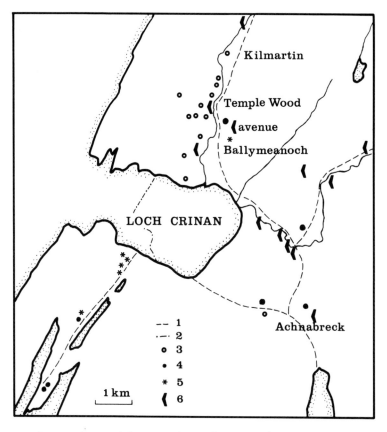

75 Kilmartin. A map of the principal Scottish ceremonial centre:

1 land route	4 main cup-and-ring carvings
2 present shoreline	5 earth or stone circle
3 cairns	6 standing stone

At Kilmartin, on one of the Temple Wood circle stones, there is a spiral with cups-and-rings not far away. Many different explanations have been offered. They may have functioned as altars, with the cups as receptacles for offerings of grain. The Ilkley ladders may be a symbolic link between this world and the next or between earth and the heavens, with the rings representing the movements of stars or planets. Possibly the cup-and-ring symbolises rain falling on water. It has been suggested that it is a tattooist's show-case, a prospector's trade mark, a metal-casting mould, a lamp. It is more likely to be a smaller version of the circle symbol that we can see in the earth and stone circles; as such, it is best seen as a multiple symbol – of the sun, the clan, the world, the territory, the margin from which spiritual journeys might begin. There is an overlap in meaning with the spiral; the Cauldside Burn symbol is a perfect composite symbol, including the shapes and metaphysical contents of both in a single design.

The ornamentation on pottery comprises a fairly narrow range of simple patterns, although re-oriented and re-combined in many different ways. The patterns include chevrons, triangles, hatched triangles, dots, parallel lines, spirals, cross-hatching: much the same vocabulary that we find on the plaques, tablets and megaliths. We can interpret these devices in the simplest way and regard them as ornament only, but the narrow range of patterns used and their persistence geographically suggest that they are something more. It is more likely that they are ideograms. Some seem to be schematised representations of natural features or man-made objects. The chevrons on Ebbsfleet pots may represent rippling water, rivers, seas or streaming rain. The hatched triangles on Fengate and Durrington Walls pottery have a texture reminiscent of basketwork. The dots on a West Kennet long barrow pot represent sown seeds. The parallel lines on a Meldon Bridge pot represent ard furrows and the cross-hatching on a Waterford pot is cross-arding.

From this starting-point, we can venture a little further and tentatively decipher some of the compound designs. Let us take, as an illustration, the design on the three-spiked object from Skara Brae (Figure 76A). Its purpose is unknown, but the design is very clear, consisting of two areas of cross-hatching with an area of

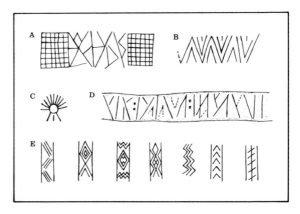

76 Proto-writing

A Symbols on spiked object, Skara Brae
B Zig-zag symbol outside House 7, Skara Brae
C Sun symbol in chamber at Newgrange
D Symbols on bed in House 7, Skara Brae
E Symbols on the Brodgar Stone, Stenness

triangles and lozenges in between. It can be deciphered as 'cross-arding, fields, fields, streaming rain, cross-arding'. Another Skara Brae carving seems to be saying, 'cross-arding, cross-arding, barley in the fields, empty fields'.

Not far from Skara Brae, between the two stone circles of Brodgar and Stenness, a barrow burial was surmounted by a slab with markings along one edge. The Brodgar Stone carries twelve separate carvings, all different and arranged in a row reminiscent of later runic writings. They might mean 'fields, arding, sown fields, water on the sown field, dry field or growing field?, streaming rain, crops gathered into heaps, empty fields'. The fundamental compatibility of these ideas in juxtaposition implies that we are indeed on the right track.

The primitive runes in Hut 7 at Skara Brae are much closer to modern writing than anything so far found anywhere else in Britain (Figure 76D). Archaeologists tend to put from their minds the idea that writing may have been evolving in northern Europe in the neolithic, so deeply intrenched is the idea that writing came from the Middle East as an import. Yet the evidence we are looking at all points in the same direction: in Britain, the Stonehenge people were making the earliest attempts at writing in the third millennium BC or earlier. The runic scratch-marks at Skara Brae dating from the late neolothic consist of a few simple verticals and diagonals punctuated by colons. It is tempting to interpret the colons as separations between words. There are even recognisable letters but the excavators could not decipher them and, as far as I know, no one else has succeeded either.

As more of the inscriptions are discovered and collated, each will tend to shed light on the meanings of the others. They will become clearer. Whilst the late neolithic quasi-runic inscriptions appear to be very close indeed to writing, the symbols on the earlier plaques and tablets are much simpler communications, yet they amount to a form of proto-writing. There were proto-literate societies in the Near East by 3500 BC and something very close to writing was emerging in Romania in 3000 BC: the Tartaria tablets carry up to eleven symbols and they were obviously intended to amount to a statement of some kind. The chalk tablets of Wessex and Sussex seem crude by comparison but only, really, because they usually consist of a single symbol. An exciting recent discovery in a long barrow in the Downs north of Chichester has revealed symbol-tablets arrayed in a row like Scrabble tiles. But, even so, the much commoner single ideas come through to us like distant longbow shots, terse utterances that are as urgent, as poignant and as evocative as any of the more evolved writings of later cultures. These were the first stirrings of a literary tradition in Britain that has culminated, five thousand years later, in the complex utterances of the present millennium.

CONCLUSION

CHAPTER 16

CHILDHOOD'S END

Remove not the landmark at the boundary of the arable land,
Nor disturb the position of the measuring cord;
Covet not a cubit of land,
Nor throw down the fences of a widow.
Beware of throwing down the boundaries of the fields,
Lest a terror carry you off.
Better is poverty in the land of the god
Than riches in a storehouse;
Better is bread, when the heart is happy,
Than riches with vexation.

Ancient Egyptian, 'The Teaching of Amenemope', *c.* 1300 BC

THE END OF THE NEOLITHIC

The strength and spiritual wealth of the culture were such that it may seem surprising that it ever came to an end. Yet eventually the earth and stone circles fell silent for the last time and the great timber roundhouses collapsed in ruins. The temple-barrows at the arable boundaries were ploughed down or allowed to decay. The megalith-bearing sledges were left abandoned, their rawhide hawsers thrown down in the grass. Christchurch Harbour was empty, deserted by the sea-going craft that had brought in salt, pottery and greenstone axes for Durrington Walls. The fires went out for ever at Skara Brae and the salt wind blew over the cold stone hearths. Silt and grass gradually filled the ditches of barrow and henge, while the special numinous relationship between sky, earth and Stonehenge people petered out.

The simplest explanation for these changes, and the oldest, is that new people came in from mainland Europe with a superior culture and imposed it on the natives, but the archaeological evidence for waves of invaders in prehistoric times is not very good. Although Beaker people did come into Britain from 2200 BC onwards, bringing new customs and technology, there is no evidence that they arrived in large numbers, no evidence that they all came at once, and no evidence of any kind of imposition.

Even so, over a period of three or four centuries beginning in 2200 BC, important new ideas were abroad. During that time, nearly every aspect of the way of life that had slowly evolved over the previous two-and-a-half thousand years was altered. Changing social conditions and technology brought with them new economic practices and somewhere – whether at the beginning or at the end of the complex chain reaction – a new religion and a new philosophy emerged. Stone circles, for instance, were built during this transition period but became smaller in diameter and were made of smaller stones: eventually the practice of building circles petered out altogether.

The bronze age has attracted a great deal of attention and interest among archaeologists and the general public. It is easy to see why. The bronze age produced glittering gold treasure hoards and the warrior-hero cults that survived to be written down in Celtic and Homeric sagas; it threw up princes, palaces and pyramids. It is probably easier for us to recognise how such societies worked, with their clear division of labour, social stratification, legal and administrative systems. It is also easier for us to focus on individual people, on kings, princes and heroes who wanted, perhaps more than anything else, the immortality of being remembered for ever in song and fable. In the neolithic there were no kings, nor was there any literature in which individual self-glorification would have been possible.

We might wonder how the very durable way of life of the Stonehenge people allowed itself to be superseded. Was the bronze age way somehow better? Fred Hoyle, believing that Stonehenge was a device for predicting eclipses, suggested that the priests of Stonehenge became complacent and that with time the monument became inaccurate. After a few wrong predictions, people lost faith in the priests and, once the religion crumbled, the foundation of the entire culture collapsed. But I have already argued against this interpretation of Stonehenge and in favour of the monument as a ceremonial salutation to various astronomical and calendrical events. This would not imply that faith depended in any significant sense on the precision of an observation. Even so, the monument *could* have been used to fix the summer solstice with equal precision throughout the neolithic, bronze age and iron age (see Chapter 10).

The arrival of quite small numbers of strangers with strikingly unorthodox views could have sown the seeds of a deep-seated spiritual, intellectual and social disquiet that finally, after a long period of germination, loosened the foundations of the culture. Static cultures may in time grow brittle through rigidity; if the basic assumptions go unchallenged for too long, outmoded practices cannot be justified except in terms of custom. Unity of view and purpose may have sustained and strengthened the culture through two millennia, but once different and divergent views were strenuously expressed cracks began to open up in the monolithic edifice and disintegration was under way.

The very different bronze age orientation, towards heroes, chiefs and kings, may have developed partly as a result of population growth. The population density in the neolithic was low enough for neighbouring groups to maintain friendly relations with one another and for disputes over land and other resources to be kept to a minimum – perhaps averted altogether. With higher population densities in the bronze age, territorial disputes would have become more frequent and strife as a means of resolving them may have become the norm. It would then be natural for a warrior ethic to develop. We saw that in late neolithic Wessex a type of tribal nation had begun to emerge. With the expansion of this type of organisation across the whole of Britain in the bronze age, men were required increasingly to fight for causes remote from their own immediate concerns. It was probably at this developmental stage that such destructive innovations as vassalage and the concept of patriotism evolved, to supply the stimuli to risk life in an alien cause. A class of professional warriors may then have begun to emerge. It is easy to see how individuals might come to the fore as charismatic warlords and heroes, how personality-cults might develop, how rich individual graves, palaces, forts and an aristocracy would lend an entirely new texture and quality to the British way of life.

With this scenario in mind, we might speculate on the density of people in Britain in the late neolithic. In lowland areas we know that territories of 4-5 square kilometres were normal and each of these would have held an estimated fifty people. Information on the highland zone is less reliable, but we may assume provisionally that densities were about one-third those of the lowland zone. This would mean that Britain as a whole had a population of $1\frac{1}{2}$ million, which seems very high. Even if we assume that the highlands were rather emptier than our initial estimate, we are still forced to visualise a neolithic island inhabited by a million people.

The neolithic economy may therefore have been operating close to the limits of its resources and techniques. If we add into the equation the soil depletion that we know resulted from neolithic farming in some areas, we can see an economy heading towards either famine or reorganisation. There is no need to suppose that the bronze age approach represents a superior culture – just one that was appropriate to the conditions. The emergence of exploitative landlords in the London slums of the 1950s was not an evolution towards a greater good, simply a manifestation of a social ill. The bronze age culture was produced by the circumstances: an aggressive, stratified, authoritarian response to a crisis.

This, at least, is the likelihood that we should keep in view. The neolithic culture, though intrinsically rock-strong, had not the flexibility to deal with the severe economic emergency and still retain its social, ethical and spiritual character intact. Unfortunately, the more volatile conditions and social inequalities that went with kingship and personality-cults seem to have been unavoidable. The new capacity for radical and rapid change brought instability with it.

THE LOST BEGINNING

The small scale of neolithic society produced great strength, with economic activity based almost entirely on local resources and tiny social groups. With something approaching ecological balance and communities as a matter of routine living peacefully within their means, it is possible to see in the neolithic culture an object lesson for modern industrial economies and societies in the west. They show few signs of outlasting the Industrial Revolution by more than two or three centuries, whilst the neolithic subsistence economy lasted ten times as long.

There is a danger that such small social and territorial units might become too parochial and narrow in outlook, yet cultural implosion was averted by frequent contacts and exchanges with neighbouring cells and also intermittent contacts with groups living much further afield. Objects have been found that came from Ireland, Brittany and even Germany. Contacts like these stimulated and refreshed the culture, preventing it from collapsing in on itself.

The stone circles are testament enough to the greatness of spirit and breadth of vision possessed by the Stonehenge people. Again and again we are drawn back to the magnetic image of Stonehenge, because it tells us so much about the skills, values and preoccupations of the people who made it. These were not people whose efforts we can dismiss as a mere prelude to the more serious history that came afterwards. They built an astonishingly rich and multi-faceted culture and managed to sustain it in a secure and stable condition for a much longer time than any subsequent culture – a great achievement in itself. Who knows what might have been achieved if the slow evolution of this extraordinary indigenous culture had been allowed to continue without the disruptions and intrusions of later centuries? This is how we should view the Stonehenge people; they were the aboriginal people of our island and their culture is our native culture. Even though we can now only pick our way among the ruins of that culture, it is well worth the attempt, if only to catch occasional glimpses of its monumental greatness, be moved by the determination of its creators and reflect on what we have lost. There is a tendency to assume that as one phase of history gives way to the next the condition of man automatically and necessarily advances, but this essentially Darwinian approach is suspect; it can be a defence for conquest and empire, a rationalisation of cruelty and exploitation.

In some important ways the neolithic world was a superior world to those that followed, with not only more stability, security and continuity, but more leisure and equality. No man was a serf, no woman a servant. The Stonehenge people were more concerned than modern men with eternal values, as they have proved by the sheer durability of their monuments. The great cathedrals of the middle ages, regarded by many as the highest achievements of the last two millennia, are already reaching the end of their design-lives after less than a thousand years. But for the deliberate depredations of later cultures, Stonehenge and Avebury would even now be completely intact over four thousand years after they were built. The Stonehenge people thought and built for all time, which is hard for us today even to imagine.

But this neolithic world, with its equality and stability, its powerful ideology and its sense of the everlasting, was it a civilisation? Does it display the hallmarks by which we recognise civilised societies of the ancient world? Normally, we would expect such a society to be complex, with well-defined strata and specialised occupations. In this respect we could not regard Britain as civilised, since it had a simple, unstratified and largely unspecialised society. There is no archaeological evidence of the sort of class system we find among the North American Indians; the Natchez Indians, for instance, used to divide themselves into four strata – Suns, Nobles, Honoured People and Stinkers.

Normally, following Colin Renfrew's criteria, we would expect an ancient civilisation to produce palaces and temples. Although there were no palaces, there were temples in profusion in the form of chambered tombs, earthen barrows, earth circles and stone circles. A civilisation would normally be both urban and literate. Neolithic Britain was predominantly rural, but the late neolothic superhenges of Wessex count as towns. We can therefore say that the late neolithic was proto-urban, but no more than that. The ideograms represent the first steps towards literacy and literature, yet we can still think of them as proto-writing. Civilisations have an evolved infrastructure. We saw in Part 2 how the trackways and seaways brought the peoples of the various regions of Britain into systematic contact with one another. Civilisations generally display an evolved philosophy and it is very clear from the number, elaboration and consistency of the ritual objects and monuments that a true philosophy, an ideology, pervaded neolithic Britain. The human energies that had previously been tied up in the struggle for survival were freed by farming and released in an eruption of cult activity never seen before.

So, out of the seven diagnostic hallmarks of civilisation that we have proposed – complex society, palaces, temples, towns, writing, infrastructure, philosophy – we can recognise three with certainty and two with reservations. The simplicity of the society and lack of palatial civic buildings disqualify our culture on the remaining two counts. I am not going so far as to suggest that the British neolithic amounted to a civilisation, but it was sufficiently evolved for terms such as 'uncivilised' or 'precivilised' to be inappropriately pejorative. Instead we should think of the culture as 'proto-civilised', with many of the characteristics of the civilised way of life already achieved and the remainder well on the way, although we need not regard such developments as palaces and social differentiation as improvements.

Indeed, instead of asking how far short of civilisation neolithic Britain fell, which inevitably involves us in a measure of temporal chauvinism, we should ask what positive character it had. If we use the term 'simple society' to emphasise the lack of vertical stratification, we risk implying that there was no horizontal differentiation among people, when in fact all kinds of subtle distinctions may have existed in this area. Some writers describe this sort of society as 'non-literate' but, in view of the trend of the evidence, I do not feel we want to use such a pre-emptive term. 'Primitive' is another of the negative and dismissive terms that we would want to avoid in a description of this or any other society.

'Archaic' seems to suit the culture best. Eric Carlton defines an archaic society in terms of nine characteristics, most of which are clearly visible in neolithic British society. Administrative control, though minimal and very local, was in the hands of a nominal specialist, the bigman. There was a pervasive theocratic ethic that controlled many other aspects of the society. Intellectual enquiry was circumscribed and focussed mainly on the ideology, a limitation that produced a concentration on relatively few problems and a near-hysterical obsession with quite a small complex of ideas. The enormous scale of some of the projects, such as the 21 million man-hours invested in Silbury Hill, and what seems to our eyes the disproportionate ingenuity of megalithic technology are clear proofs of this.

There was minimal differentiation of social roles and, probably, an emphasis on the ethnicity of the group. The society was oriented to long-established and enduring values or, as Carlton puts it, to the past. From these characteristics sprang three more: political inflexibility, stasis and permanence. These last are closely related and give us that monolithic quality that we have already seen as a possible cause of the culture's final destruction. It was simply unable to absorb or adjust to the simultaneous challenges of severely new and heterodox ideas introduced by Beaker people and increasing pressures on economic resources.

Carlton's description of an archaic society accords very closely indeed with what we are learning about the British neolithic. More fundamentally still, it was a congruent system, a culture in which the social and cosmic orders were indivisible. Society, nature, religion and economy were undivided and universal in the minds of the Stonehenge people. But even if a society is something universal in relation to its individual members, it is nevertheless an individuality itself, with its own physiognomy and idiosyncrasies, and it is these details of form, character and behaviour that in this book I have been striving to bring into sharper focus. A society is not just a collection of people, a nominal being created out of academic convenience as a shorthand for the many. It is a system of active and dynamic forces and we should always see it as a significant unit of behaviour. In a culture gripped by a powerful ideology, it is the optimal unit of behavioural study, the best way of explaining people.

THE LITTLE PEOPLE

But what sort of people? Tippett's laughing children, the chorus in *The Midsummer Marriage* that acts out the ancient ritual dances, come close, with their bright, playful, intelligent ways and their preoccupation with ritual, dance and song. There may even be clues to this collective personality in folklore. The stories we hear of pixies, fairies, leprechauns and little people are an inheritance from the distant past, very possibly a bronze age memory of the smaller people who went before and whose unearthly spirits still inhabited the large, mysterious monuments that lay silent and deserted. From these stories we can infer that the little people were delicately made, with child-like faces, beautiful, benign, playful, strange and often mischievous: by night, they danced in their magic rings.

On a darker note, we learn that they were kidnappers. This recollection of child-stealing may be a distorted folk-memory of the child sacrifices. Most pervasive, though, is their reputation for limitless supernatural powers. To suggest that the Stonehenge people were pixies or fairies may seem fanciful, but the various characteristics that are attributed to these delightful creatures of legend do correspond startlingly closely with what we have learned through archaeology. We should not reject out of hand this useful mental image of them, at once appealing and infinitely strange and unsettling.

Pursuing a different and equally tentative line of thought, we may look to astrology for clues to the collective personality of the Stonehenge people. According to astrologers, each Great Month, a period of some two thousand years, is dominated by the influence of a particular zodiac sign. The Age of Pisces, just ended, was a mild and unworldly age of indecision and change but, because of the gradual precession of the spring equinox, which heralds the start of each solar year, it has not always been so. From 2000 BC until the birth of Christ it was the Age of Aries. The dominant influence of warfare and aggression was to an extent softened by the secondary astrological influence, the opposing sign of Libra, which may account for the symmetry and equilibrium manifested in both the social structures and architecture of the classical era.

The Age of Taurus, the Great Month stretching from 4000 to 2000 BC, was governed by the most striking polarity of all the zodiac signs, Taurus and Scorpio. Taurus is associated with beauty and solidity, grace and massiveness. It is a powerful earth-sign associated with farming, management, surveying and building. Taurus brings permanence, resistance to change, determination, persistence, tenacity and an obsession with routine: characteristics we have, in fact, already come to associate with neolithic society and personality. It may be no more than a curious coincidence, but Taurus was the age of bull-gods in Europe, the period when the famous bull-cult evolved on Crete and, here and there, more obscure proto-Dionysian ox-cults in Britain. The secondary zodiacal influence of Scorpio is even more striking in its relevance to our study, for Scorpio is associated by astrologers with a preoccupation with death and the after-life, a preoccupation that, perhaps more than anything else, gives the Stonehenge people their distinctive character.

We might well dismiss non-material evidence like this as fanciful, but there is a harmony that gives pause for thought between the astrologers' view of the Age of Taurus and our own conclusion, arrived at quite independently, about the spirit of the age. Jung was aware of an association between the psychic changes now under way in the population at large and the imminent end of the Age of Pisces. He drew attention also to the awareness that existed in the ancient world of the significance of these ages and their psychic dominants. The ancient Egyptians knew of the major psychic changes that accompanied the transition from one age to the next. It may be that myths involving successive generations of gods were a means of expressing the general concept of shifting emphases in the archetypes over very long periods. The whole complex of issues arising from this train of thought has a particular relevance because we are now on the brink of the Age of Aquarius.

No doubt when the character of the new age emerges and new gods reign, we shall see the Age of Taurus in a new perspective, but for the moment I like to think we have been able to glimpse its realities relatively undisturbed from the threshold of the ages, our perceptions sharpened like the heightened awareness of the solitary initiand. We are out on the boundary, where we can hover fleetingly alongside cultures that have gone before and are yet to come, and from which we can see with tantalising clarity the beauty of a way of life long since lost.

APPENDIX

CONVERSION TABLES FOR RADIOCARBON DATES

The radiocarbon dating method depends on the inclusion in the remains of all living things of the isotope carbon-14. When an organism dies, the carbon-14 it contains decays at a constant and predictable rate. The dating method uses precise laboratory measurements of the amount of carbon-14 remaining to calculate the date of death (see Column A). A complication arises because other methods of dating, notably the one that uses the annular rings of the bristlecone pine, indicate that the levels of carbon-14 in the atmosphere have fluctuated with time. 'Raw' radiocarbon dates thus need correcting. Column B shows the best available conversion of radiocarbon dates, resulting mainly from the evidence of the long-lived bristlecone pine. The corrected dates are significantly older, and they lengthen the neolithic by several centuries. It should be remembered, though, that even the corrected dates are only approximate and may prove to be in error by as much as two hundred years.

COLUMN A Radiocarbon date bc (5568 years half-life)	COLUMN B Corrected date BC = Mean calendar date (Arizona/Pennsylvania)
1600	2070
1800	2270
2000	2540
2200	2830
2400	3080
2600	3340
2800	3510
3000	3730
3200	4040
3400	4240
3600	4420
3800	4640
4000	4850

Source: Renfrew, C. (1974), *British Prehistory: a New Outline*, Duckworth.

REFERENCES

British Archaeological Reports abbreviated as *BAR*.
Council for British Archaeology abbreviated as CBA.
Proceedings of the Prehistoric Society abbreviated as *PPS*.

Four sources in particular proved invaluable in several chapters:
Burgess, C. (1980), *The Age of Stonehenge*, Dent.
Forde-Johnston, F. (1976), *Prehistoric Britain and Ireland*, Dent.
Piggott, S. (1954), *The Neolithic Cultures of the British Isles*, Cambridge University Press.
Whittle, A. W. R. (1977), 'The earlier Neolithic of southern England and its continental background', *BAR Supplementary Series*, 35.

The following select bibliography is not intended to be exhaustive. Hundreds of archaeological site reports were utilised in the preparation of the book and space does not permit all the site references to be included here. Readers should nevertheless find what they need within the texts or reference lists of the following publications.

2 HERE IN THIS MAGIC WOOD

Ashbee, P. (1978), *The Ancient British*, Geo Abstracts.
Barker, G. and Webley, D. (1978), 'Causewayed camps and early neolithic economies in central southern England', *PPS*, 44, 161-86.
Barnatt, J. (1982), *Prehistoric Cornwall: the Ceremonial Monuments*, Turnstone.
Bell, M. (1977), 'Excavation at Bishopstone', *Sussex Archaeological Collection*, 115, 1-291.
Fox, A. (1973), *South-West England, 3500 BC – AD 600*, David & Charles.
Laing, L. and J. (1980), *The Origins of Britain*, Routledge & Kegan Paul.
Limbrey, S. and Evans, J. G. (1978), 'The effect of man on the landscape: the Lowland Zone, *C.B.A. Research Report* No. 21.
Pennington, W. (1969), *The History of British Vegetation*, English Universities Press.

Renfrew, C. (1979), *Investigations in Orkney*, Society of Antiquaries and Thames & Hudson.

Simmons, I. G. and Tooley, M. J. (1981), *The Environment in British Prehistory*, Duckworth.

Simpson, D. D. A. (1971), *Economy and Settlement in Neolithic and Early Bronze Age Britain and Europe*, Leicester University Press.

3 HEARTH AND HOME

Field, N. H., Matthews, C. L. and Smith, I. F. (1964), 'New neolithic sites in Dorset and Bedfordshire, with a note on the distribution of neolithic storage pits in Britain', *PPS* 30, 352-81.

Fox, A. (1973), *South-west England, 3500 BC – AD 600*, David & Charles.

Laing, L. and J. (1980), *The Origins of Britain*, Routledge & Kegan Paul.

MacKie, E. (1977), *Science and Society in Prehistoric Britain*, Elek.

Simpson, D. D. A. (1971), *Economy and Settlement in Neolithic and Early Bronze Age Britain and Europe*, Leicester University Press.

4 THE BROKEN CIRCLE

Ashbee, P. (1978), *The Ancient British*, Geo Abstracts.

Barnatt, J. (1982), *Prehistoric Cornwall: the Ceremonial Monuments*, Turnstone.

Burl, A. (1976), *The Stone Circles of the British Isles*, Yale University Press.

Burl, A. (1979), *Prehistoric Avebury*, Yale University Press.

Case, H. J. (1962), 'Long barrows and causewayed camps', *Antiquity*, 36, 212-16.

Childe, V. G. (1940), *Prehistoric Communities of the British Isles*, Kegan Paul.

Evans, J. G. (1971), 'Notes on the environment of early farming communities in Britain', in *Economy and Settlement in Neolithic and Early Bronze Age Britain*, ed. D. D. A. Simpson, Leicester University Press.

Hedges, J. and Buckley, D. (1978), 'Excavations at a neolithic causewayed enclosure, Orsett, Essex', *PPS* 44, 219-308.

Renfrew, C. (ed.) (1974), *British Prehistory: a New Outline*, Duckworth.

Simpson, D. D. A. (1971), *Economy and Settlement in Neolithic and Early Bronze Age Britain and Europe*, Leicester University Press.

Smith, I. F. (1971), 'Causewayed enclosures' in *Economy and Settlement in Neolithic and Early Bronze Age Britain and Europe*. ed. D. D. A. Simpson, Leicester University Press.

5 OF THE EFFECTE OF CERTAINE STONES

Dyer, J. (1982), *The Penguin Guide to Prehistoric England and Wales*, Penguin.

Fox, A. (1973), *South-West England, 3500 BC – AD 600*, David & Charles.

Houlder, C. H. (1961), 'The excavation of a neolithic stone implement factory on Mynydd Rhiw in Caernarvonshire', *PPS* 27, 108-43.

Jessup, R. (1970), *South East England*, Thames & Hudson.

Laing, L. and J. (1980), *The Origins of Britain*, Routledge & Kegan Paul.

MacKie, E. (1977), *Science and Society in Prehistoric Britain*, Elek.

Renfrew, C. (1979), *Investigations in Orkney*, Society of Antiquaries and Thames & Hudson.

Seligman, C. G. (1910), *The Melanesians of British New Guinea*, Cambridge University Press.

6 CLAY CIRCLES: THE FIRST POTTERY

Smith, I. F. (1974), 'The neolithic', in *British Prehistory: a New Outline*, ed. C. Renfrew, Duckworth.

Hedges, J. and Buckley, D. (1978), 'Excavation at a neolithic causewayed enclosure, Orsett, Essex', *PPS* 44, 219-308.

Fox, A. (1973), *South-West England, 3500 BC – AD 600*, David & Charles.

7 BY WHAT MECHANICAL CRAFT

Atkinson, R. J. C. (1979), *Stonehenge: Archaeology and Interpretation*, Penguin.

Burl, A. (1979), *Prehistoric Avebury*, Yale Univerity Press.

Clark, J. G. D. (1963), 'Neolithic bows from Somerset, England, and the prehistory of archery in north-west Europe', *PPS* 29, 50-98.

8 BY THE DEVIL'S FORCE

Barker, G. (1982), *Prehistoric Communities in Northern England: Essays in Economic and Social Reconstruction*, University of Sheffield.

Coles, J. M., Heal, S. V. E. and Orme, B. J. (1978), 'The use of wood in prehistoric Britain and Ireland', *PPS* 44, 1-45.

Coles, J. M. and Hibbert, F. A. (1968), 'Prehistoric roads and tracks in Somerset, England', *PPS* 34, 238-58.

Cummins, W. A. (1980), 'Stone axes as a guide to neolithic communities and boundaries in England and Wales', *PPS* 46, 45-60.

Godwin, H. (1960), 'Prehistoric wooden trackways of the Somerset Levels: their construction, age and relation to climatic change', *PPS* 26, 1-36.

Wright, E. V. and Churchill, D. M. (1965), 'The boats from North Ferriby, Yorkshire, England, with a review of the origins of sewn boats of the Bronze Age', *PPS* 31, 1-24.

9 EARTH CIRCLES AND EARTH LINES: THE RITUAL FUNCTION

Atkinson, R. J. C. (1979), *Stonehenge: Archaeology and Interpretation*, Penguin.

Burl, A. (1979), *Prehistoric Avebury*, Yale University Press.

Taylor, J. A. (1980), 'Culture and environment in prehistoric Wales: selected essays', *BAR British Series*, 76.

10 THE OLD TEMPLES OF THE GODS

Atkinson, R. J. C. (1979), *Stonehenge: Archaeology and Interpretation*, Penguin.

Balfour, M. (1983), *Stonehenge and its Mysteries*, Hutchinson.

Burl, A. (1976), *The Stone Circles of the British Isles*, Yale University Press.

Burl, A. (1987), *The Stonehenge People: Life and Death at the World's Greatest Stone Circle*, Dent.

Burl, A. (1988), '"Without Sharp North ..." Alexander Thom and the great stone circles of Cumbria', in *Records in Stone: Papers in Memory of Alexander Thom*, ed. Ruggles, Cambridge University Press.

Hadingham, E. (1975), *Circles and Standing Stones*, Heinemann.

Hawkins, G. (1966), *Stonehenge Decoded*, Souvenir Press.

Heggie, D. C. (1981), *Megalithic Science: Ancient Mathematics and Astronomy in Northwest Europe*, Thames & Hudson.

Krupp, E. C. (1984), *In Search of Ancient Astronomies*, Penguin.

Thom, A. (1967), *Megalithic Sites in Britain*, Oxford University Press.

11 DIALOGUE WITH DEATH

Ashbee, P., Smith, I. F. and Evans, J. G. (1979), 'Excavation of three long barrows near Avebury, Wiltshire', *PPS* 45, 207-300.

Barnatt, J. (1982), *Prehistoric Cornwall: the Ceremonial Monuments*, Turnstone.

Coles, J. M. and Simpson, D. D. A. (1965), 'The excavation of a neolithic round barrow at Pitnacree, Perthshire, Scotland', *PPS* 31, 34-57.

Daniel, G. (1963), *The Megalith Builders of Western Europe*, Hutchinson.

Drewett, P. J. (1975), 'The excavation of an oval burial mound of the third millennium bc at Alfriston, East Sussex, 1974', *PPS* 41, 119-52.

Helm, P. J. (1971), *Exploring Prehistoric England*, Hale.

Henshall, A. (1974), 'Scottish chambered tombs and long barrows', in *British Prehistory: a New Outline*, ed. C. Renfrew, Duckworth.

Jessup, R. (1970), *South East England*, Thames & Hudson.

MacKie, E. (1977), *The Megalith Builders*, Phaidon.

Manby, T. G. (1976), 'Excavation of the Kilham Long Barrow, East Riding of Yorkshire', *PPS* 42, 111-59.

Renfrew, C. (1979), *Investigations in Orkney*, Society of Antiquaries and Thames & Hudson.

Vatcher, F. (1961), 'The excavation of the long mortuary enclosure on Normanton Down, Wiltshire', *PPS* 27, 160-73.

12 THE LAUGHING CHILDREN

Bock, P.J. (1969), *Modern Cultural Anthropology*, Knopf.

Burl, A. (1979), *Prehistoric Avebury*, Yale University Press.

Fox, A. (1973), *South-West England, 3500 BC – AD 600*, David & Charles.

Jessup, R. (1970), *South East England*, Thames & Hudson.

MacKie, E. (1977), *The Megalith Builders*, Phaidon.

Renfrew, C. (1979), *Investigations in Orkney*, Society of Antiquaries and Thames & Hudson.

Taylor, J. A. (1980), 'Culture and environment in prehistoric Wales: selected essays', *BAR British Series*, 76.

13 THE PEACEFUL CITADEL

Ashbee, P. (1978), *The Ancient British*, Geo Abstracts.

Barnatt, J. (1982), *Prehistoric Cornwall: the Ceremonial Monuments*, Turnstone.

Bock, P. J. (1969), *Modern Cultural Anthropology*, Knopf.

Burl, A. (1979), *Prehistoric Avebury*, Yale University Press.

Carlton, E. (1977), *Ideology and Social Order*, Routledge & Kegan Paul.

Childe, V. G. (1940), *Prehistoric Communities of the British Isles*, Kegan Paul.

Curwen, E. C. (1936), 'Excavation in Whitehawk Camp, Brighton', *Sussex Archaeological Collection*, 77, 60-92.

Hogbin, H. I. (1938), 'Tillage and collection: a New Guinea economy', *Oceania*, 9, 286-325.

Howard, A. (1971), *Polynesia: Readings on a Culture Area*, Chandler.

Limbrey, S. and Evans, J. G. (1978), 'The effect of man on the landscape: the Lowland Zone', *C.B.A. Research Report* No. 21.

Lorenz, K. (1966), *On Aggression*, Methuen.

MacKie, E. (1977), *The Megalith Builders*, Phaidon.

Mair, L. (1962), *Primitive Government*, Scolar Press.

Pierpoint, S. (1980), 'Social patterns in Yorkshire prehistory', *BAR British Series*, 74.

Renfrew, C. (1979), *Investigations in Orkney*, Society of Antiquaries and Thames & Hudson.

Seligman, C. G. (1910), *The Melanesians of British New Guinea*, Cambridge University Press.

Strathern, A. (1979), *Ongka: A Self-Account by a New Guinea Big-man*, Duckworth.

Stukeley, W. (1740), *Stonehenge: a Temple Restored to the British Druids*.

14 THE GREAT MYSTERY

Burl, A. (1979), *Prehistoric Avebury*, Yale University Press.

Castleden, R. (1983), *The Wilmington Giant: the Quest for a Lost Myth*, Turnstone.

Dames, M. (1976), *The Silbury Treasure*, Thames & Hudson.

Dupré, W. (1975), *Religion in Primitive Cultures*, Mouton.

Durkheim, E. (1915), *The Elementary Forms of Religious Life*, Allen & Unwin.

Eliade, M. (1979), *From Primitives to Zen*, Collins.

Frazer, J. G. (1922), *The Golden Bough: a Study in Magic and Religion*, Macmillan.

Herskovits, M. J. (1955), *Cultural Anthropology*, Knopf.

Jung, C. G. (1956), *Symbols of Transformation*, Routledge & Kegan Paul.

Mendelssohn, K. (1974), *The Riddle of the Pyramids*, Thames & Hudson.

O'Kelly, M. J. (1982), *Newgrange: Archaeology, Art and Legend*, Thames & Hudson.

Shorter, B. (1982), 'Border People', *Guild of Pastoral Psychology Lecture* No. 211.

15 THE SPEAKING STONES

Childe. V. G. (1931), *Skara Brae*, Kegan Paul.

Hadingham, E. (1975), *Circles and Standing Stones*, Heinemann.

Renfrew, C. (1966), 'The Tartaria Tablets, *Nestor*, 469-70.

Thompson, A. (1983), Institute of Archaeology: personal communication.

16 CHILDHOOD'S END

Carlton, E. (1977), *Ideology and Social Order*, Routledge & Kegan Paul.

Durkheim, E. (1915), *The Elementary Forms of the Religious Life*, Allen & Unwin.

Jung, C. G. (1970), *Civilization in Transition*, Routledge & Kegan Paul.

Renfrew, C. (1973), *Before Civilization: the Radiocarbon Revolution and Prehistoric Europe*, Jonathan Cape.

INDEX